AF860435

A NEW RHETORIC of SOCIAL MOVEMENTS

Dana L. Cloud
University of Cincinnati

cognella
SAN DIEGO

Bassim Hamadeh, CEO and Publisher
Todd R. Armstrong, Publisher
Susana Christie, Senior Developmental Editor
Zoe Flores, Project Editor
Abbey Hastings, Senior Production Editor
Jessica Delia, Graphic Design Associate
JoHannah McDonald, Licensing Coordinator
Natalie Piccotti, Director of Marketing
Kassie Graves, Senior Vice President, Editorial
Alia Bales, Director, Project Editorial and Production

Copyright © 2026 by Cognella, Inc. All rights reserved. No part of this publication may be reprinted, reproduced, transmitted, or utilized in any form or by any electronic, mechanical, or other means, now known or hereafter invented, including photocopying, microfilming, and recording, or in any information retrieval system without the written permission of Cognella, Inc. For inquiries regarding permissions, translations, foreign rights, audio rights, and any other forms of reproduction, please contact the Cognella Licensing Department at rights@cognella.com.

Trademark Notice: Product or corporate names may be trademarks or registered trademarks and are used only for identification and explanation without intent to infringe.

Cover images:
Copyright © 2017 Depositphotos/Forgem.
Copyright © 2020 iStockphoto LP/jacoblund.
Copyright © 2021 iStockphoto LP/mustafahacalaki.
Copyright © 2023 iStockphoto LP/Budi yanto.

Printed in the United States of America.

cognella® ACADEMIC PUBLISHING
3970 Sorrento Valley Blvd., Ste. 500, San Diego, CA 92121

Detailed Contents

Preface

From the Movement for Black Lives to the eruption of campuses in support of Palestine and against war, from the proliferation of academic unionization drives and labor actions to the resurgence of the national labor movement, it is clear that we are witnessing a new era of movements for social justice.

How are we to understand the emergence of such movements and their unfolding? Rhetorical scholars have long been interested in movements for social justice. There are a number of excellent books on the rhetoric of social movements, but there is not a recent textbook in the field that systematically addresses the formation, rise, and fall of contemporary social movements. There is an urgent need for an updated, comprehensive, and systematically theorized textbook on the rhetoric of movements for social change.

Those of us teaching movements to both undergraduate and graduate students find ourselves collecting pieces of theoretical, historical, and analytical writing to concatenate a coherent perspective and body of knowledge for our students. The present historical moment has galvanized me to take the narrative I have constructed in my courses and develop it as a framework for a comprehensive and useful textbook on this subject.

This book covers the rhetoric—visual, aural, verbal, and technological—of social change actors across a range of U.S. social movements from a theoretical perspective that emphasizes the interrelationship of hegemony and struggle and the spectrum of movement activities from the reformist to the revolutionary. The book is based on a Gramscian approach to the mutual engagement of struggle and control.

The book is geared toward upper-division undergraduate and graduate students. It offers a framework that can help to explain a movement's motives, successes, failures—its mobilization, growth, and pressure on the establishment—as well as periods of retreat and quiescence.

Gramsci's conceptualization of the interaction of hegemony (control) and counterhegemony (resistance; although this is not a term he coined) and his distinction between the war of position—a struggle in culture and politics—and the war of maneuver—a strategic challenge to an oppressive system as a whole—allows us to theorize, describe, and explain social movements both past and present.

A New Rhetoric of Social Movements introduces students to the tasks of describing and explaining social movements in an accessible way. There is extensive consideration of how media, including social media, serve as affordances of social movement actors and organizations. Each chapter, while providing multiple current examples, features one extended case study for continuity and clarity—and an opportunity to appreciate the creativity and genius in our shared rhetorical history.

The book develops two new theoretical models, the first being a "two-axis" model of social movements that disentangles questions of politics from questions of tactics such that we can get beyond conceptualizing movements on a spectrum from moderate to militant as if those terms capture both politics and tactics. If we put moderation to militancy along one spectrum and degrees of political radicalization on the other, we end up with a quadrant model that admits the possibility of movements being complex: ideologically radical but tactically moderate, ideologically reformist and tactically militant, and so on. A related contribution on this point is an emphasis on the radical flank effect, identified by sociologist Herbert Haines as the influence a militant split in a movement can have on the movement's more moderate elements. In situations of high polarization and peak movement influence, that effect can be positive in enhancing the influence of the mainstream movement.

The second theoretical framework that makes this book a *new* rhetoric of social movements is the Hegemony-Formation-Pressure model. This model conceives of movements as operating in and against a framework of established hegemonic social relations. Then, it describes a cycle of movement formation and public pressure that incorporates multiple tensions in the field of rhetorical studies. Rhetoric scholars have asked the questions: Are social movements "phenomena" or "meaning"? Are they constitutive in character—emphasizing the creation of identities and consciousness—or instrumental—aimed at pressuring the establishment for concrete institutional change? Should we emphasize whether they are geared toward internal movement audiences or external, extra-movement audiences? Should we rely on sociological accounts of movements or develop distinctly rhetorical ones instead? Should we emphasize the role of moments in the war of position instead of anticipating the war of maneuver?

These need not be either-or questions. The Hegemony-Formation-Pressure model puts the moments of formation—identity- and consciousness-forming rhetorics—in a dialectical cycle with the tactics of pressure—instrumental action demanding institutional change. Both moments in the cycle are mutually determining and reinforcing in a process that is not linear but cyclical. The idea of a circuit of formation and pressure captures the totality of movements and their complexity. It recognizes the relevance of both sociological and rhetorical traditions; of both internally-oriented rhetorics and externally-oriented ones; of both the constitutive and the instrumental moments; and both the war of position and the war of maneuver.

The Organization of This Book

The chapters of this book explore the rhetoric of movements for social justice, starting with theoretical frameworks from sociology and rhetorical studies and the introduction of key theoretical concepts. Although examples from many social movements appear throughout the book, each conceptual chapter features a single primary movement case study to illustrate the chapter's key concepts. The book does not cover every U.S. social movement but rather focuses on just a few signal movements in the past that are clear examples of the characteristics each chapter explores and analyzes.

Most of these examples are from the 20th century, and for a reason: Those movements won significant—albeit sometimes impermanent—institutional and political change and shifted cultural narratives justifying oppression in significant ways. The turn to the study of social movements in the late 20th and early 21st century—"new" social movements—was a turn away from valuing the effective, systematic, sustained mass organizing that characterized the movements of the 19th and 20th centuries. New social movements are important and fascinating, characterized by (increasingly digital) networks rather than broad organization, a reliance on prefigurative politics (in which a movement constitutes an ephemeral model of democratic practice without making demands on society's structure and institutions), and a focus on the local, the identity-oriented, the ephemeral, and the short-term.[1] Yet, we still need the knowledge of how large-scale, instrumental, organized, and effective movements have worked—in addition to understanding the multitude of knowledges, cultures, actions, and worlds made by the oppressed.[2]

When it comes to building a *model* of social movements, it is important to not only look at what is, but also to recall what was—and could be again. When the next tidal wave of movement for change swells, it will be useful to have historical knowledge and conceptual tools to both ride and study that wave.

(There is a companion volume to this book, *Rhetorical Histories of Social Movements in the U.S.* [Cognella, 2024], co-authored by Dana Cloud, Jim Cherney, David Cisneros, Constance Gordon, Theon Hill, Kristen Hoerl, and Mary Triece. That book covers most U.S. movements from the early Republic, suffrage, and abolition movements; to the labor, communist, and socialist movements; the Black Freedom Struggle; 1960s student and anti-war movements; Latine and immigrant movements; disability rights and justice movements; gay rights and queer liberation movements; and environmental and environmental justice movements. The authors of that book's chapters are deep, current experts on specific movements, their variations, rhetors, tensions, organizations, methods, and results.)

Chapters in Part I cover introductory material explaining why social movements arise and why they are still necessary; the part also lays out key concepts and the theoretical perspective of the book, which is grounded in the theory of hegemony as it was developed by Italian philosopher and revolutionary Antonio Gramsci. Then, Part II provides overviews of the two major traditions of scholarship informing the study of social movements: sociology and rhetoric. Coverage of the rhetorical tradition will consider the multiple rhetorical repertoires—sets of communicative actions (like speeches, demonstrations, art, and music) that operate strategically to achieve a movement's goals. Part III introduces a new model of social movements that combines the two dominant perspectives in rhetorical studies on social movements, the constitutive (or identity-focused) and instrumental (or pressure- and goal-focused) paradigms. The chapters integrate these two dimensions of movements in a Hegemony-Formation-Pressure model that can be used to understand many movements, both historical and unfolding today.

The first thing to do is to explore why social movements happen and why they are still necessary today. To that end, Chapter 1 describes the injustices faced in U.S. society today. These injustices are based on race, gender, sexuality, class, and ability. We must examine the rhetoric that legitimizes such injustice and how these injustices are the fuel for movements for social change.

Chapter 2 lays out the theoretical perspective of the book, based on the ideas of Antonio Gramsci, in more detail. It offers more specific and detailed definitions of the basic concepts in understanding social movements: social movement, social justice, resistance, reform, revolution, rhetoric, strategies, and tactics. The chapter covers the two sides of hegemony, agitation and control. It also defines the concepts from Gramsci of "war of position" and "war of maneuver" to help us describe social movements. Finally, the chapter considers the crucial role of the rhetorical production of consciousness—identity and ideology—in social movements.

Chapter 3 describes how much of what we know about how social movements work comes from the field of sociology. The chapter summarizes this work on social movement organizations and activity. This research gives us a number of core concepts for the study of movements including organization, leadership, identity, framing, and repertoires of action. The chapter describes how this research is different from studies of social movements from rhetorical perspectives. These concepts are illustrated through an extended case study of the radical feminist movement.

Chapters 4 and 5 review existing literature in the fields of communication and rhetorical studies on social movements including the field's controversy over the value of confrontation, research on the strategies of agitation and control, rhetoric's critique of the sociological tradition, the rhetorical criticism of movements, and the turn toward theorizing "resistance" as an expression of social movements that do not take on traditional organizational and methodological formats. In addition, the chapters define how ideological and tactical flanking operate in social movements to press more moderate activists toward more radical goals and to make the goals of moderate movements seem more realistic and reasonable. As a primary case study, The AIDS Coalition to Unleash Power (ACT UP) illustrates a number of the strategies identified in rhetorical scholarship on social movements.

Chapters 6, 7, and 8 lay out a new model of the rhetoric of social movements. This model integrates hegemony theory, sociological research, and rhetorical studies of movements in the *Hegemony-Formation-Pressure* model. This model describes a new, useful theory of the stages of social movements, from initial consciousness-raising and identity formation to concerted pressure on establishment institutions, through movement success, maintenance, decline, or failure. A key insight of this model is that all struggles for social change are challenges to hegemonic power; this struggle takes place in economics, politics, and culture. The model posits a dialectical (interdependent) relationship between the internally-oriented rhetoric of consciousness-raising and identity-creating, on the one hand; and the rhetorical strategies of public pressure on society's institutions, on the other. In the process of formation and pressure, movements can galvanize adjustments in hegemonic power relations, lead to revolutionary change (in which a new hegemony is established), meet with both repressive and cultural resistance from hegemonic standpoints, maintain themselves in a holding pattern over time, and/or decline and fail. Chapter 6 covers the first part of the model: the formation cycle. Chapters 7 and 8 continue the development of the Hegemony-Formation-Pressure model with an explanation of the pressure cycle, the stages and strategies of activists and organizations that pressure established institutions and elites. The U.S. civil rights and Black Power movements are developed as cases in point for these chapters on the Hegemony-Formation-Pressure model.

The Appendix describes how students can get involved in movements for social justice. In addition to providing step-by-step advice for students seeking opportunities for activism, it lays out some key principles for such involvement, including intersectionality, solidarity, and coalition. This part advises readers in discovering movement organizations or people in their area that they can commit to as a participant, engaging in real, significant conversation with established activists about their experiences and goals, and listening to potential criticisms of privileged students entering the cause. It offers suggestions for doing the work of building and supporting the movement, including publicity, logistics, and democratic organization.

Features of the Book

- Writing that is direct and clear for undergraduates, with extensive footnotes for undergraduate and graduate students who want to take a deeper dive into the literature
- Two new, comprehensive models for understanding the rhetoric of social movements, as described above
- Discussion of the role of social media in movements for social justice
- Discussion of right-wing movements and their role in disciplining agitation for change
- Chapters with helpful lists of key terms (bolded, with sub-terms in italics), suggestions for further reading, suggestions for viewing,

questions for discussion, and suggested exercises to make teaching the textbook an engaging experience

- An appendix that offers a "how-to" create and get involved in social movements for students interested in taking their knowledge on the road
- A glossary of key terms, figures, events, and organizations
- A list of suggested potentially semester- or term-long exercises for students as individuals and groups
- A companion volume, *Rhetorical Histories of Social Movements in the U.S.* (by Dana L. Cloud, James "Jim" L. Cherney, Josue David Cisneros, Constance Gordon, Theon E. Hill, Kristen Hoerl, and Mary E. Triece) that includes nine movement-specific, historical, analytical, and detailed chapters

Welcome to *A New Rhetoric of Social Movements*! I hope that you and your students find the work engaging and rewarding as we move further into what is turning out to be a century of struggle.

Acknowledgments

Many thanks to the reviewers of this book: Stephen Howard Browne (The Pennsylvania State University), Nathan Crick (Texas A&M University), Christina Foust (Metropolitan State University of Denver), Phaedra C. Pezzullo (University of Colorado Boulder), Matt Sobnosky (Florida Atlantic University), and M. Elizabeth Thorpe (SUNY Brockport). The time and attention you gave the work has made it stronger and more thorough. (Remaining shortcomings are still, of course, my own.)

Todd Armstrong, Susana Christie, Zoe Flores, and Abbey Hastings at Cognella have been amazing, supportive, and patient collaborators. Thank you.

I offer profound thanks to my family for their support: my wife Nina Maria Lozano, a powerful scholar of rhetoric in their own right, a source of constant and unwavering support, and a generous reader of my work; our kids Dylan, Sarah, and Ben, who have been patient with my hiding out in my study to work for days on end; my daughter Samantha Cloud-Miller and my grandson Keith, both inspirations for understanding how the world can—and why it must—become a better place; and my mother Lana Cloud, my role model for strong womanhood and career success and source of loving support.

I am grateful for my longtime friends Cindy Rigg, Karin Wilkins, Diane Wiener, and Raka Shome and for my activist colleagues and organizations past and present—most recently in the Tempest Collective—from where much of my practical knowledge and passion for movements springs. I thank all of my superstar graduate students over the course of my career and my undergraduates, including those at the California State University, Fullerton, who engaged this work with both interest and constructive advice. My dog Hugo and cat kittyfoods (long story) are sources of hilarity and perspective. Thank you all, very much.

I

Preliminaries

Introduction

The Rhetoric of Social Movements

KEY TERMS

social movement
rhetoric
hegemony
counterhegemony
war of position
war of maneuver
agitation, control

In May 2020, police officer Derek Chauvin choked a Black man in Minneapolis to death. George Floyd had been arrested for passing a counterfeit twenty-dollar bill. The circulation of a video of this event reignited the Movement for Black Lives, which had arisen in 2013 after the revelation of a spate of police killings of people of color. In particular, the police killing of youth Trayvon Martin in 2013 motivated organizers to build a concerted movement against racism in the criminal justice system and beyond.

Even during the quarantines imposed during the 2020 COVID-19 pandemic, activists (most wearing protective masks), erupted into the streets in the hundreds of thousands across the United States and beyond. From large cities to small, rural, towns, diverse groups of protesters again proclaimed, "Black Lives Matter." Despite concerns over the spread of the novel coronavirus, the movement was characterized by militancy and diversity across the lines of gender, race, sexuality, class, nation, and more.

Through the spring and into the summer, activists took over streets and highways chanting the names of those killed by police: George Floyd, Breonna Taylor, and dozens more. The movement demanded and won surprising reforms: the defunding of the police in cities across the nation, the resignations of police chiefs and other city officials in multiple metropolises, the removal of Confederate and other racist statues and monuments, the removal of the Confederate flag from sites in the South, the renaming of sports teams like the Washington Commanders,

FIGURE 0.1 A protest for Black Lives Matter in New York City, November 28, 2014.

and more. Activists in anti-racist movements had worked for decades on each of these separate reform projects with little progress.

Even before the events of May 2020, there was a vibrant resurgence of social movement activity on both right and Left in the United States. For example, in 2017 a wave of resistance to sexual harassment and assault under the hashtag #MeToo swept multiple industries from Hollywood to banking. Teachers in North Carolina, Arizona, and West Virginia mobilized and struck in the tens of thousands in 2018, winning significant gains not only for teachers but also for other public employees. Donald Trump's presidency was the context for these movements. At the time of his inauguration and for three years following, enormous protest marches, "Women's Marches," filled the streets with outrage over what his election signaled for women, racial minorities, and the poor.

The present moment has witnessed the emergence of another social movement, that of the far- and Alt-right (fascist and neo-fascist groups both on- and offline), in the streets, in mass culture, and, significantly, on our university campuses. The ranks of the right have swelled under Trump; today there are more than 600 extreme-right-wing hate groups, according to the Southern Poverty Law Center, 121 of which are open neo-Nazi organizations.[1] Between 2017 and 2019, the number of white nationalist groups increased by 55 percent. The SPLC notes that Trump's anti-immigrant stance and apparent condoning of extreme right organizing has emboldened members of these movements. Campaigns of hate have targeted intellectuals in an alignment with neoliberal professionalization of curricula. Anti-immigrant and anti-Muslim sentiment have produced violence across the country as well.

How are we to describe this unfolding? How might we explain it? What should students, scholars, and activists take away from these events, and indeed, from the many powerful protest movements across history? These questions and their answers are the subject of this book: the rhetoric of movements for social justice.

While not all contemporary social movements seek social justice, students and others are demonstrating a renewed interest in social change and how they can participate in its processes. For example, as I write, students at Columbia, Yale and universities across the nation are occupying campus spaces, building encampments, and facing arrest and disciplinary action. They are protesting Israel's war on Gaza and U.S. support for the Israeli action.[2]

As another example, on my former campus of Syracuse University, a combative movement exploded in defense of the oppressed and exploited on campus in the wake of the revelation of horrifying videos taken by members of a fraternity on campus. In the videos, young men are shown engaging in simulated sexual assault against a disabled person and using racist epithets. However, hundreds of students flowed into the quad, demanding university reforms and a town hall with the Chancellor.[3] The Chancellor acceded.

And likewise, at California State University, Fullerton, students and faculty were shocked in spring, 2022, when the administration unilaterally and without notice closed the University's Women's Center, gutting its office and leaving nothing behind. Like centers for Black and Latine students, the Women's Center had been in place since a social movement demanding space for women's community and organizing won it. Undergraduates, graduate students, student organizations, and faculty—particular those in Women's and Gender Studies—mounted a movement asking the administration to re-instate the Center—with more resources and staffing. Some faculty worked inside the University Senate to put pressure on the administration. A group called WAGE—Women's and Gender Equality—formed and planned meetings and demonstrations. By the end of the Spring semester, the Center had been re-instated, rehoused, and provided funding and staffing.[4]

In 2022 and 2023, a wave of labor actions swept U.S. campuses, organizing graduate workers, faculty, and staff demanding raises,

FIGURE 0.2 Rutgers University faculty on strike on April 10, 2023.

changes in fee structures, job security for part-time faculty, increases in graduate fellowships, and more. At Rutgers in April 2023, a one-week strike pressured the system to grant an astonishing 40 percent raise and job security for adjuncts (part-time, contingent faculty, which at Rutgers and around the country, account for more than 60 percent of undergraduate instruction), large gains for graduate students, and raises for tenured and tenure-track faculty.[5]

There are dozens of other such examples, perhaps on your own campus, showing how relevant the study of the rhetoric of social movements is—right where you are.

Social Movements: A Rhetorical Perspective

This book is designed to help you understand these events and many other instances of social movements. **Social movements** are collective, concerted, organized, and strategic campaigns to win social change. Such movements have been studied by sociologists, historians, geographers, anthropologists, and more. Here we take a particular perspective in order to describe, explain, and participate in social movements: a rhetorical perspective. To study the **rhetoric of social movements** is to focus on how social movement actors employ words, sounds, images, and bodies as symbolic resources in the struggle for influence. It is also to focus on how established institutions and interests also deploy words, sounds, images, bodies—and violence—in attempts to limit the influence of agitation.

The Book's Theoretical Perspective

This book is focused on the **rhetoric** of social movements. Rhetoric is the practice and study of how human beings strategically use the resources language, image, sound, and more to achieve their purposes with audiences. Thus, a rhetorical perspective on social movements emphasizes strategic communication in the service of social change. This book covers the rhetorics—visual, aural, verbal, and technological—of social change actors across a range of U.S. social movements. Our theoretical perspective emphasizes the interrelationship of agitation and control and the spectrum of movement activities from the reformist to the revolutionary. One useful way of conceptualizing social movements comes to us from the 20th-century theorist Antonio Gramsci.

Gramsci's perspective—about the mutual engagement of struggle and control—lends itself well to this project. Gramsci's conceptualization of the interaction of **hegemony** (political and economic control by established powers) and **counterhegemony** (resistance to and organization against established powers, although this is not a term Gramsci coined) and his distinction between the **war of position**—a limited struggle in culture and politics—and the **war of maneuver**—a strategic challenge to an oppressive system as a whole—allows us to theorize social movements along a spectrum from reformist to revolutionary. His emphasis on the significance of culture in the process of social change helps us take struggle in political and popular culture very seriously.

This theoretical perspective is quite useful in understanding movements as the production of counterhegemonic rhetoric and social movement activity to challenge hegemonic power in struggles for social justice. The process of counterhegemony includes both ideological (cultural/rhetorical) work and the deployment of political and economic clout. Movements are not simply a matter of ideas taking off or ideas failing to reach others; rather, they are a matter of taking advantage of opportunities and weaknesses in the hegemonic order to insert agitational rhetorics, build opposition groups, and, ultimately, challenge institutions to change. But if the window of opportunity closes or if the powerful crush movements with force, no amount of the best possible rhetorical effort can sustain a movement, and it will go into decline or hibernation.

From this perspective, the point of studying social movements is not only to describe them but also to explain them: why they succeed and using what means, why they fail and in what contexts and conditions, and in whose interests they operate. The story of social movements is a story of both **agitation**—the organized activity and rhetoric of collectives engaged in challenging established institutions, norms, practices, laws, and more—and **control**—attempts on the part of established institutions and leaders to limit the influence of agitation.[6,7]

This book presumes the value of the struggle for social justice as a common good. As the next chapter shows, the injustices facing oppressed and exploited groups in the United States are real and significant. Historically, movements for social change have emerged to challenge injustice and to win gains for such groups. In the recognition of real injustice, this book is not only about understanding social movements but also about how you, the student, can use this information to become an agent of transformation yourself. It is an exciting time when you can see how fruitful movements for social justice can be. It is a moment of great opportunity and great peril for those who seek freedom and justice. It is not an exaggeration to say that the shape of society to come depends upon what you, along with others, do today.

Questions for Discussion

1. What movements for or against social justice have happened on your campus? Who were their organizers? What were their messages? What effects did these movements have on campus?
2. Have you participated in any social movement activities? What, when, where, and why? What is your overall assessment of the success or failure of that event or movement?

Credits

Fig. 0.1: Copyright © by The All-Nite Images (CC BY-SA 2.0) at https://commons.wikimedia.org/wiki/File:Black_Lives_Matter_Black_Friday_%2815742148387%29.jpg.

Fig. 0.2: Copyright © by SeichanGant (CC BY-SA 4.0) at https://commons.wikimedia.org/wiki/File:Labor_Strike_at_Rutgers_University_104.jpg.

1

Why Social Movements?

The Realities and Rhetorics of Injustice

KEY TERMS

social justice
injustice
oppression
racism
rhetoric of family values
Latine
First Nations
Islamophobia
sexism
misogyny
gender
gender oppression
transphobia
gender identity
gender expression
cis-gender
homophobia
heteronormativity
exploitation
class/social class
disability
ableism
intersectionality
hegemony

Social movements don't arise out of nowhere. There are some scholars who consider protest to be irrational and ineffective, and sometimes you might look around and wonder why groups of people are agitating loudly and challenging established institutions and ways of life. However, most of the time, organized movements are understandable, laudable, and effective collective responses to perceived and experienced injustice on the part of social groups. Rhetoric is an important factor in the perpetuation of and challenges to injustice. This chapter briefly defines justice and injustice and surveys the major axes along which injustice occurs: race, gender, sexuality, class, and ability. It also describes the rhetorical practices used to justify ongoing injustice.

This information credibly represents the harms faced by oppressed and exploited groups in society. We need to be aware of these realities to understand the conditions to which social movements respond and recognize the reasonableness and necessity of groups of people taking action to defend their identities, interests, well-being—their very lives. This list of injustices is comprehensive but not exhaustive; as you read, you might think about injustices you would add to this list. This chapter aims to provide this context so that you might remember the real social conditions affecting ordinary people in our society as you move forward through the subsequent chapters.

Defining Justice and Injustice

Scholars from many disciplines including philosophy, religion, sociology, political science and government, social work, race and gender studies, and communication (among others), have refined our ideas about what constitutes justice and injustice. In brief, **social justice** is the state of fairness and equal treatment across the domains of social life: the nation-state, the economy, the culture, social settings, and private life. Justice is an ideal that calls for enforcement of its terms.

There are many different kinds of justice. We most commonly think about justice in terms of *corrective justice*, in which an individual who has done harm to another is punished for wrongdoing. However, advocates of social justice often reject the idea that harm is only a matter of individual wrong action addressable through the law. *Distributive justice* demands actual redress of inequality in the form of distribution of economic and other goods. *Substantive justice* is met when institutions and people are held accountable in meaningful ways for their actions and ideas. *Reparative and restorative justice* attempts to sustain community by enabling perpetrators of injustice to atone for their actions and re-establish trust in their communities while still being held accountable for harm. *Participatory justice* ensures that those directly impacted by harm are included in decision-making processes about conditions that affect them the most. *Procedural justice* is when the process to resolve disputes is fair.

One particular form of injustice of special relevance to rhetorical studies is *epistemic injustice*, defined by Miranda Fricker, José Medina, and others as the condition of not having one's voice, experience, and reality recognized or included in the prevailing common sense of society.[1] An example of epistemic injustice is when a Black person is told that they are "imagining things" or "exaggerating" when they critique racism. Today's right-wing denial (taking the form of an attack on "Critical Race

Theory") of the relevance of historical oppression, including slavery, represents epistemic injustice.[2] Thus, epistemic injustice occurs on a societal level: Establishment discourses that deny the realities of oppression contribute to epistemic injustice. In contrast, *epistemic justice* is achieved when groups, often in social movements, make themselves heard and their claims recognized by broader society. Every group discussed below faces epistemic injustice when the realities of their oppression are denied in society. Every group discussed below has challenged epistemic injustice by making its voices heard in social movements. Finally, *recognition justice* is the state of affairs in which the dignity and humanity of oppressed and exploited groups in relation to dominant groups are recognized.[3]

Injustice is, then, the opposite of justice: the lack of fairness and equal treatment and lack of the enforcement of those goals. It is the failure of society to redress the wrongs of violence and inequality. It is the failure of accountability for harmful and discriminatory ideas and actions. Injustice is related to **oppression**, or the systematic subjugation of and discrimination against particular groups of people based on their identity. Injustice is also related to processes of *dispossession*, or the systemic theft of land and property and the denial of access to life-sustaining resources like food, water, housing, and more. Injustice

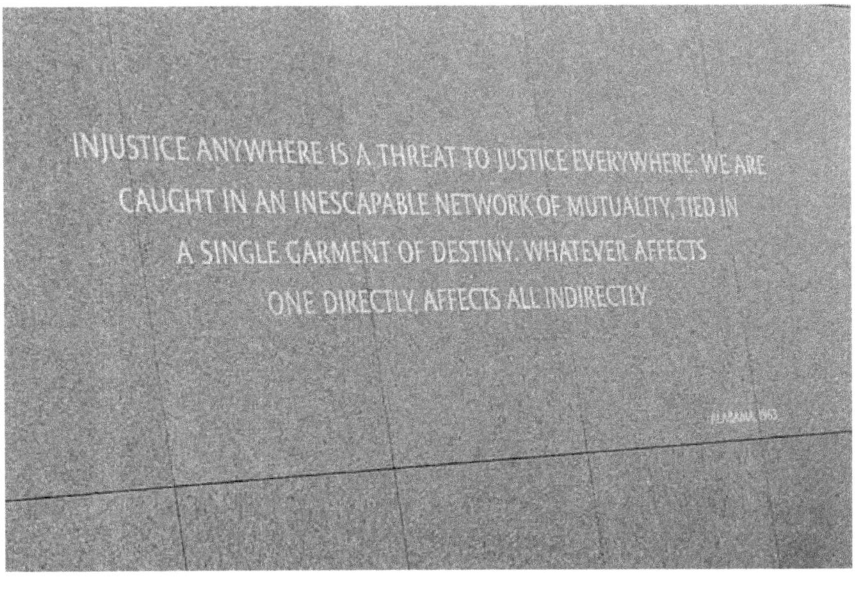

FIGURE 1.1 A wall inscribed with a quotation from Dr. Martin Luther King's Letter from a Birmingham Jail stands in West Potomac Park next to the National Mall, Wahington DC.

and oppression are real and affect many different groups of people. Injustice prompts social movements whose goals include fairness, equality, freedom from violence, and the rejection and revision of stereotypical and demeaning cultural ideas. Oftentimes, these goals are sought and won in tandem. If we are to understand the rhetoric of social movements, we must examine *why* they arise in response to injustice.

Injustices of Race

Racism is a set of institutional exclusions of, routine violence against, and cultural defamation of racialized minority groups in society motivated by hatred and/or fear of racial and ethnic difference. It is also motivated by the desire to maintain the privileges afforded to white people. In addition, it is motivated by the desire of dominant groups to maintain their power and wealth in society.

Black people in the United States lag behind white people in homeownership, wealth, and income. Black people are at least twice as likely as whites to be poor or unemployed, and workers in Black households earn around half of what the average white household brings in. Black people are more than twice as likely than white people to live in poverty. In addition, white households maintain ten times the wealth of both Black and Latine[4] households. This figure includes the fact that white people are far more likely to own their homes than other racial groups.[5]

The Brookings Institute reports that, with regard to education, there are massive disparities in education levels between Black and white students. Just as in the middle of the 20th century, schools are largely segregated (although not by law) and public schools spend twice as much on the education of white, suburban students than they do in Black and other racial minority communities. While rich schools have pools and computer labs, poor ones lack safe facilities, current textbooks, well qualified teachers (who gravitate toward the higher salaries afforded by affluent schools), small (and more effective) class sizes, and many other resources.[6]

The COVID-19 pandemic that began in 2020 intensified these differences. American Progress reported in 2021 that the pandemic hit when gaps and wealth were already at their widest.[7] The report summarizes the situation:

> Black households suffered more in the pandemic in large part because they needed more but had much less wealth than white households. Wealth, both as an emergency

> buffer and as a means to invest in people's futures, became critically important.
>
> Millions of households, especially African American and Latino households, faced unemployment and multiple health emergencies more or less from one day to the next. Yet many of these same households had few or no emergency savings to fall back on during this time. When people lost their jobs, many needed to rely on emergency savings, leaving them with less financial security as the pandemic unfolded. For example, in 2020, 46.7 percent of unemployed white households could not come up with $400 in an emergency, while 65.2 percent of unemployed Black households lacked access to $400 in such situations.

We might also ask ourselves how it is that more than 45 percent of white families, who are relatively privileged, also have too little wealth to weather emergencies. But the gaps in wealth by race are stark. How are such disparities justified? As Bryan McCann, Michelle Alexander, Stuart Hall, and other scholars have noted, contemporary anti-Black racism is justified in portrayals of Black men as defined by criminality. In the news media, Black Americans are overrepresented as perpetrators of crime, which stokes fear and racial tension among white citizens.[8] The perception of Black men as automatically criminal warrants violent policing and disparate incarceration and sentencing rates. In the United States, Black men are 2.5 times more likely to be killed by police than white men.[9] Black men are also subject to vigilante violence, in which white groups like the Ku Klux Klan and today's white supremacist organizations harm or kill Black people as a form of discipline and retribution.

The representations of Black people as dangerous, lazy, sexually aggressive, and unintelligent come down to us from the time of slavery. Then, these ideas justified the treatment of slaves as sub-human and undeserving of the rights and freedoms laid out in the U.S. Constitution and Declaration of Independence.

Another set of ideas that warrants unequal treatment is the **rhetoric of family values**. White citizens and policymakers often attribute the struggles of Black Americans to succeed to some families' allegedly "pathological" households headed by single women. The ideal of "family values" implicitly justifies the exclusions of Black people from equal housing, education, employment, and wealth.[10] A modern form of discourse legitimating ongoing racist discrimination is "post-race racism," which denies the continuing force of racism in society.[11]

Of course, racism is not a problem that only Black people face. Discrimination against Mexican-Americans and other **Latine** groups is most pronounced at the U.S.-Mexico border, where migrants seeking entry to the United States are detained (including children) and deported, subjected to violent treatment by immigration enforcement agencies. Latine communities face the same kinds of discrimination in housing, education, and wealth that Black Americans bear. Public discourse about immigrants features images of "exemplary assimilated individuals" while the racist, discriminatory policies and institutions of neoliberal capitalism carry on.[12]

People belonging to the **First Nations**—tribal societies of North America colonized by Europeans starting in the early 17th century—also face racist discrimination with material consequences: "Based on the data from the 2018 U.S. Census cited by Poverty USA, Native Americans have the highest poverty rate among all minority groups."[13] Motivated by colonialism and ideologies of racial superiority, and later by the doctrine of Manifest Destiny, European colonizers engaged in genocide against indigenous tribes and displaced their peoples while occupying land previously held by native peoples. The discourse of settler colonialism includes romantic stereotypes of Indians as "noble savages," while omitting stories of the historical oppression and hardships they face.[14]

The dominant culture's portrayal of Muslims (especially men) as terrorists to be reviled and feared (in a discourse called **Islamophobia**) has justified violence against Muslims, barriers to immigration, and, ultimately, wars in the Middle East.[15]

The ideological division of society into "races" has served throughout history to prevent exploited groups across racial divides to unite in common struggle against oppression. In addition, the denunciation of the Black family as "pathological" justifies the broader privatization of social responsibility. In other words, the mainstream family ideal tells every family, not just Black families, that they are on their own and should not count on support from their employers or from the government.

What do all of these factors mean for the study of and participation in social movements? Participants in movements against racism have demanded changes in all of these spaces and institutions throughout our nation's history. The antislavery movement of the 19th century, the civil rights and Black Power movements of the 1950s and 1960s, the Chicano rights movement, the American Indian Movement, and the movement for Black lives today all have struggled for civil rights,

Image 1.1

resources, freedom from violence, and the elimination of racist ideas circulating in culture. To understand their actions and ideas, it is important to know what they are fighting against and fighting for. To look for how these movements make shifts in culture and ideas (against rhetorics of criminalization and family values, for example) requires that we understand the cultural and ideological contexts of these movements.

Injustices of Gender

Sexism is a set of institutional exclusions of, routine violence against, and cultural defamation of women in society motivated by the hatred and fear of gender difference, also called **misogyny**. It is also motivated by the desire to maintain the privileges afforded to many men. In addition, it is motivated by the desire of dominant groups to maintain their power and wealth in society. Injustices rooted in sexism are functions of oppression based on **gender**, the social construction of one's identity as masculine or feminine, often assigned a birth according to anatomical differences.

According to a Pew survey, 42 percent of American women have faced discrimination in the workplace, including exclusion from high-paying career options and certain kinds of jobs and inequality in wages. Indeed, in 2019, women on average earned only 79 cents for every dollar made, on average, by men.[16] The #MeToo movement that arose in 2018 has called attention to the rampant against sexual harassment and abuse of women in the workplace.

One in four women experiences severe intimate partner violence in the forms of physical abuse, sexual assault, and stalking. One in ten women has been raped by an intimate partner. One in five women has been raped in her lifetime, compared to one in 71 men. Women lack equal representation among corporate and economic elites. Despite increasing gains over the past 100 years (since women won the right to vote), there are three men for every woman elected to Congress.[17] Among industrial nations with democratic political institutions, the United States is unique in never having elected a woman to executive office.

As with racism, there are sets of cultural ideas with deep historical roots that justify these injustices. One is the belief that women's place is in the domestic or private sphere. Women, the argument goes, are less suited to the rough-and-tumble of politics. When women do enter the political fray, they walk a tightrope between the expectation to be feminine and the need to be powerful.

Even though most women must and do work outside the home, there is still a strong ideology (again, related to the rhetoric of family values) that women should take care of every need of the private family from food, clothing and shelter to education and socialization. Indeed, women in the United States do more than two-thirds of household labor on average, performing what some researchers have called the "double shift." The idea that taking care of families is women's work justifies the neglect of families' needs by employers and the government (for example, the provision of free or subsidized childcare).

The other significant rhetoric justifying women's oppression is the idea that women's bodies should be controlled and disciplined. This discourse includes the treatment of women and their bodies as sex objects (for example, in advertising, and pornography, including pornographic "deep fakes" created by AIs) to be used and abused by men at will. Images of women as sex objects cultivate a culture in which rape is normalized. In addition, the control of women's bodies extends to the regulation of pregnancy and abortion. The abortion rights (or pro-choice) movement emerged in the 1960s to win women's right to control their reproduction.

Gender-based oppression is not only felt by women whose bodies are anatomically female. Such oppression also affects gender non-conforming persons, including transgender and gender non-binary people.

Injustices of Gender Identity and Expression

Gender oppression is a set of institutional exclusions of, routine violence against, and cultural defamation of gender non-binary persons in society motivated by the hatred and fear of gender diversity and fluidity, also called **transphobia** when referring to transgender persons. It is also motivated by the desire to maintain the privileges afforded to many cisgender people. In addition, it is motivated by the desire of dominant groups to maintain their power and wealth in society.

The question of gender discrimination and violence are complicated by the realities and experiences of transgender and gender non-binary persons. Increasingly, people whose biological anatomy/gender assignment at birth does not match their felt gender identities are becoming visible and legible to society. In addition, there are growing numbers of people who are coming out as not wanting to belong to either restrictive side of the culturally enforced gender binary (male/female, masculine/feminine). Some people do not want to be "boxed in" in this way. **Gender identity** refers to the felt identity of a person in terms of their gender; **gender expression** refers to how that person presents themselves to others. Gender identity and expression do not necessarily match. In contrast, those whose felt identity corresponds to their gender assignment (based on anatomy) at birth are referred to as **cis-gender**.

There is an ongoing, partial culture shift to recognize transgender and non-binary persons, for example, in using a person's chosen pronouns to refer to them. Major dictionaries and presses have accepted the use of the plural pronouns "they" and "them" as singular pronouns referring to persons who are neither "he" nor "she." There are other pronoun systems adopted by persons who do not wish to be labeled as either male or female, masculine or feminine.

Despite such recognition, the oppression of transgender and non-binary persons is intense. One in five transgender and non-binary people is denied medical treatment, when access to hormones and specific medical expertise are crucial. Transgender people have difficulty in finding and keeping jobs; unemployment rates for transgender people are twice as high than for cisgender people. This difficulty is especially pronounced for transwomen and transwomen of color. Transgender and nonbinary persons are also subject to intense violence. The Human Rights Campaign reports that in 2019, there were at least 27 deaths of transgender or gender non-conforming people, most of whom were Black transgender women. As of July 2020, there were 22 reported murders of transgender and non-conforming people in that year.[18]

The stigmatization of and violence against gender divergent people is connected to the same sets of ideas that justify the oppression of women: A fixed gendered order sustains the normative family and the privatization of social responsibility. Violations of the capacity to "fix" gender are threatening to this ideology. In addition, in a society and

FIGURE 1.2 A June 2016 vigil in Portland, Oregon, commemorating the Pulse Nightclub massacre in Orlando, Florida.

language that is dependent on binary concepts to understand reality (me/you, self/other, man/woman, black/white, citizen/noncitizen, and so on) the recognition of fluid identities and meanings might call into question many patterns of discrimination and injustice.

Injustices of Sexuality

Oppression based on sexual orientation and practice is a set of institutional exclusions of, routine violence against, and cultural defamation of lesbian, gay, bisexual, asexual, pansexual, and others whose sexuality does not fit a heteronormative social order motivated by hatred or fear of sexual difference (**homophobia**). Most of the time, scholars and activists use the acronym LGBTQ to refer to sexual minorities who face similar oppressions. Sometimes, the letter "A" is added to represent asexuals and other letters are added to make the acroynym more and more inclusive. If you see the acronym LGBTIA, it might refer to "lesbian, gay, bisexual, transgender, intersex, and/or asexual." Sometimes the word *queer* is added—LGBTQ—and used as an umbrella term encompassing multiple sexual orientations and identities. The "queer" label also signals a more critical and radical stance toward sexual liberation. Rather than seeking equal rights for gays and lesbians, queer activists also affirm what is unique about their different identities and experiences. In addition, when LGBTQ communities embraced the term "queer" to describe themselves, they were appropriating what had been once used as a term of derision and shame and using it in an emancipatory, or freeing, way. The movements for LGBTQ liberation have challenged homophobia and heteronormativity.

Heteronormativity refers to the widespread assumption that heterosexuality is the only normal and correct sexual orientation. It refers to how being heterosexual is automatically assumed and valued. LGBTQ oppression is motivated by the desire to maintain the privileges afforded to many heterosexual people. In addition, it is motivated by the desire of dominant groups to maintain their power and wealth in society. Some queer scholars have criticized how LGBTQ people uncritically adopt the conventional norms of family and nation, calling those practices "*homonormativity*."[19]

Movements on behalf of lesbian, gay, bisexual, transgender, and other sexual minorities' rights have met with success, for example, with the 2015 Supreme Court ruling legalizing same-gender marriage across the United States. Moreover, on June 15, 2020, the Supreme Court of the United States ruled that the Civil Rights Act of 1964 protects employees from discrimination on the basis of sexual orientation or gender identity. This means that workers across the U.S. cannot be fired for being LGBTQ. As of 2020, 93 percent of Fortune 500 companies had non-discrimination policies that include sexual orientation. Ninety-one percent had non-discrimination policies that include gender identity. Many companies also provide other benefits. Fifty-three percent include domestic partner benefits, and 65 percent include transgender-inclusive benefits.

Despite such gains, discrimination in the workplace against people whose sexual orientations and practices diverge from heteronormative expectations is ongoing. Twenty percent of LGBTQ people reported employment discrimination based on sexual orientation and/or gender identity. The problem is more pronounced with regard to LGBTQ people of color. Research has found that 37 percent of these people face workplace injustice.[20]

More telling are the rising numbers of hate crimes committed on the basis of sexual orientation. The 2016 massacre at the Pulse nightclub in Orlando targeted Latine LGBTQ people. The shooting left 50 people dead. It was, at the time, the deadliest mass shooting in the United States and remains the deadliest attack on LGBTQ persons to date.

While extreme, the Orlando massacre was not an isolated incident. *USA Today* reported on FBI data showing that hate crimes based on sexual orientation rose each year from 2014 to 2017, when 1,130 incidents were reported, the majority against gay men.[21] Violence and discrimination in the workplace and other domains are closely linked in a reciprocal way: Public hatred against oppressed groups is a response to gains made in institutional settings. At the same time, widespread hateful ideas toward particular groups justifies injustices in institutional settings. Hate crimes in the context of sexuality, gender, or race create cultures in which discrimination becomes acceptable and can be understood as attempts to keep groups making gains toward justice "in their place."

By blaming particular minority groups for social problems and setting groups of ordinary people against each other, political and economic elites distract citizens from institutional and systemic problems and weaken the capacity of social movements to organize across lines of difference. Oppressions based on race, gender, and sexuality often serve a broader class divide in contemporary society by encouraging separation and blaming particular groups for social problems.

Injustices of Class

In 2011, the "Occupy" (originally "Occupy Wall Street") movement called attention to the significant divide between the well-being and interests of a wealthy elite in society (dubbed by the movement as "the one percent") and the rest of the people (whom the movement called "the 99 percent"). The symbolic value of these labels was their ability to call attention to how a small elite in the United States and around the world relies upon the labor and cooperation of the vast majority of people in order to sustain profitability and the security of those elites in power. Movement activists laid out what is essentially a Marxist critique of class-based exploitation.

Social class refers to the economic layer or position held in the economy by a group of people. In Marxist thought, there is a

FIGURE 1.3 Amazon warehouse workers at four Amazon warehouses on Staten Island rallied outside the National Labor Relations Board petitioning it to authorize a union vote on October 25.

fundamental divide between a *ruling class*, which owns and controls the production, distribution, and cost of goods in the capitalist market, on the one hand; and a *working class,* which consists of all people (across race, gender, and sexuality) who must work for a wage in the economy and who do not control their workplaces, on the other. On this view, the working class is exploited by the ruling class in order to secure the latter's profits.

Related to the concept of oppression, **exploitation** refers to the process by which corporate owners rely upon the labor of ordinary people to create commodities—the necessities and luxuries of life that are bought and sold. If workers were paid the entire value of their labor, by definition the employers would see no profit. It is the difference between what workers are paid and how much value they create for employers that defines the concept of exploitation. Employers pay the minimum necessary to sustain workers (although only just barely in many cases) and take the remainder of what the workers produce as profit.

Marxist critics understand exploitation to be another kind of injustice motivated by the drive for profitability and economic growth in capitalist society. In July, 2021, Amazon owner Jeff Bezos built a rocket ship and took it briefly into space with several other wealthy people.

Upon his return to Earth, Bezos thanked his customers *and* employees, telling them: "You paid for this."[22] The use of profits derived from the labor of hundreds of thousands of people for a luxury adventure is the very definition of exploitation.

Whether one believes that capitalism and the profit motive are harmful, the class divide in the United States is quite stark. According to sociologist Geoffrey Wodtke, the distribution of personal income in the U.S., already profoundly unequal, has become substantially more unequal since the early 1980s.[23] Following the sociological research of Eric Olin Wright and others, Wodtke asserts that there are several social classes in contemporary capitalist society: the owners and employers of corporate firms, the employees or workers in those firms, managers and bureaucrats who enable the operation of corporate firms, small-business proprietors and others who own and operate their own small-scale operations, and the unemployed.

Income inequality is closely tied to one's place among these categories. From the 1980s through the 2000s, income for proprietors of large firms increased by 60 percent while the incomes of managers and small proprietors remained stagnant and the incomes of working people and the unemployed fell sharply.

Income inequality in the United States is the highest among all of the G7 nations, according to a Pew study.[24] And the gap in wealth between America's richer and poorer groups more than doubled between 1989 and 2016 such that by 2016, the top five percent of the United States population held 248 times as much wealth as those at the median, up from 114 times in 1989.

The richest families are also the only ones whose wealth increased in the years after the start of the Great Recession in 2008. From 2007 to 2016, the median net worth of the top twenty percent increased by 13 percent to $1.2 million. For the top five percent, it increased by four percent, to $4.8 million. In contrast, the median net worth of families in lower tiers of wealth decreased by at least twenty percent.

According to the Urban Institute, average wealth has increased over the past 50 years, but it has not grown equally for all groups. Between 1963 and 2016, poor families went from having no wealth on average to being $1000 or more in debt. While those in the middle of the spectrum doubled their wealth, those at the top—in the 90th percentile) increased their wealth by 500 percent. Moreover, those at the *very* top—in the 99th percentile) had seven times as much wealth at the end of that time period than before.[25]

Families of color will soon make up a majority of the population, but most continue to fall behind whites in building wealth. In 1963, the average wealth of white families was $121,000 higher than the average wealth of nonwhite families. By 2016, the average total wealth of white families ($919,000) was more than $700,000 higher than the average wealth of Black families ($140,000) and of Hispanic families ($192,000). Put another way, white family wealth was nearly eight times greater than Black family wealth and five times greater than Hispanic family wealth in 2016.[26] Despite some fluctuations over the past five decades, this disparity is as high or higher than it was in 1963.

These differences have serious consequences for the quality of education, housing, health care, retirement, and more. In addition, the divergence of income and wealth between classes is exacerbated by race and gender, as women and racial minority workers are disadvantaged more greatly than white working men. These complicating factors illustrate how oppression and exploitation happen along intersecting vectors of injustice.

FIGURE 1.4 Amazon workers picket a warehouse in Ontario, CA, on October 14, 2022.

Injustices of Ability

Economic injustice is connected to discrimination against people based on their abilities and disabilities. **Disability** is a cultural construct or ideological definition of people whose bodies don't conform to social ideals of "able-bodiedness." People defined in our society as disabled often are stigmatized as lacking the capacity to labor at capitalist ideals of productivity. Injustices affecting people with disabilities (including physical, intellectual, and psychological disabilities) include lack of access to education, employment, housing, healthcare, transportation, and public spaces. Historically, a rhetoric of **ableism** has defined people with disabilities are inferior and held that meeting culturally-defined bodily ideals are determining measures of human worth.[27] Keith Rostenthal lays out the consequences of oppression based on disability:

> Disabled people in the U.S. today experience a poverty rate of approximately 30 percent; comprise 40 percent of the total homeless population; have an active labor market participation rate of less than 20 percent, despite self-reporting a preference to do so at a rate well over 60 percent. Hundreds of thousands of disabled people remain today living in institutional or carceral environments, such as nursing homes or prisons, where conditions tend towards the cruel or barbaric.[28]

Ableism has variously defined the disabled as objects of pity and charity, medical cases requiring medical intervention and institutionalization, and heroes who have overcome their disabilities, among other ideas. Movements for disability rights have challenged ableism and argued for inclusion of disabled people in political, economic, urban/architectural/spatial, and cultural domains and have won major legislative reforms.[29]

Movements for disability justice have gone further to demand respect for the autonomy, integrity, cultural identity, and uniqueness of people with disabilities and their capacity to determine their conditions of life and futures.[30] Disability justice asks society to adapt to the needs of all *body-minds* (a term that recognizes the interconnection between our thinking, feeling, and physical bodies) in the processes of learning, working, communicating, and moving. Disability justice puts disability in an intersectional context, recognizing that capitalism and systems of racial and gender-based oppression are systematically woven together with disability-based oppression.

Intersectionality and Injustice

Increasingly, scholars of injustice and challenges to injustice have called attention to how people do not suffer oppression along only one identity axis. Black feminist scholar Kimberlé Crenshaw coined the term **intersectionality** to describe this feature of social reality.[31] A Black lesbian, working-class person experiences more and different kinds of violence, hardship, and inequality than a white male, heterosexual worker, on average, for example.

As an example of intersectionality, I am struck by a June 26, 2020 account in *The New York Times* by Caroline Randall Williams. In an essay called, "My Body is a Confederate Monument," Williams opens the narrative with the chilling statement: "I have rape-colored skin."[32] This beginning signals an intersectional analysis: Williams and her female ancestors were not only oppressed as slaves on the basis of race. They also faced racialized gender oppression, a situation in which white slaveowners regularly raped their Black slaves, leading to an involuntary mixed-race genealogy and heritage that Black women today understand as a product of race, gender, and the historic violation of both. She writes,

> *I am proof.* I am proof that whatever else the South might have been, or might believe itself to be, it was and is a space whose prosperity and sense of romance and nostalgia were built upon the grievous exploitation of black life.

Williams' body is, in this way, the site of intersecting identities, oppressions, and history. She mobilizes this bodily knowledge in support of the movement for Black lives.

Conclusion: Injustice and Social Movements

What do these stories mean for the study of and participation in social movements? Participants in movements against oppression, exploitation, sexism, heterosexism, homophobia, and transphobia have demanded changes in all of these spaces and institutions throughout our nation's history. The women's suffrage movement, movements against harassment and violence such as the #MeToo movement, movements for gay rights and liberation, and emerging movements for transgender justice all have struggled for rights, resources, freedom from violence, and the elimination of racist ideas circulating in culture. The labor movement has challenged exploitation and fought for higher wages, greater workplace protections, and the inclusion of all groups in various domains of work. To understand the actions and ideas of participants in these movements, it is important to know what they are fighting against and fighting for. To look for how these movements make shifts in culture and ideas (against rhetorics of criminalization and family values, for example) requires that we understand the cultural and ideological contexts of these movements.

The next chapter introduces our framework for understanding how rhetoric and other forms of influence contribute to both injustice and challenges to injustice in social movements. That framework is based on the concept of **hegemony**, defined by Italian Marxist Antonio Gramsci as the balance of economic, political, and cultural power at a given moment in history. This balance is often stable, favoring the interests of political and economic elites. However, the entire history of social movements is the history of how, time and again, ordinary people organize themselves to rise up and challenge the balance of power, often resulting in dramatic change. Rhetoric is at the core of that process.

Questions for Discussion

1. After reading this chapter, do you understand the terms "justice" and "injustice"? Define them in your own words.
2. Define and explain the key concepts of justice, injustice, oppression, exploitation, and intersectionality. Give examples.
3. Are you convinced by this chapter that institutional, group, and interpersonal injustices are real? Why or why not?
4. Do you think groups of people are right to rise up against injustice?
5. What other injustices have you heard of and would like to discuss?
6. Describe an instance from your own experience, the experience of your family, or the experience of the communities to which you belong when you felt injustice, oppression, or exploitation. How does your experience relate to the general descriptions of oppression and injustice in this chapter? *There is no obligation to share your experience if you are uncomfortable doing so for any reason.*
7. Has the situation for the groups discussed in this chapter changed? Has it improved, gotten worse, or stayed the same? What events led to change, if any? How do you know? Provide evidence for your answer.
8. In your experience, is there evidence on your campus of inequality and injustice? Of movements in response and meaningful change?

Credits

Fig. 1.1: L. Cunningham, "Racial Injustice," https://nara.getarchive.net/media/a-wall-inscribed-with-a-quote-from-dr-martin-luther-9e719a, 2013.

IMG 1.1: Copyright © by Anne Marie Champagne (CC BY-SA 4.0) at https://commons.wikimedia.org/wiki/File:TRANS_RIGHT.jpg.

Fig. 1.2: Copyright © by sarahmirk (CC BY-SA 4.0) at https://commons.wikimedia.org/wiki/File:Vigil_to_mourn_Orlando%27s_pulse_shooting.jpg.

Fig. 1.3: Copyright © by Joe Piette (CC BY-SA 2.0) at https://commons.wikimedia.org/wiki/File:Amazon_warehouse_workers_outside_the_National_Labor_Relations_Board_01.jpg.

2

Social Movements and Hegemony

KEY TERMS

social movement
agitators
controllers
establishment
strategy
tactics
ideology
hegemony
avoidance
counter-persuasion
suppression
adjustment
capitulation
fascism
civil society
reform
revolution
war of position
war of maneuver
populism

Consider the following scenario: On your campus, hundreds of activists have occupied the main mall or plaza, erecting tents, banners, and signs indicating that they are protesting the war conducted by Israel in Gaza and that they are defending Palestinian rights. You don't know much about the conflict but would like to know more, so you go out to visit the encampment. You listen to speakers at the ongoing rally/teach-in talk about their reasons for protesting. You also learn that the previous night, the university administration had turned the sprinklers on, soaking the encampment in near-freezing temperatures. The encampment is still there, and people are going in and out, bringing food and supplies —until authorities close the entry. Campus police, backed up by city police in riot gear, arrive and demand that the activists evacuate.

When the activists refuse, the police move in and make arrests while the demonstrators chant, "Free Palestine!" and "Whose university? Our university!" Some demonstrators surround a police car demanding that the person who was taken into custody be let go. The police let the arrestee go but carry on with efforts to evacuate the space. The students in the encampment are debating what to do next. They want

FIGURE 2.1 The demands of the University of California, Los Angeles Palestine solidarity encampment, May 18, 2024.

to continue to put pressure on the University administration to allow the protest and to divest financially from corporations whose activities support or profit Israel. The administration is calling the demonstrators violent and antisemitic; the demonstrators are calling the administration dictatorial and complicit in the deaths of tens of thousands of Palestinians.

Regardless of your position on this or any other issue, you wonder, what is happening here? How can we understand this conflict between administrators, police, and students? How are the demonstrators making decisions about what to do and what to say? What will happen next?

You are witnessing one expression of a social movement. The purpose of this book is to give you some conceptual tools and vocabulary to understand this and any other movement in a particular framework based on the theory of hegemony. First, we need some basic definitions, beginning with "social movement."

Defining Social Movements

Sociologists Charles Tilly and Sydney Tarrow define **social movements** simply as "contentious politics."[1] For Tilly and Tarrow, social movements happen when people are organized around common interests, who make claims based upon those interests, and engage challenges, common purposes, identities, and when they are engaged in an antagonism with elites.[2] Here we build on these authors' observations to define a *social movement as a collective, concerted, purposeful, and strategic campaign on the part of non-establishment actors targeting establishment actors and institutions with the goal of reforming or revolutionizing parts or all of a social system*. The parties in a social movement are **agitators**, who organize to challenge established forces, who, in turn attempt to assert control over the direction of the conflict. John Bowers, Donovan Ochs, Richard Jensen, and David Schultz are rhetoric scholars who have written extensively about social movements. They define agitators as people outside the normal decision-making establishment who advocate significant social change and encounter resistance from the establishment.[3] Agents of the establishment who attempt to quell agitation are **controllers**, on this model. Both sets of agents engage in rhetorical strategy and innovation over the course of a movement's existence.

In the scenario above, we can determine that what is happening involves agitators who are doing something concerted, purposeful, and strategic to pressure an established institution to make change; there are controllers, in the form of the University administration and police. The agitators are ordinary students without inherent authority, and they are facing resistance. It is fair to conclude that the encampment is part of a social movement.

Although movements can be instigated by, informed by, or inspired by individuals, movements themselves are collective or group phenomena. To say that something is "concerted" means that it is organized. Tarrow writes, "Contention always brings together subjects, objects, and claims.[4]" Movements exhibit various degrees of organization at different moments of their evolution, so even a somewhat haphazard effort can count in this definition. Social movements have the purpose of influencing establishment representatives and institutions to make changes of various scales, from the smallest reform to total revolution. The **establishment** is simply the group of people, organizations, and institutions who currently possess the preponderance of resources of and determine the direction of an organization, institution, or society as whole.

It is clear that the University administration is the establishment here, and that the demonstrators have engaged in concerted, organized work. (By definition, operatives and actions of the establishment cannot constitute a social movement, because they are determined to prevent movement, or change, from happening.)

Strategy and Tactics

In every case, movements are strategic, which is to say that their members consider not only what they intend to accomplish, but also how best to do so. A **strategy** refers to a broad plan or goal on the way to achieving a purpose. For example, in a war, a nation state might have the strategy of acquiring footholds in important launching points for ships and troops. In the case of our scenario, we can say that a strategy of this movement is to call attention to the consequences of the war and to pressure the University to act.

Tactics are the smaller units of the "how" picture: the specific means of enacting the strategy. For example, in the case of war, tactics would be the specific means by which an army (or navy, or air force) can acquire the foothold they seek. A tactic in this case might be to deploy a group to occupy the site via sea in the middle of the night. In the case of our demonstrators, their tactics have included occupying a public space, developing arguments, slogans, and chants, and resisting arrest, all of which serve the broader strategy of pressuring the university. They are in a position to determine what their next tactical choice will be: Retreat? March to the administration building to occupy those halls? Demand a meeting with the university president? Call on people from outside the university for support? Choices regarding strategies and tactics depend upon what resources—financial and other material means, membership, morale, and other goods—are available to a movement and to the establishment.[5] That means that the university is also weighing its options, one of which would be to let the encampment play out.

It is in the area of strategy and tactics that the crucial rhetorical character of social movements becomes evident. One resource available to most agitators and controllers is the capacity to influence others through communication. Controllers most often have the benefit of having already established the basic frames for rhetorical action, sets of common-sense ideas dominant in society without which we could not make sense to one another. For example, in modern democratic societies, most social movements have necessarily and wisely couched their aims in terms of the ideals of liberty, equality, and justice. In the case of our scenario, the university and society at large are invested in the rhetoric of order and civility; other common-sense ideas may be about the value and validity of Israel's actions in Gaza. Agitators then need to use rhetoric to challenge the establishment's common sense, which they are doing with their signs, slogans, and speeches.

FIGURE 2.2 Police confront the encampment at California State University, Irvine.

Sociological definitions of social movements are helpful to understanding what is playing out. Another framework that is particularly useful in understanding of how movements and their opponents struggle to challenge existing power and shape public discourse comes to us from the ideas of early-20th-century Italian theorist Antonio Gramsci who used the term "hegemony" to describe to struggle over power and influence in contemporary society.

Antonio Gramsci and the Theory of Hegemony

Antonio Gramsci was an Italian thinker and activist who came of age under the rule of the fascist dictator Benedetto Mussolini. He was educated at the University of Turin, where he joined a heady mix of intellectuals and activists in critical conversation. He left his studies in favor of growing commitments to activism, wartime journalism, and eventual leadership in both the Socialist Party and the Communist Party of Italy. The seizure of power by fascists in 1922 led to the destruction of most oppositional organizations and presses. The Communist Party was operating clandestinely during this period, and activists were continually harassed and jailed. In 1926, Mussolini finished the consolidation of power by abolishing all democratic institutions in Italy. Inspired by socialist thinkers and other anti-fascists, Gramsci became a leader in the struggle against Mussolini's rule. For that reason, the government imprisoned him and all of his fellow leaders in 1926. Gramsci was tried, convicted, and spent most of his time as a prisoner in Turin, from 1928 to 1935, after which he was transferred to a prison clinic, gravely ill (as he had been all of his life). He died in April 1937.[6]

Gramsci's intellectual work and activism did not end when he went to prison in spite of his severe illness and isolation. Instead, he continued to write and agitate from his cell and the prison yard. In addition to educating other prisoners and plotting future courses of action, Gramsci produced around 2500 pages of political theory. He had to smuggle his work—written in a kind of code to get around the censors—out of the prison with his wife Julia and Julia's sister Tatiana. During his time in prison, Gramsci was understandably preoccupied with questions of power and resistance. How did fascists rise to power in the modern society of democratic institutions? And how can the people organize against authoritarian rule and for their own control over society? The answers to these questions lay in a model of power that recognizes the importance of ideas, consciousness, and culture in the processes of both dominance and resistance.

Ideology

The concept he employed to describe to the dynamics of power he had witnessed is that of hegemony. In other contexts, you might have heard this term defined as something like "the dominant ideology," "common sense," or "rule by consent." These ways of understanding the term are partially correct. But the value of the idea lies in a more fully rounded way of understanding the term, which should be distinguished from the concept of ideology.

There are a number of different definitions of the term "ideology" by theorists representing various intellectual standpoints. In the original critical usage of the term, Karl Marx defined ideology simply as "the dominant ideas, which are the ideas of the ruling class."[7] Literary critic Terry Eagleton is also direct: Ideology is composed of "the ways in which people may come to invest in their own unhappiness."[8] Ideology consists of the language, beliefs, values, rules, norms, codes, and scripts that guide a population's knowledge and action. For Eagleton, ideology legitimates established power by making the social order seem natural, necessary, and permanent. Both Marx and Eagleton stress the capacity of ideologies to mask or mystify social reality; in other words, ideology convinces us that we are living in a good and fair society and live our lives according to our own free will. In fact, we are raised up in societies whose ideologies inculcate in us the values, beliefs, and narratives that lead to our thinking that we are free and that the world is fair. This insight was developed in the work of French theorist Louis Althusser, who said that our feeling that we are human individual subjects who have agency over our futures is the very first operation of ideology.[9] Althusser was pessimistic about our capacity to resist dominant ideologies. However, under the pressure of social movements, ideologies justifying the social order start to crack.

Out of these definitions of ideology we can craft one for our purposes here: **Ideology** as a concept refers to a set of relatively stable and broadly accepted shared ideas, motivated by the preservation of power, operating in multiple domains of society, and shaping our consciousness, identities, and actions without our conscious decision to comply. We all come to be who we are inside of idea systems that serve these functions. Ideology shapes our consciousness. Not all ideology is composed of lies, but ideologies cultivate ways of being and thinking that may or may not be in our own best interest. They form a collective "*common sense*" that seems natural, pre-given, and permanent.

For example, in modern society there is a longstanding popular narrative about "family values" that influences millions of people to form private nuclear families with the ideal (rather than the actual reality) of caretaking performed by women. It is taken for granted by many people that the "proper" biographical narrative of a citizen moves from birth through childhood and youth, through romantic involvements and education, to employment, marriage and children (who follow the same cycle), leading ultimately to retirement and death. To the extent that we hold these values and engage this narrative largely without conscious thought as to its purpose, viability, or desirability in varying circumstances, we can call it an ideology.

A critic of family values notices that participation in this narrative absolves any social institution (like nation-states and corporations) from responsibility for humans' well-being. Thus, "family values" justifies the separation of domestic, economic, and political domains, an arrangement that benefits dominant institutions in the cost-savings of caretaking, the availability of cared-for and trained-up labor, and the liberty to operate without commitments beyond their own power. Ideologies are part of hegemony. They establish what is taken-for-granted common sense until a movement comes along to destabilize them and the kinds of power they justify. Ideologies constitute only one part of the formation and maintenance of power, or hegemony.

Hegemony

For our purposes, **hegemony** is the achievement of stability in economic, political, and cultural power by a particular class. The first key part of the definition is that hegemony is an *achievement*. It is not the equivalent of dominant ideology or "false consciousness." Rather than being a static monolithic form of domination, it is something that a class of people—any class (in the Marxist sense) of people—can struggle for and win on economic, legal, political, and cultural levels, all of which are interdependent.[10] The achievement of hegemony is something that takes place through social movements. The established social order, as a structure of political alliances, is a form of hegemony, but it is always subject to disruption and contestation, which is where movements come in. Gramsci's writing in the notebooks emphasized hegemony as, in part, the production of ideas in culture and politics to win a public's "consent" to the social order in the stories that constitute society's common sense.

Of course, when we look around today, established power, social divisions, and many injustices seem to be permanent fixtures, the way things are, just "common sense." But Gramsci asked the question, how did *these people* with *what resources*, at *what point in time* use *which strategies and tactics* to come to a position of leadership? Who are the forces that can contest the hegemonic order from below, and how may they go about it? This is the key question of this book.

Every established government emerged from history. Every one of them came into being on the heels of massive revolts from below. The control of the economy by an elite class of business owners may seem wrong to many people, but also seems like "the way things are." These elites "have" or "hold" hegemony over and against us, right? Well, not exactly. They have held power for a long time, but their power, like anyone's power, is temporary, vulnerable to challenges, and in need of constant maintenance.[11]

For Gramsci, economic power, political power, and cultural influence are interdependent such that work on culture and communication (rhetoric) becomes an important element of movement action. Thus, hegemony refers to economic, political, and cultural power altogether. The authority of a nation-state or corporate elite depends upon the credibility of political institutions like Congress and the capacity of elites to dominate culture with ideas justifying their rule.

Hegemony is achieved by particular classes of people, for example the merchant class in the American colonies during the late 18th century. The reign of the market was a revolutionary idea in the 1770s when the American colonists took issue with the British monarchy. The King thought that his hegemony was not in question. But the ideals of liberty, equality, and justice were championed by a class of merchants who wanted to be free of British rule and to engage in commerce as they saw fit. The American War for Independence was a revolutionary war that put a new class of people—merchants and agriculturalists—in charge of society. It took a bloody revolution for that class to achieve its hegemony.

In one form or another, since that time, democracy as an ideology has been tied to the idea of the "free market." Capitalism is an

FIGURE 2.3 George Washington during the U.S. War for Independence.

economic system in which today, corporate owners still appeal to the ideal of liberty to justify their management of the economy. That class, the owning class, has maintained its hegemony for more than 240 years. But Gramsci remained a revolutionary thinker who looked forward to a time when another class, a class made up of ordinary people, would rise up just like the merchants did, and achieve its own hegemony.

Strategies of Hegemonic Control

Those who control the economic, political, and cultural operation of society exercise two kinds of power, the power to repress challengers with force, and the power to win the people over to the legitimacy of established control. Gramsci called the latter kind of rule by

> the "spontaneous" consent given by the great masses of the population to the general direction imposed on social life by the dominant fundamental group; this consent is "historically" caused by the prestige (and consequent confidence) which the dominant group enjoys because of its position and function in the world of production.[12]

"*Consent*" on this view should generally be thought of in quotation marks, because in capitalist society, very few people have the freedom to refuse to adhere to the demands of their employers and the state, and so cannot fully consent. In addition, people are won to the terms of a given order through rhetorical and ideological means that they do not control. Those at the top of society (what Karl Marx called "the ruling class") control the mainstream ideas of a society, what Karl Marx "the ideas of the ruling class." Established powers circulate ideas justifying how and why society works to the point that they become invisible, given, automatically assumed to be shared in common as "common sense." The ideology of family values is one common sense narrative that justifies the status quo.

"Common sense" becomes visible when it is challenged. Often, that challenge comes from social movements. During the United States revolutionary era, the "founding fathers" created and intentionally circulated a new set of ideas to become the common sense of society. Indeed, Thomas Paine's pamphlet *Common Sense* was a direct appeal to the public to support the war against the monarch on the basis of a new idea: liberty. As the leaders of the new nation consolidated their power, the terms liberty, equality, and justice entered the documents we know as the Constitution and the Declaration of Independence. These documents constituted (that's why it's called the Constitution) the common sense of the new society.[13]

Thus, no particular version of society (nor its common-sense justifications) is natural, given, or permanent. It is helpful to know that the word *hegemony* described the state of a balance of power or alliance among Greek city-states.[14] Any historian of ancient Greece can tell you that that state of balance was always unstable and subject to challenge. Just as between Athens and Sparta, the collective peace is always fragile. Movements can challenge established power at the system's crisis points.

Hegemonic struggles are not only about conflicts among nation states or revolutionary wars. Every social movement can press against hegemonic institutions, power, and ideology. The not-so-hypothetical pro-Palestinian encampment has set itself to challenging hegemonic ideas, both about war and foreign policy, the role and authority of the university, the place of antagonism and conflict over and against civility and cooperation, and more. Because such encampments have erupted at dozens of universities and because popular opinion about the war is shifting, a crisis has emerged, and they are in a place to challenge established power by using the opportunity that crisis creates.

As another example, since 2020, the hegemonic position held by the owning class is fractured at the site of race and policing. In other words, the police murder of Black people exposes a weakness or contradiction in a system that depends upon the public acceptance of the government or state—including the police—as legitimate. Movements pressing on that weak spot are calling the system into question. They may not go as far as a revolution, but already this pressure has caused key powerful actors—police, politicians, and celebrities—to demand, make, and enact reforms. The achievement of stability in systems of economic, political, and cultural power is always subject to challenge by others who also want to achieve hegemony—to run society in the interests of their people. Hegemony is both the achievement of power and the process of its diminution and replacement.

It is when social movements begin to exert pressure on established institutions and leaders that the establishment undertakes efforts to control, end, or moderate the impact of agitation. Nation states and corporate elites are compelled to resist counterhegemonic agitation in order to protect the security and legitimacy of the state, profitability, and social and economic stability. Attendant ideologies of racism, sexism, gender discrimination, ableism, anti-immigrant sentiment, and so on are buttresses of state and corporate sustainability. Ideological discourses like family values, meritocracy, and conservative religious narratives are resources for ideological containment of the impact of struggle. Why does the establishment resist change? Why does a university call the police on demonstrators? That is a simple question with multiple answers, including the basic fact of elites' investment in the way things are.

Investment in the Status Quo: Establishment Motives

The refusal of establishment institutions and leaders—including those of governments and corporations—to entertain the demands of social movements has its roots in the vested interests of established elites in the systems, institutions, and resources of the status quo. There is a small layer of people in the United States and around the world who directly benefit from the operation of society as it stands. Along with economic interests, established elites also have stakes in structures of political power and influence. To be the president, a senator or congressperson (at state and federal levels), a governor, or a delegate to a political convention—all of these positions come with credibility, authority, prestige, and decision-making power. People in these positions become used to running society in particular ways and object to movements that would like to see change.

For example, in the 1960s, Fannie Lou Hamer and fellow activists in the Mississippi Freedom Democratic Party built a parallel political party structure to the mainstream Democratic Party because the mainstream party would not grant rights or representation to Black citizens. Their call to be acknowledged as the legitimate delegation to the Democratic National Convention in 1964 was refused because the elites in the Democratic Party apparatus did not want to cede control—especially if granting these rights would mean that the economic interests of their powerful allies in the corporate world would be threatened.

There is a profound intersection between economic interests—corporations, their heads, their investors, and other stakeholders—and political power because politicians rely heavily on funding from those stakeholders to win elections.[15] The Supreme Court's *Citizens United* decision in 2010 permitted corporations to give as much money to politicians as they liked through Political Action Campaigns (PACs), allowing unlimited donations for activities in support of particular campaigns.[16] Corporate lobbyists—for example, the insurance industry and the pharmaceutical industry—also pressure politicians in office by promising votes, perks, and financial support. So when a political body, be it a city council or the U.S. Senate, faces appeals from social movements that would limit their economic profitability or that of their friends and supporters, they are unlikely to give in to movement demands.

There is a third reason that institutions deny appeals for change: the existence of social norms and values that have been in place for so long

FIGURE 2.4 Occupy Wall Street, March 15, 2012.

that they seem natural, permanent, and inevitable. Even people who don't run the country or lead corporations resist change because how things are is (wrongly) understood to be the way it always has been. Ideologies propagated by the mainstream media and politicians can convince people to abide by "normal" identities and roles, for example with regard to gender, sexuality, race, and so on.

People can hold psychological investments in the way things are. Following the ideas of W.E.B. Du Bois, historian David Roediger explained how even poor and working-class white Southerners opposed equal rights for Black Americans because they perceived themselves as benefiting from racial oppression in what Roediger calls the "psychological wage."[17] In the South during the Civil Rights Movement, ordinary white people engaged in harassment, exclusion, and violence against Black people: To admit equality would undermine a whole way of life, which led President Lyndon Johnson to proclaim that there were two societies, separate and unequal, one white, and one Black.

When faced with agitational threats, establishment authorities have a number of options. In democratic societies, the establishment will not usually make immediate recourse to outright suppression through policing, incarceration, and other violence. On the other hand, in authoritarian societies without a vibrant public sphere and defined constitutional rights, the move to suppression is more immediate.

Attributions of Violence

One nearly universal strategy of the establishment is to preemptively label protesters as violent threats to order and safety. This was a common response during the global justice movement of the early 2000s, when police and city leaders would conduct careful media campaigns warning citizens about protesters (characterized as violent, anarchist, and foreign) about to descend on a city where an international trade meeting was to be held. These narratives of violence justified massive police mobilization and militarization in advance, near or total lockdowns on cities, and thus served to mitigate the persuasive impact that a large demonstration against corporate greed would have.

Because movement activists are often tarnished with accusations of violence, it is important to note that on the whole, social movements in the United States have not been violent. Violence is a label for activities that harm human beings or other living things. Confrontation, disruption, and even vandalism and property damage, while sometimes dramatic, do not constitute violence.

Avoidance

Bowers, Ochs, Jensen, and Schulz lay out some of the options available to establishment forces when facing sustained agitation.[18] Based largely on their analysis of student protest movements, they write that the establishment has three general options: avoidance, postponement, and suppression. Under the heading of **avoidance**, establishment actors engage in counter-persuasion, working with movement leaders to see whether and on what terms the movement would de-escalate.

In addition to those efforts, **counter-persuasion** involves media framing that attempts to demean, discredit, or otherwise minimize the significance of the movement. In general, the routines and norms of mainstream journalism privilege the voices and perspectives of the establishment with an emphasis on order—they serve a hegemonic function. When faced with a crisis, mainstream media engage in a number of framing tactics: trivialization (making light of movement identities, style, and goals), polarization ("balancing" movement coverage with the perspectives of ultra-right and even neo-Nazi groups as if both sides were "extreme"), focusing on internal conflict and dissension inside the movement; marginalization (portraying activists as deviant), disparagement by numbers (undercounting attendance at demonstrations and other events), and disparagement of the movement's effectiveness. In addition, corporate media rely on the statements of government and other authorities, emphasize any real or imagined presence of communists in the movement, emphasize (and exaggerate) any violence at movement events, and pay inordinate attention to right-wing opposition to the movements.[19]

Such efforts at counter-framing and counter-persuasion redefine movements in the eyes of the public—changing "peaceful" to "violent," "reasonable" to "irrational," and so on. They can build public perception of movements as threats—especially with regard to movements of people of color. They also can come to affect the internal dynamics of movements, who may adjust their strategies in order to garner greater media attention.

Another strategy of avoidance is evasion: when politicians, university leaders, and other bureaucrats use bureaucratic roadblocks and delays to "give protesters the run-around." This strategy can stretch out "negotiations" to cool off the movement and dodge accountability. This strategy is closely related to that of postponement, when representatives of the establishment suggest that they form a committee, hold a meeting, or charge a commission with investigating the problem the movement is calling attention to.

The establishment can also withhold information necessary to the movement, claiming that secrecy is warranted by security or other concerns. Denial of means is another tactic of postponement when establishment representatives refuse movements the space, funding, media, equipment, and other resources they might need to build successful events. Denial of means is common on university campuses, where activists must undertake a complex process of obtaining permits to use campus spaces and are often forbidden the use of amplified sound. We can add court trials and the legal process to the strategy of postponement as agitators take on lengthy and expensive court battles to the detriment of immediate movement building.

Suppression

If avoidance and postponement are unsuccessful to curb a movement's escalation, an establishment will turn to **suppression**, one form of which is harassment, including surveillance and infiltration. The FBI's Counterintelligence Project (COINTELPRO) is the most significant example of such efforts in the United States. COINTELPRO involved decades (from 1956 to 1971, even with the approval of President John F. Kennedy) of secret and illegal surveillance, infiltration, discrediting, and disruption of movement organizations that the government designated as "subversive." These included the civil rights movement, feminist organizations, communist movements, anti-war movements, Black Power movements, environmentalist and animal rights movements, the American Indian Movement, Chicano and Mexican-American rights movements, much of the New Left, and some white supremacist and other right-wing groups. Conspiring with police departments and the military, COINTELPRO agents provoked tension and splits in the civil rights and anti-war movements, often using "red-baiting" (accusations of communism) to do so; operatives urged violence in order to discredit movements.

COINTELPRO tactics attempted to discredit its targets using fabricated stories, forged documents, and false reports; they engaged in wrongful imprisonment, illegal violence, and assassination. COINTELPRO's violence targeted Black Panthers, harassing, imprisoning, humiliating, and assassinating members (including Fred Hampton).[20]

FIGURE 2.5 Taking a stand in Baton Rouge by Jonathan Bachman has become one of the most iconic images of the Black Lives Matter Movements. Ieshia Evans, dressed in a light flowing dress, stands in front of police officers in full riot gear. Her calm, confident demeanor is in stark contrast to the officers' aggression. For many, this photo is emblematic of the issues facing BLM activists: rampant militarization of police forces and disproportionate, often violent responses to peaceful protests (especially those led by black people). Like the nonviolent protests of the 20th-century civil rights movement, this confrontation dramatizes the Black Lives Matter movement's claims with regard to racist policing in the United States. Evan's arrest immediately after this photograph only served to reinforce this reading.

Bowers, Ochs, Jensen, and Schulz include in their inventory of suppression tactics banishment (excommunication, expulsion, academic suspension, firing, forcible removal from space, confinement) and purgation (killing leaders and members of an agitative movement). We might add to that list the infringement on academic freedom which has characterized much reaction against critical intellectuals on university campuses since the World Trade Center attacks in 2001.

Academic repression escalated with the rise of the alt-right in the mid-2000s, with multiple academics targeted for their outspoken criticisms of war and racism and support, in particular, for Palestine resistance. Tactics of this repression include viral smear campaigns, doxxing, public harassment, and threats of violence, including sexual assault, and actual violence. The right has mounted campaigns that resulted in the dismissal of professors for their views.[21] The pressure has escalated again during Israel's war on Gaza beginning in 2023, when public pressure forced the resignation of Harvard President Claudine Gay and others.[22] Far right organizations got a foothold on a number of campuses as the organization Turning Point USA—a group recruited, trained, and funded by Christian nationalist and white supremacist organizations—established chapters at hundreds of universities and high schools.[23]

The suppression of protest through policing was particularly intense during the early-2000s' movement against corporate globalization. Mass protests at meetings of the World Trade Organization, the International Monetary Fund, and the G8 around the world threatened the credibility of transnational economic elites' control over the world economy. These drew an increasingly militarized police response, with a particularly egregious example in Miami in 2003 at a meeting of the Free Trade Area of the Americas, when the city was emptied, garrisons of militarized riot police in full armor guarded streets around the site of the meeting, a tank rolled onto the grounds of a permitted demonstration, and police fired rubber bullets into unarmed crowds, including elderly labor activists.

Luis Fernandez, in his study of policing in the global justice movement, mentions the 2003 Miami protest as an example of how, especially after 2001, an economy of training militarized police, fueled by war on terrorism funds, engaged in planning, surveillance, infiltration, control of space, beatings, shootings, and arrests. Aggressive patrolling, the fortification of spaces, and preemptive arrests effectively curtailed the effectiveness and credibility of protests.[24]

Policing of protest used an escalation of force model through the 1960s, a strategy designed to suppress dissent by all means possible, violating freedoms and inflicting injury, all without negotiation. The police setting dogs and firehoses upon youth in the civil disobedience in Birmingham in 1963 is a case in point. However, images of this event, captured on camera, circulated the globe and ended up generating moral outrage and a publicity backlash against the policing of the civil rights movement. The negative publicity created sympathy for the protesters.

This backlash, along with the urban unrest, largely fueled by police, of the late 1960s led to a shift in policing toward negotiated management, in which police departments offer movement leaders concessions in exchange for an agreement to self-police and share the scale, route, and timing of demonstrations, for example, in obtaining legal permits. On this model, police remain in constant communication with protesters. This negotiated model still favors the police and acts a form of soft-line control, allowing the police to surveil organizing as organizers become complicit in making their actions less contentious.

Since the late 1990s, and especially after 9/11, there was a return to hard-line policing of protest including the use of "non-lethal" weapons

FIGURE 2.6 In November 2003, riot police turned Miami, Florida, into a war zone during a protest against the trade policies of the Free Trade Area of the Americas.

(like chemical agents and rubber bullets) against activists. The "new forms of multitudinous resistance" represented in the global justice movement triggered new forms of control in legal, physical, and psychological spheres.[25] Alongside the work of active policing, states and their agencies hire public relations firms to systematically discredit such protests as anarchist and violent in a highly resourced process not available to protesters themselves.[26] Another example of suppression through policing comes from the recent movement among Atlanta environmentalists, anti-racist activists, anarchists, and others to stop the construction of a massive police training center in the middle of a protected forest—to stop what has been dubbed "Cop City." Constance Gordon discusses how the defenders of the land were punished by anti-protest policing and the passage of "critical infrastructure" laws that defined the police facility as necessary and critical. These laws warranted the sweeping criminalization, harassment, and arrests of activists, who, at the same time, built their own "critical infrastructures" of mutual care and solidarity.[27]

Adjustment and Capitulation

Returning to the general strategies of control, another option for the establishment faced with escalating protests is **adjustment**: the adaptation, modification, or alteration of their structures, activities, and personnel. Adjustment can include changing the names of agencies and offices or sacrificing personnel (for example President Lyndon Baines Johnson's withdrawal from the 1968 Presidential race in the wake of anti-war protests and University of California President Clark Kerr's stepping down during the student movements in Berkeley). Another kind of adjustment is when the establishment allows some disorder to happen such that the energy has nowhere to go without opposition and dissipates. The establishment can incorporate some of the leaders of the movement, which can constitute a victory but also risks co-optation. The establishment can also incorporate some of the dissidents' ideas and ideology.

Failing to curtail a movement at this point, institutions and leaders of the establishment may be compelled to engage in **capitulation**: the acceptance of movement demands and institution of desired reforms. At the far end of the capitulation spectrum, the movement's goals, policies, beliefs, and personnel replace those of the establishment in what is essentially, a revolution. Rarely does the establishment capitulate entirely.

The Rise of Counter-Movements

The control of social movements does not only come from official, establishment institutions and leaders. This fact can be a source of confusion in the analysis of social movements, because it seems that sometimes social movements are not battling the establishment but rather are contending with other social movements made up of ordinary people outside the regular halls of power. It is important to understand, as Gramsci did, the rise of counter-movements against movements for social justice as part of the hegemonic struggle—in defense of the broader social order. As a whole—even when those movements hold aims that do not completely align with the official positions and policies of established institutions.

Christian nationalism, "prepper" movements, and movements against the affordances of the welfare state (for example, the anti-vaccine movement) can thus be understood broadly as expressions of hegemonic reaction against forces of social justice. The influence of conservative Christianity is an anachronism that layers a pre-modern ideological veneer onto modern struggles against the empowerment of racial minorities, women, and LGBTQ people. The Christian right struggles, in Gramsci's terms, for moral and intellectual leadership over what counts as truth just as Left-wing intellectuals and culture creators do.[28]

The abortion rights and anti-abortion movements are good cases in point. In the latter case, opponents of the right to abortion were, for decades, at odds with established law, in the form of the court decision *Roe v. Wade*, which legalized abortion, with some restrictions, in 1973. While the anti-abortion movement was at odds with the state until the 2022 *Dobbs v. Jackson* decision reversed *Roe*, the movement could be understood as a hegemonic effort to govern women and their role in the reproduction of people and care in contemporary society.[29] When proponents of abortion have confronted anti-abortion activists, for example, in clinic defenses, they have been, in fact, contending with an establishment-adjacent movement defending hegemonic social relations in a broad sense.

This function of right-wing movements explains why representatives of such movements often end up leading establishment institutions such as the presidency. Indeed, conservative and far-right social movements (including fascism) usually arise in response to broader social crisis and uprisings for social justice and therefore must be included in the repertoire of control.

White Supremacist Movements

For example, white supremacist movements in the United States have served the function of disciplining movements for racial justice, starting with the Ku Klux Klan and other vigilante movements of the turn of the 20th century. These groups were a reaction against the end of slavery and the newfound rights of former slaves—and, indeed, against a whole host of social changes unfolding in U.S. society.[30] After a lull, the Klan resurged after the *Brown v. Board* decision of 1954 mandating the integration of public schools. The Klan, like other white-supremacist organizations, distributed mass amounts of racist propaganda and included hosts of police and politicians in its ranks.

In response to the civil rights movement of the 1950s and 1960s, white citizens' councils formed to campaign stridently against anti-racist reforms, often on behalf of white businesses in Southern cities. The councils used economic intimidation to retaliate against integrationist activists and voting rights. It is not an accident that the Klan bombed four Black churches and multiple homes in Montgomery, Alabama after the success of the Montgomery Bus Boycott. The Klan also attacked freedom riders and other demonstrations in the 1960s. While the governments of both states and the nation were under pressure to grant civil rights reforms and did not openly support white supremacist action, efforts at preserving a racist social order still served broader hegemonic power relations in which the oppression of Black Americans divided the working class and undercut its power while also legitimating increases in the resources of the police state. Brutal racism serves psychological functions for oppressed and exploited white people in times of change, but it also serves the broader functioning of a society riven by class and race.[31]

More recently, white supremacist groups gained members, strength, and influence during and in reaction against the Black Lives Matter Movement, fueled by the Internet and the rise of the Internet-based alt-right. The alt-right had been seeking to normalize racism in the United States and advocated the formation of a white ethnostate. After protests erupted after the killing of Trayvon Martin, Michael Brown, Eric Garner, and George Floyd, "there was a notable increase in the number of Patriot and militia groups in operation. By 2012, the Southern Poverty Law Center had identified 1,360 such groups, up from 149 in 2008, a growth of over 800 percent."[32]

The alt-right radicalized murderous extremists Dylann Roof, a 21-year-old white supremacist who shot and murdered nine Black worshippers in Charleston, South Carolina; and Robert Bowers, who

FIGURE 2.7 The Ku Klux Klan on parade in Washington, DC, in 1926.

killed eleven and injured seven others in an October 27, 2018 attack on a synagogue in Pittsburgh. There are numerous other examples of how a white-supremacist movement mobilized individuals to discipline groups who had been rising in rebellion against racism. The alt-right also espoused reaction against women's movement agitation in rampant misogyny. We can understand the 2017 "Unite the Right" rally and murder of activist Heather Heyer in Charlottesville as an effort to discipline both the women's movement and the Movement for Black Lives and to reinforce the racist discourses and social relations that remain hegemonic in the United States today.

Fascism

We can understand fascist movements and regimes in a similar way. **Fascism** is a modern movement on the far right of the political spectrum. Beyond being conservative, fascism is a method of governance that mobilizes paramilitary forces out of the middle class to suppress working-class organizations and other movements in times of economic and political crisis. In rhetorical studies, scholars have defined fascism in terms of its rhetorical tropes and political style. Fascism in rhetorical practices can be identified, according to Nathan Crick, by its efforts to offer redemption and rebirth to a social group cast as victims through violence.[33] This analysis is helpful in identifying potentially fascist rhetoric in, say, the discourse of a president like Donald Trump whose slogan "Make America Great Again" is a prime example.[34]

At the same time, it is important to situate an analysis of fascism in material and historical context to see what its broader functions are in sustaining social order in the face of agitational challenge. A study of fascist movements across time (since the early 20th century, specifically) and geography shows how their political (authoritarian, nationalist, imperialist), ideological (anti-liberal, anti-communist), and stylistic (committed to masculine aesthetic choreography and spectacle) forms

FIGURE 2.8 Adolf Hitler and Benito Mussolini in June 1940.

correspond to moments of existential crisis in populations disturbed by defeats in war, economic crisis, and rapid, disorienting modernization.[35] Fascism is a movement rising in developed industrial societies, triggered by socio-economic crisis and focused on eliminating the organizations of the working class.[36]

In Italy, Gramsci writes, fascism was a response to the "real transfer of wealth" upward to the rich and the threat of the workers' movement in the form of mass strikes.[37] Fascist leaders like Mussolini impose order artificially on a situation of disorder through the figure of a charismatic leader and military organization grounded in the disaffected "small producer" class, or petit bourgeoisie. This group is tasked with defending "order, property, and the state."[38] In this light, fascism appears as primarily a tool of establishment control of democratic movements in situation of broader social crisis.

In summary, the rising of movements for social justice routinely provokes efforts on the part of the establishment to control them and contain their impact on the status quo. These efforts range from avoidance and suppression through reactionary counter-movements, including white supremacy and fascism. Hegemony is a useful frame for understanding the interconnected work of all of these responses and explains how, when movements seem to be engaged in battling other movements and not the official institutions of the establishment, they are still engaged fundamentally in counterhegemonic struggle. The hegemonic order as a whole is what constitutes the establishment, beyond particular agencies, organizations, and political leaders. For Gramsci, the alternative was to build genuine movements of ordinary people from below to offer actual solutions to disorder and privation.

Strategies of Counterhegemonic Agitation

Just as there are two kinds of power in a class's hegemonic achievement (coercive and ideological), there are two interdependent orientations toward power on the part of social movements. One is oriented toward **reform**, the making of changes within the system while leaving the system itself intact. An example is the movement goal that police officers wear body cameras so as to be accountable for their actions. The other is toward **revolution**, or the overturning and replacing of the existing system by something else. An example of a potentially revolutionary orientation is the demand to abolish the police.

Reform and revolution are not separate orientations. They are more like interrelated moments in a struggle. Movements toward reforms often end up urging more wholesale change. Winning reforms builds confidence. At the same time, for a movement to reach a revolutionary moment is rare, not a decision to destroy society overnight, but the product of the organization for reforms followed by a crisis in the legitimacy of the state. Nor are militant tactics like civil disobedience and the destruction of property limited to revolutions. As will be explained later in this book, tactics are not the same thing as ideology. Peaceable people have worked toward wholesale social transformation. Confrontational and unruly people and groups have been part of movements for reforms.

For example, the movement to abolish slavery worked unflaggingly in the United States over a period of decades beginning in the 1830s. Speaking tours, the publication of tracts and treatises, the pressuring of politicians and others more powerful—all built a social movement that could achieve only modest reforms, for example, the abolition of slavery in one state or compromises over the conditions of slaves. There was one famous eruption of militancy in the actions of John Brown, who is best known for his raid on an ammunitions stockpile at Harper's Ferry, Virginia in 1859. He intended to free and arm slaves so that they could lead a revolution, but after a failed battle, he became the first American to be executed (by hanging) for treason. Brown had revolutionary ideas and attempted to "jump-start" a revolutionary process. But the moment at hand was not a revolutionary one. He had only a few men and limited weapons that were inadequate against the slavers, the police, and the military. (However, the movement to end slavery did become revolutionary in the form of the Civil War, in which one class, Northern industrialists, achieved hegemony over the Southern plantation economy.)

War of Maneuver and War of Position

In addition to defining and describing hegemony and the process of establishing common sense, Gramsci distinguished between two kinds of struggle in society (or wars, although the word war is not completely literal here): the war of position and the war of maneuver. The **war of maneuver** is the mobilization of large forces to make a wholesale challenge to the existing social system including both the state and the economic system; it is potentially revolutionary in character. In contrast, the **war of position** is the process of slowly gaining and holding ground primarily in the realms of ideology and culture (rather than targeting the economy or the state directly). Gramsci likened this strategy to "trench warfare," or establishing and holding ground in incremental steps.[39] Social movements engage continually in the war of position. Challengers to an existing system may engage in education, cultural production (like media making), and social organization in order to win potential members of a movement away from reigning "common sense."

Pro-Palestinian encampments are literally engaged in trench warfare, occupying actual ground and trying to hold it. They are also engaged in holding ideological ground as they engage in tactics of both position and maneuver, the latter exemplified by the student's direct pressure on the university administration.

Ideologies attempt to make the interests of a ruling elite seem to be everyone's interests, universalizing its claims on power. However, societies experience a crisis of hegemony when the operation of the basic institutional and economic structures—such as the nation-state, governments, official institutions, and economic activity—become increasingly divorced from the ideologies that are supposed to be justifying those structures, or ideologies.[40] When police are routinely murdering people of color, for example, ideas justifying the police as protectors and helpers become nonsensical. The contradiction between the institution and its practices is a gap for the development of new interpretations of social reality. People doing organizing, community service, and media work have an opportunity to insert new visions for society into that gap, to assert their knowledge and needs as part of what circulates as "common sense." The war of position can take hold in such times and places.

In these spaces, like school, college classes, social media and in-person socializing, religious observation, political meetings, popular culture, and other community-building sites, organizers of social movements may prepare the way for broader movement by circulating new ways of thinking. Gramsci scholar Peter Thomas notes that Gramsci referred to all of these sites as belonging to *civil society*, a place of gathering, discourse, and action independent of both the state and corporate power.[41] Teachers, scholars, union organizers, anti-racist activists, groups organizing for women's liberation and the recognition of trans and

FIGURE 2.9 A 1958 strike organizing meeting of the International Ladies Garment Workers Union.

queer lives—all of these groups prepare the way for political action in the mutual education and persuasion taking place in these spaces. These are sites of potential "counter hegemony" where ordinary people can organize, educate, and mobilize themselves. As movements form, they generate their own media and perceptions of reality, challenging dominant knowledge and ideology, which, in turn, can influence political processes and institutions.

That said, it should be noted that it is not only challengers who engage in the war of position and the war of maneuver. The nation-state and its forces—such as the military and police—defend the existing system and are always busy at the war of position: creating and reinforcing a body of knowledge and opinion congruent with the aims of those at the top. Society's elites produce their own intellectuals in think-tanks and universities, in newspapers and other media, and in social and political groups. For example, conservatives (those who would conserve the established order) have control of news outlets like Fox news. The Koch Foundation, a conservative think-tank and set of resources held by the Koch family, has invested millions of dollars into university business schools to influence the philosophy and business and economics taught there.

Other conservative organizations have attempted a foothold on university campuses by establishing externally-funded student organizations like Turning Point. Political and economic elites work diligently to refute and discredit oppositional ideas. Social movements engage in the war of position to attempt to disrupt this process. At each step communication—particularly rhetoric as communication designed to influence others—plays a key role. Throughout history, communicators inside of movements frame up causes and organize people around the purpose, meaning, and identity of the group.[42]

Communication Studies and Hegemony

Because of the centrality of communication to the theory of hegemony, communication studies and all of its subdisciplines have taken up Gramsci's ideas.

In cultural studies Gramsci's theories of ideology and hegemony are used to critique, dominant cultural narratives, including racism. Cultural studies scholars appreciate the idea of the war of position—in which cultural work and critique have a central place. Cultural studies make hegemony central as a concept in explaining how the discourses surrounding us are articulated, or connected, to changes in economics, culture, and politics, or "conjunctures."[43] Although resonant with Gramsci's Marxism, cultural studies thinkers have extended Gramsci's thought to questions of how identities beyond class, particularly with regard to race, are constructed in popular culture.[44] The study of conjunctures might lead us to see race and policing as a site of contestation over race and racism. In the wake of continual police murders of Black people, hegemonic ideas about race and crime, for example that Black men in particular are all criminals, start to fracture. An opportunity emerges for movements to call both hegemonic ideas and hegemonic institutions like the police into question.

Arguing against the concept of hegemony as top-down domination, organizational communication scholar Dennis Mumby argued for us to regard hegemony as dialectical—involving both control and agitation in attempts to win, preserve, and challenge power.[45] Ordinary people engage in struggle over the terms of their lives in everyday and significant ways. The dialectical approach is the one featured in this book.

There is important work on the hegemonic discourses—the ones circulating as common sense—justifying identity-based oppression, for example hegemonic ideas about ability and disability or hegemonic ideas about gender identities and roles. These ideas include hegemonic masculinity. The hegemonic cultural prescription for ideal masculine behavior emphasizes toughness, physical strength, heterosexuality, control over women, and the rejection of anything feminine. The alarming consequences of this ideal are, for men, a constrained subjectivity that expects violence and disdains care and vulnerability, and, for women, a culture that fosters the acceptability of violence against them.[46] Other work in rhetorical studies has analyzed dominant culture's capacity to create and sustain oppressive ideas and practices regarding race and racism, while also noticing counterhegemonic resistance in culture and social movements to those ideas. And, importantly, communication scholars have taken up Gramsci for the study of social movements.

Gramsci for the Rhetoric of Social Movements

One more concept from Gramsci's thought is helpful to understand how social movements work as counterhegemonic agents of change: civil society. **Civil society** refers to the spheres of communication, culture, education, social life, groups and organizations, deliberation, debate, dialogue, and controversy—all of the areas of our lives that are not under the control of economic power (employers) or the state (the government and all of its functions, including the prerogative of violence). Civil society is where the war of position is conducted and the war of maneuver begun. In civil society, people struggle over the narratives that govern shared reality, or ideologies. Civil society is where culture work happens—the production and performance of literature, art, dance, media, and other forms of collective expression. Civil society is where social movements come into being and do their work.

Gramsci's concepts are especially important to communication scholars who analyze social movements. Marco Briziarelli and Susana Martínez Guillem argue that Gramsci offers an integral model of social power and transformation in which the war of position (cultural, political, and symbolic work) must join with the war of maneuver (a frontal attack on society and the state itself) if movements are to achieve counterhegemonic force.[47] On this basis, they criticize the Occupy Wall Street Movement of 2011. Provoked by the economic collapse of 2008, the activists in Occupy took over streets, sidewalks, city squares, plazas outside city halls, corporate spaces, and other venues and established long-term encampments challenging the control over politics by a moneyed elite. Instead of listing concrete demands and engaging in mass action to pressure the system to give in to those demands, the movement built a "prefigurative" political space—in which the encampments became a model for a more democratic society to come. The problem for Briziarelli and Guillem is that this movement failed to mount the war of maneuver.

Briziarelli and Guillem posit fundamental questions for social movements and scholarship about social movements:

> What are the conditions that (do not) allow for social mobilization and its specific communicative strategies to develop? How do these same conditions influence the extent to which these practices are successful? What is the relationship between a particular movement's objectives and its participants' rhetorical means to achieve such goals? How can particularistic and individualistic economic interests be translated into a collective and ethical-political project? How does the tension between progressive and regressive interests and practices both produce and constrain social movements?[48]

These are questions guiding this textbook as well.

All of this scholarship on hegemony makes the key point that influential communication serves to bring movements together; make their arguments public; convince others to join their causes; orient people toward an establishment; educate its members in history, strategies, and tactics; create and distribute media of all kinds and on all platforms; create and share common histories and feelings; and craft identities for activists and the movement as a whole. Ultimately, they create a culture of movement is created—a situation when the identities, feelings, arguments, and media of movements catch on to others and spread in opposition to national and global hegemonies.

It is a situation when the crises in the hegemony of the establishment become apparent and an opportunity for movements to enter the crisis with a real hope for gaining material and ideological leadership of society. In the United States and in parts of Europe, the late 1960s and early 1970s marked a time like that, when movements both discredited a U.S. war and made enormous gains in civil rights for women, ethnic and racial minorities, sexual minorities, and others. These gains included access to health care, housing, education and careers, and protections from discrimination and abuse.

For Gramsci, all society is born of, preserved in, challenged by, and remade in struggle. This perspective allows us to see social movements in a new way: Rather than there being a set "system" with a permanent "establishment" that withstands challenges of movements without fundamental change, we recognize that the evolution of society around the world is dynamic and shifting. The world is always in movement.

Conclusion: Social Movements in a Gramscian Frame

You now have some basic conceptual tools to begin to make sense of social movements, including the scenario that opened this chapter. First, you have definitions of social movement, establishment, agitators and controllers, and strategies and tactics. Second, you have been introduced to a broad framework to understand how established and movement forces employ strategies of maneuver and of position to vie for leadership in a situation where social justice is at stake.

We are about to learn additional ways of thinking about, analyzing, describing, and undertaking these processes in ways that allow us more refinement and clarity. From sociology, we take insights about organization, structure, opportunities, and resources. From rhetorical studies, we refine our way of talking about a movement's rhetoric: language, identity, meaning, ideology, and feeling, among other elements that communication can produce. Through the careful study of social movements, we equip ourselves to say something meaningful about the processes of permanence and change.

So that we will have common reference points when talking about social movements, the next chapters include examples of modern U.S. movements with an emphasis on their rhetorical character. Because movements occur in historical contexts that afford them constraints and opportunities, knowing these histories allows us to understand their strategies and tactics as responses to established power in moments of particular possibility.

Suggestions for Further Reading

Marco Briziarelli and Susana Martínez Guillem, *Reviving Gramsci: Crisis, Communication, and Change* (New York: Routledge, 2016).

Dana L. Cloud, *We Are the Union: Democratic Unionism and Dissent at Boeing* (Urbana: University of Illinois Press, 2011).

Terry Eagleton, *Ideology: An Introduction* (London: Verso, 2007).

Antonio Gramsci, *Selections from the Prison Notebooks*, edited and translated by Quintin Hoare and Geoffrey Newell Smith (New York: International Publishers, 1971).

Questions for Discussion

1. How would you advise the activists in the scenario at the beginning of the chapter to proceed, and why?
2. Explain the distinction between "ideology" and "hegemony."
3. What are ways that a Gramscian framework gives us insights about social movements?

Credits

Fig. 2.3: Copyright © 2017 Pixabay/ParentRap.

Fig. 2.4: Copyright © by Michael Fleshman (CC BY-SA 2.0) at https://www.flickr.com/photos/fleshmanpix/6840361918.

Fig. 2.5: Jonathan Bachman, "Taking a Stand in Baton Rouge," https://widerimage.reuters.com/story/taking-a-stand-in-baton-rouge. Copyright © 2017 by Reuters.

Fig. 2.6: Kaldari, https://commons.wikimedia.org/wiki/File:Riot_police_at_FTAA_protests_in_Miami_01.jpg, 2003.

Fig. 2.7: Library of Congress, https://picryl.com/media/ku-klux-klan-parade-washingotn-dc-on-pennsylvania-ave-nw-birds-eye-view, 1926.

Fig. 2.8: National Archives, https://www.flickr.com/photos/pingnews/442013867, 1940.

Fig. 2.9: Copyright © by Kheel Center (CC BY 2.0) at https://commons.wikimedia.org/wiki/File:Members_of_the_International_Ladies_Garment_Workers_Union_on_strike_gather_in_a_meeting_hall,_March_15,_1958._%285279689582%29.jpg.

II

Traditions

3

Sociological Traditions in Social Movement Studies

KEY TERMS

social movement
repertoires of contention
social movement organization
leaders
resource mobilization theory
cultural turn
collective identity
collective action frames
narratives
emotions
affect
music
media frames
new social movements

The social movements of the 1960s in the United States transformed society, and along with changes in the world at large came shifts in academic disciplines, including sociology. In the civil rights movement (begun in the 1950s), women's rights and liberation movements, LGBTQ movements, student movements including the free speech movement, and the movement against the Vietnam War revolutionized many aspects of society. Black activists were demanding power; women were demanding access to public life and control of their private bodies; LGBTQ people were squaring off against police—and against shame and secrecy. Students were taking over their campuses. And opposition to the war in Vietnam shamed the nation. People were marching, rioting, and dancing in the streets.

Sociologists—scholars of society itself—were provoked to ask: Why did these movements begin? Who joined and built these movements? What kinds of organization did they employ? What were their strategies and tactics? What achievements (both immediate and lasting) did they make in politics, law, social relations, culture, public opinion, and consciousness and identity? When and why did some decline and fail? When and why did they resurge?[1] In answering these questions over a period of decades, sociologists have developed the most extensive set of theoretical perspectives on social movements available to us today.

Sociologists are interested in identifying the common mechanisms and processes that cut across social struggles to not only describe movements but to figure out the variables leading to success or failure. These perspectives have deeply informed work by rhetoric scholars on movements for social change and remain valuable to anyone interested in the rhetoric of social movements.

This chapter explores the sociological research on movements. First, it covers the big-picture work of Sidney Tarrow, who, along with Doug McAdam and Charles Tilly, coined a famous and useful definition of social movements as contentious collective politics. They also define an important concept: repertoires of action, referring to the protest skillsets both inherited from previous activists and innovated by current ones. Second, it covers a number of specific authors and concepts related to the activities of movements, including their forms of organization and the life cycle of movements. Third, the chapter turns to research on the more qualitative question of how movements engage with issues of identity, culture, thought, feeling, and meaning. In the 1980s, sociologists moved away from the utilitarian and instrumentalist theories that had been prominent, and questions of identity and meaning came to the fore, explored through the concept of framing. Movements' affirmative framing of their identities and purposes often ran up against the framing of protest in mass media, where it became a struggle for popular opinion. This chapter uses the example of the radical feminist movement as an example as it explores these ideas. After a discussion of the achievements and failures of movements, the concepts introduced here will be organized into a method of analyzing movements.

Social Movements: The Basics

Definitions of Social Movements

Sydney Tarrow is an American sociologist and historian who, alongside such sociologists as Charles Tilly and Doug McAdam, defined **social movements** as instances of *contentious collective politics*: "when ordinary people—often in alliance with more influential citizens and with changes in public mood—join forces in confrontation with elites, authorities, and opponents."[2] Social movements involve the mounting, coordinating, and sustaining of collective contentious politics "used by people who lack regular access to representative institutions, who act in the name of new or unaccepted claims, and who behave in ways that fundamentally challenge others or authorities." Contentious collective action is often the only recourse that ordinary people possess to make effective demands for justice.[3] We have that capacity when we engage with others and act collectively. Uniting with others is the greatest source of power for ordinary people.

Rooted in networks and traditions, social movements create sustained campaigns of "claim making" on the broader society, employing a set of performative protest events.[4] Contentious collective action is defined by confrontation, but not confrontation regarded as random, extremist, irrational violence. In movements, confrontation is defined by purpose, reason, and solidarity—or common cause—and aimed at actually oppressive and exploitative groups and institutions.

Movements face the challenges of authoritarian government and other forms of repression that make action through regular channels impossible. Ordinary people can't control politicians with money. We don't usually have access to the means of mass communication. Individually, we don't control our workplaces, bosses, politicians, or judges. But when people recognize that they share grievances with others (and that, therefore, there is a problem with the system, not just themselves), the potential for movement becomes real. Tarrow summarizes:

> People engage in contentious politics when patterns of political opportunities and constraints change, and then by strategically employing a repertoire of collective action, creating new opportunities, which are used by others in widening cycles of contention. When their struggles revolve around broad cleavages in society; when they bring people together around inherited cultural symbols; and when they can build on—or construct—dense social networks and conceptive structures, these episodes of contention result in sustained interactions with opponents in social movements.[5]

Opportunities, Repertoires, and Cycles of Contention

Opportunities include crises or gaps in an establishment's leadership, shifts in popular consciousness, and other historical events that make openings for social movement actors to make their claims. They do so by engaging in various forms of protest and organization discovered in their struggle or inherited from the past.[6]

These forms of action comprise **repertoires of contention**.[7] These are the set of skills and actions that constitute a toolkit for movements: voting, petitioning, asserting, claiming, meeting, demonstrating, striking, marching, occupying, performing, obstructing, sabotaging, and (rarely) violently attacking. Tilly and Tarrow define repertoires as "inherited forms of collective action" that guide the performances of collectives making claims on established social relations.[8] Activists use established forms of protest, such as striking, demonstrating, and so on, but they also innovate new practices, for example the organizing of "die-in" protests against police murders in the Movement for Black Lives. In these protests, participants fall to the ground for a period of time, during which others draw chalk outlines around their bodies to symbolize murder. The events build upon established modes of protest in a compelling way.

Such activities are enabled by networks and other connective structures like workplaces and other institutions that bring people together. Then, activists develop a set of cultural and ideological messages that bind people together and communicate their grievances and identities. Printed information including newspapers, and later, electronic and social media, enable this communication. Over time, movements exhibit a cyclical dynamic in which they emerge, struggle, and recede.

This process is called the *cycle of contention*: the evolution of movements through the stages of diffusion, or the spread of conflict, ideas

FIGURE 3.1 A die-in to protest racist policing in Austin, Texas, in December 2014. The die-in is an element of the protest repertoire innovated by ACT UP in the movement to fight AIDS in the 1980s, subsequently adopted by other movements whose causes are matters of life and death.

and actions; radicalization, or institutional change; exhaustion, or weariness and disillusionment; restabilization, or when society returns to "normal" by repression, facilitation (compromise or adjustment) and other actions of established powers; or, escalation, when movements gain ideological hold and militancy even unto revolution, which is rare in the United States. Movements often begin in small, specific episodes of contention and open up in phases of opportunity and constraint during which participants create new ways of challenging hegemonic authority.[9] Movements also rise and recede in waves that repeat their history in new times and ways.

Tarrow and Tilly updated their conceptual apparatus after the murder of Michael Brown in 2014 by police and the emergence of the Movement for Black Lives. Working from that and other examples, they lay out the steps for movement analysis: Identify the political actors (people who participate in movements), political identities (how these actors conceive themselves and their cause), contentious performances (all of the actions of protest and resistance), contexts and opportunities, and repertoires (the skillsets with regard to types of movement activity) leading to cycles of contention. David Meyer and Tarrow also brought the sociology of social movements up to date in a collection of studies of movements responding to the right-wing populism of Donald Trump's presidency (2017–2021).[10] They noted that the rise of populism and resistance to it still requires an account of the agents, organizations, and repertoires of social movements. In addition to describing these features of movements, sociologists have explored the elements of organization and resources in movements.

Case in Point: The Radical Feminist Movement

The radical feminist movement in the United States during the 1960s and 1970s exhibited these dynamics of contentious collective action. Radical feminism was a movement composed primarily of women (defined in traditional terms by anatomy at that time). Arising out of other feminist movements at the time, *radical feminism* was critical of mainstream, or liberal, feminism for failing to recognize, indict, and transform a systematic form of oppression, known as patriarchy, or "rule by men." There were various tendencies among radical feminists, but for our purposes, radical feminism may be understood as a movement of women targeting patriarchy, its institutions (including the church and family), its expressions in the forms of violence against women and in cultural discourse that demeaned them, and its consequences—the violation of women in general and the restriction of identities and roles for women in broader society.[11] Radical feminists amplified the message "the personal is political,"[12] emphasizing how a great deal of sexism and misogyny took place in interpersonal relationships and the family. One offshoot of radical feminism was lesbian feminism, since women in the movement identified with other women and sought alternatives to the heterosexual family.[13] It is important not to dismiss the ideas of radical feminism when we are aware of ongoing systemic violence against women and girls and restrictive gender roles, even today.

In the terms of the work on social movements done by Tarrow, Tilly, and other sociologists, radical feminists engaged in contentious collective action on behalf of their interests. Lacking access to regular institutions of power—from which women were largely excluded and routinely denigrated, and which were dismissive of their claims—radical feminists fundamentally challenged elites and authorities in the making of claims on the broader society. Specifically, radical feminists sought the elimination of violence against women and the ending of restrictive gender roles and the objectification of women in hegemonic culture. They engaged in contentious collective action when they held meetings, protests, and performances.

For example, they used the opportunity of the Miss America Pageant in 1968, an "obvious target" of feminist challenges. In their words, they protested "the image of Miss America, an image that oppresses women in every area in which it purports to represent us." The protest

FIGURE 3.2 The Miss America swimsuit competition (here, from 1953) prompted concerns among radical feminists over the objectification of women.

engaged a number of repertoires of action, including the innovative "'freedom trash can,' into which women could throw away all the physical manifestations of women's oppression, such as 'bras, girdles, curlers, false eyelashes, wigs, and representative issues of *Cosmopolitan, Ladies' Home Journal, Family Circle*, etc. The organizers also proposed a concurrent boycott of companies whose products were used in or sponsored the pageant."[14] (Contrary to popular memory, they did not burn their bras.)

Radical feminists employed printed information to build their movement. In particular, they made grassroots newsletters like *The Ladder*, which included stories, analysis of society, invitations to the movement, and promotion of events. *The Ladder* was mimeographed in small quantities and distributed hand-to-hand among women looking for material that explained their experience and offered alternatives to the limits of their lives.[15] Because of the movement's emphasis on personal politics, this intimate form of publicity suited the growing numbers of women drawn into its analysis and activity. Radical feminists also established bookstores in cities across the nation. These were urgent sites of contact for women who otherwise could not find support and analysis.[16]

Radical feminism was part of the cycle of contention of feminism in general, which has taken place in a number of "waves." The first wave in the United States was the women suffrage movement of the late 19th century, which led to the 19th amendment giving women the right to vote. The second wave took place in the 1960s, when the economic prosperity of the post-war period led to growing opportunities and expectations. The civil rights movement had exploded into prominence, and women of all races and backgrounds had been active participants in that movement. They were influenced by the ideas of equality and freedom for oppressed groups. Yet the male leadership of that movement largely denied women leadership and intellectual roles.

Experience in that movement and the ideological openings it provided in society were opportunities for feminism. Frustration with the lack of inclusion in the civil rights and Black liberation movements generated the momentum for the second wave, radical feminism in particular. The movement went through the stages of diffusion when activists spread their ideas and organizations formed all over the country. Radicalization resulted from the limits of previous frameworks and growing awareness of rampant violence against women and the constraints of the domestic role.

Radical feminism has been rightly challenged by feminists of color who have insisted on an intersectional analysis of how gender and race are layered oppressions; the identities of Black feminists could not be reduced to the category "woman." In addition, in some of its variants, radical feminism has been essentialist—reducing gender power to the relationship between biological men and biological women as a function of biological differences. The movement has been more diverse than these criticisms suggest, but they remain important cautions.[17]

The second wave receded after the passage of *Roe v. Wade*, the Supreme Court case legalizing abortion in the United States. One platform of the radical feminist movement was reproductive freedom so that women could have a say over when and whether they wanted to occupy a maternal role. They did not want to be domesticated. The failure of the Equal Rights Amendment in 1984 marked the end of the second wave of contention, as a backlash against the gains of the 1960s, including civil rights and women's liberation, emerged in law, culture, and politics.[18] The exhaustion of the movement gave way to the restabilization of gender roles, although not all of the women's movement gains were erased. Women continued to enter educational institutions and professions at increasing rates; women's bookstores and crisis centers remained, although in waning numbers. The radical feminist movement is useful as a case study for how it exemplifies and contests the terms of the sociological tradition, beginning with the core concept of organization.

Social Movement Organizations and Resource Mobilization

Doug McAdam and W. Richard Scott have defined **organization** as the process in which "resources must be mobilized and momentum sustained," both of which "require instrumental activities and coordination of effort: in short, organization."[19] Institutional actors (participants) in organizations are agents of power and carriers of belief. Institutional logics provide the organizing principles for movements. Governance structures are the means by which power and authority are exercised.[20] In addition, organizations are sites of mobilizing structures and political opportunities.[21] Opportunity structures are the openings for movements to advance their claims against authorities. For example, the radical feminist movement created organizations, mostly small groups because of the movement's emphasis on personal connection. Many cities had multiple such groups. The movement was decentralized, non-hierarchical, and collectively governed. Its activists mobilized to perform actions in local events in response to opportunities like the Miss America Pageant.

Other social movements have built more formal and institutionalized organizations. A **social movement organization (SMO)** is an intentional grouping with identifiable routines, structures, leaders, and activities; when multiple movement organizations form a broader movement consisting of multiple organizations, sociologists call the resulting network and set of coalitions a *social movement industry* (SMI).

A social movement organization is where the tasks of building and deploying a social movement are coordinated. Organizations bring people together as a coherent group with a shared identity expressed in the name of the organization, for example, New York Radical Feminists, National Organization for Women, or Student Nonviolent Coordinating Committee. Organizations can be locally specific or geographically broad in scale; in the latter case, organizations have a branch or chapter structure. As organizations assign divisions of labor, the tasks undertaken by organizations include finding space and holding meetings, organizing meeting content (lectures, discussions, workshops, tactical and strategic development), and locating and reserving public spaces for demonstrations, marches, lectures, or protests. Organizations plan and coordinate action. Organizations are sites for education and the development of a shared ideology and analysis of society. They then become the public face of the movement.

Leaders are the people authorized to guide and coordinate discussion and action in a social movement organization. Different social movement organizations have different forms of leadership, which can include the individual charismatic leader, elected or representative leadership, hierarchical leadership (with offices with more or less authority), lateral or non-hierarchical leadership, direct leadership (when members all participate equally in decision-making, often on a consensus basis), and informal leadership (when a group of people who are unelected control the operation of a group behind the scenes). The benefits of an individual charismatic leader are that they give the public a figure to identify as the movement; they also can tightly control and coordinate action across an organization with multiple chapters or branches. The disadvantage of this kind of leadership is its potential lack of democratic representation of the needs, interests, and wishes of the organization's membership. A direct or lateral organization, while maximizing democratic input, can be chaotic and unfocused. It is difficult to coordinate action if multiple constituencies either cannot agree on a concerted plan or decide to take action on their own (the "affinity group" model). Informal leadership may appear to be democratic because it is structureless; the organization seems to be governing itself. But structureless-ness can be authoritarian when an unelected clique of members decides the organization's path.[22]

Communication is essential to leadership and to how leaders frame the meanings, cultures, ad identities of organizations, including social movement organizations. Organizational communication scholars have called our attention to how leaders transmit information and create meanings; use communication to establish relationships among participants in an organization; guide the processes of organizing in the contexts of power relations and diversity. Good leadership communication is reflexive, morally accountable, and open to change.[23]

SMOs and SMIs must mobilize resources, including legitimacy, money, facilities, and labor. A social movement involves both adherents (participants and aligned bystanders) and constituents, or those who provide resources for the activities of adherents.[24] Investment in one or more SMOs can facility the emergence and effectiveness of an SMI as it mobilizes its resources to increase its numbers and influence established institutions and groups. It is difficult to say that the radical feminist movement constituted a "social movement industry." Indeed, many feminists would object to that corporate language to describe their organizations. However, feminist organizations proliferated in the 1960s and 1970s, with liberal, radical, and eventually socialist feminist groups that operated in tandem (though not always intentionally so) to effect reforms benefiting women. Radical feminism had the productive effect of making the more moderate demands for inclusion on the part of liberal feminists more credible, and all together, the movement "industry" moved the society in meaningful ways.

The emphasis on structure, organizations, and resources characterizes a school of movement analysis called **resource mobilization theory**. Zald and McCarthy argue that movement success depends upon organization, including factors of leadership, administration, incentives, and the means of acquiring resources, including financial resources but also including membership. In the resource mobilization framework, organizations must form to provide leadership, administrative structures and processes, incentives for participation, and a means of acquiring resources and support.[25] Movements must assess political opportunity structures, or how established political institutions can be open or closed; political elites cam be stable or unstable; authorities may or may not be willing to repress agitation. It is also a political opportunity when movements have allies within political elites.[26]

These features of a movement's situation affect social movement organizations' strategy, structure, and success.

The resources and mobilization tradition notes that organizations can be centralized, featuring strong leaders whose role is to smooth over potential divisions in the organization, or more diffuse. Leadership can serve a strategic function when their role connects the movement to constituencies and when the leader herself is a strategic innovator, what Campbell calls a "movement entrepreneur."[27]

This research on these concrete organizational features of social movements operates in an instrumental, utilitarian, and rationalistic frame that subsequent scholars found limited because it could not account for the emergent processes of organization and activity in movements.[28] In addition, the resource mobilization approach stands in contrast to investigations of the more intangible aspects of movements: identities, meanings, frames, social contexts, and feelings in the cultures of social movements. The **cultural turn** in social movements research brought in the fields of social psychology, linguistics, and critical theory to explain the formation of movement identities and the development of collective rationales for action for social change.

The Cultures of Social Movements

Framing Collective Identity

Without a shared understanding of a group's situation and purpose, none of the steps of organization, resource-gathering, or mobilization can take place. This is why a number of sociologists challenged the utilitarian organizations, resources, and mobilizations model with attempts to describe the cultural dimensions of social movements. The elements of culture are vital to the recruitment of adherents to social movements, the creation of political consciousness, the definition and expansion of their identities, the motivation of common action, and the explanation for participants' shared experiences.[29] As Johnston and Noakes explain, "Mobilizing people to action always has a subjective component—the element of perception or consciousness."[30] Collective processes of interpretation mediate—operate between—experience and action, making sense of our lives and our situations, providing a sense that we share those situations with others and the belief that we have the capacity to take action on our own behalf.

Alberto Melucci described the process of identity formation as a necessary task in any movement to establish a sense of "who we are," as opposed to "who they are."[31] Gamson argued that scholars of movements must understand group identification as a social psychological process of winning individuals to a group identity. **Collective identity** is "the mesh between the individual and cultural systems" that occurs when people participate together in shared efforts.[32] What Snow and McAdam call "identity work" occurs on a public, organized level but also on the microlevel of everyday interaction among movement members. Out of such processes, people develop a sense of collective solidarity—loyalty and commitment to the group. Social movements struggle with and against the terms of established society to navigate and challenge dominant ideologies. However, James Jasper warns that a too rigidly enforced collective identity can marginalize some members of movements and lead to splits. Also, movements must create shared identities that convince others to "come out" as different, which can be frightening and off-putting.[33] Charismatic leadership lends participants purpose and confidence, generating positive emotion and greater commitment to the cause.[34]

In the radical feminist movement (and many other movements), cultural events like music festivals have been sites where collective identities are created and shared. The Michigan Women's Music Festival became controversial when its organizers embraced a rigid identity definition of "women" as only those born with biological markers of gender—genital anatomy, hormones, and genetics. In other words, in this forum, radical feminists excluded transwomen from the identity category "woman."[35]

Identity work is core to all social movements. More recent examples include how the Movement for Black Lives reshaped the identities and perceptions of Black people—formerly defined as criminals whose lives did not matter—as proud, outraged, agentive truth-tellers about the reality of police violence. Native movements work to create an agentive identity for Indigenous activists, contesting images of Indians as lazy or helpless, constituting advocates for Indigenous justice as protectors of land, water, culture, and tradition. In rhetorical studies, as we will see in Chapters 4 and 5, the process of identity formation in movements

FIGURE 3.3 Protesters against the Dakota Access Pipeline and Keystone XL Pipeline demonstrate outside the San Francisco Federal Building in January, 2017.

is called "constitutive rhetoric," in which rhetors individually or collectively tell new stories about groups who may have seen themselves through the lenses of internalized oppression and, through shared rhetorical work, can come to see themselves as agents of self-definition and transformation.

Sociologists have identified the shared meaning systems produced in social movements as **frames**. A concept first elaborated by Gregory Bateson and Erving Goffman, frames are schemas of meaning and interpretation that people use to make sense of their world and organize responses to it. Benford and Snow define a frame as an "interpretive schema that simplifies and condenses the 'world out there' by selectively punctuating and encoding objects, situations, events, experiences, and sequences of action."[36] Like a literal frame around a window, a meaning frame shows us how to focus our attention, defining what is relevant and important.[37] Framing consists of "selecting and highlighting some facets of events or issues, and making connections among them so as to promote a particular interpretation, evaluation, and/or solution."[38]

When frames identify a situation requiring change and attribute blame for that situation (attributional frames), articulate alternatives to present conditions (prognostic frames), and urge others to act together to seek those alternatives in a "call to arms" (motivational frames), they are called **collective action frames**.[39] William Gamson defined collective action frames as communicating "the need for a desirability of some form of action."[40] These frames contain three components: the injustice component, which expresses moral indignation at mistreatment, the agency component, which is the sense that one is capable of acting for change, and the identity component, which refers to the sense of collective identity, a "we" as opposed to a "they."[41] The persuasiveness of a frame depends upon its resonance, or credibility and salience for an audience.

Radical feminists published a number of often-satirical manifestoes, a form of discourse well suited to the tasks of framing their identities and issues in terms of injustice and agency. For example, the 1967 *SCUM Manifesto* starts off with an indictment of the abusive, authoritarian, and misogynistic ideologies and practices of masculinity and patriarchy and follows up with a call to arms for women to take over the domains controlled by men through militant action, including violence against men. The call for violence is a hyperbolic and satirical condensation of outrage, moreso than an actual plan to harm men. It re-frames women's identity in terms of a morally indignant "we" calling out unjust treatment and conveying upon women identified with the movement a sense of collective agency.[42]

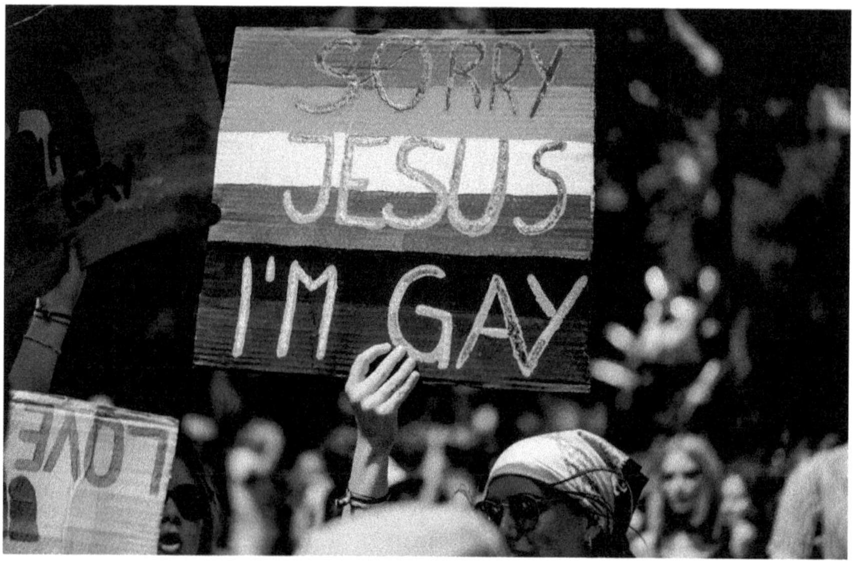

FIGURE 3.4 At a pride parade in 2021.

Frames are built in discursive processes—talk, writing, and other symbolic action that articulate and amplify the fame. Frame articulation is the process of connecting elements of a situation together in a way that hangs together out of a common set of cultural beliefs and values but does so in a new way. Frame amplification happens when movements accent and highlight aspects of the situation to focus attention, for example, in slogans like "Power to the People." Frames are also strategic: designed deliberately to achieve movement goals with particular audiences.[43]

For example, one collective action frame of the gay liberation movement, namely, that gay people are an oppressed minority group, found traction in a U.S. culture familiar with the language of civil rights.[44] The strategic use of this frame displaced the other collective action frames of the movement, especially the critique of U.S. culture as sexually repressive. This idea will become very important in a discussion of how rhetoric—the strategic crafting of public messages.

Frames are successful when they bridge the gap between movement ideas and goals and the beliefs, attitudes, and values of the broader society in a struggle over interpretations of reality. In this process, movement frames must engage *master frames*, or stable prevailing cultural narratives that define social reality for most people. These include mythic narratives like the American Dream, frontier mythology, or the association of women with domestic life. Shifts in material conditions—in the lived experience of ordinary people with relation to politics and the economy—can open up gaps in master frames, posing opportunities for movements to reframe reality. Mainstream media frames interact with and are influenced by movement frames, for example, Martin Luther King, Jr.'s civil rights rhetoric based on familiar Christian themes.[45]

Narratives

This process happens profoundly in **narratives**, or stories. If we see individuals as intersections of social relations, stories establish boundaries among identities and may bring people together in common cause and divide groups from one another in the process. Movements can be a source of non-standard stories. These stories create and convey a movement's sense of collective identity that in turns shapes the sense of identity for followers of the movement. Collective identities are socially constructed in movements in networks of groups engaged in the routines of the movement and of everyday life. In the process, individuals come to recognize themselves as part of a collective identity sharing common cause with others.[46]

In the women's movement's "cultural laboratories," two branches of the movement emerged out of conflict and struggle over identity and purpose: the equal rights feminists and the women's liberation feminists. Women participated in the "submerged networks" of previous movements, including civil rights. Then, "Isolated pairs or small groups of activist women began to voicer a sense of uneasiness to each other about what they perceived as a different and unequal role for women in the actual day-to-day activities of these movements." Facing rebuke and scorn from men in the movements, groups of radical women emerged into collective identities expressed in new activist groups.[47] These groups, such as New York Radical Women, became historic actors based on their emergent cohesive identities.

One core element of the identity-constituting element of radical feminist narrative is the idea that "the personal is political." Recasting narratives of women's place in a privatized realm of domestic and sexual servitude sealed off from political interrogation, radical feminists

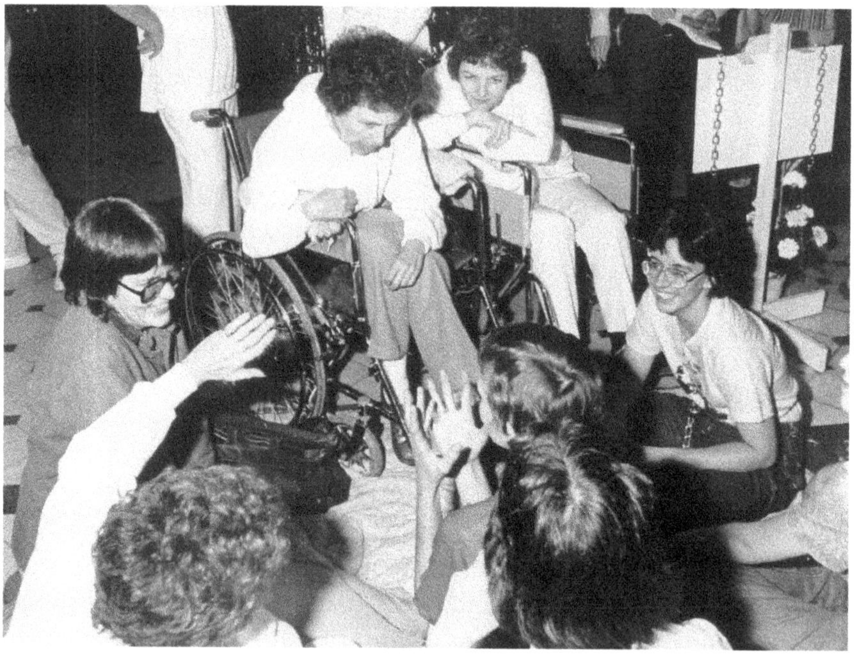

FIGURE 3.5 Women Hunger for Justice activists meet with the Grassroots Group of Second Class Citizens in support of the Equal Rights Amendment in 1982 in an example of consciousness-raising.

insisted on telling their personal stories in public to reveal the inherently political character of power and abuse in relationships defined as private and immune from scrutiny. They also moved their stories out of the therapy frame—which re-personalized these stories—to a political frame that countered women's self-blame for their own oppression.[48]

These identities become part of movement culture, and Gamson calls our attention to how "participation in social movements frequently involves enlargement of personal identity. and offers fulfillment and realization of the self."[49] Collective action frames serve as a mechanism binding individual identity to collective identity and purpose.

On this point, Alberto Melucci describes how the crafting of collective identity leads to the formation of a unified collective and self-identity for actors that sustains a movement over time. Della Porta and Diani describe how collective identity comes into being through action among new networks of relationships among movement actors in social environments who engage in symbols, practices, and rituals of identity construction. The process involves emotion that engenders feelings of solidarity toward others. As collective identities emerge from common action, the meanings of those actions become part of the identity of the collective. Thus, movement groups can enable individuals to break with their former sense of self in becoming part of a collective engaged in challenging old systems and identities. Stigmatization of movements and their members by external powers can strengthen collective identity.[50] Often, identity formation happens in a process of contrast between a movement's group identity and the identity of other groups representing the establishment.

In these ways, movements engage in identity politics, or a struggle for recognition of identity on the part of the broader society as a primary goal of movement organizing. In articulating a contrast to outside views of themselves, movement participants experience both shame and pride, the former leading to retreat and the latter leading to expansive behavior and political agency.[51] Movement activity can generate the transformation of collective identity from shame to pride.

As an example, Verta Taylor and Nancy Whitter describe how lesbian feminism as a social movement developed "counterinstitutions, a politicized group identity, shared norms, values, and symbolic forms of resistance."[52] Building on narratives of shared personal experience (of oppressive situations involving abuse by men, experiences of demeaning culture, and others), lesbian feminists established symbolic boundaries between the positive identity of autonomous women against the norms of established groups. The groups also established a new *political consciousness*: "the interpretive frameworks that emerge from a group's struggle to define and realize members' common interests in opposition to the dominant order ... an ongoing process in which groups reevaluate themselves, their subjective experiences, their opportunities, and their shared interests."[53]

However, this process can be uneven and conflicted. Writing about the LGBTQ and queer movements, Joshua Gamson has noted how debates over sexual and gender identities in these movements were destabilizing. Indeed, the destabilization of firm identities is a hallmark of social movements questioning gender and sexual identities. Queerness—a radically deconstructive vision of gender and sexual identity, "shakes the ground on which gay and lesbian politics has been built." Gamson concludes that movement studies should attend not only to how movements create and stabilize oppositional identities, but also to whether and how these identities are viable and useful.[54]

As we will stress in the next chapter, the process called consciousness-raising is accomplished through writings, speeches, and documents that create a new understanding of women's structural position, resulting in oppositional consciousness. In the case of lesbian feminism, this consciousness is built upon the insight that heterosexuality is an "institution of patriarchal control and that lesbian relations are a means of subverting male domination."[55] This new collective action frame is amplified in the slogan, "Feminism is the theory and lesbianism is the practice."

Emotions and Music

The sociological literature calls our attention to how **emotions** are integral to the processes of identity formation and consciousness-raising. Emotions are feelings given meaning and names in a rhetorical process; the feelings on which enotions are based are powerful resources for social movements. Verta Taylor summarizes this work:

> Research on the sociology of emotions suggests that the social inequalities and injustices that set the stage for social protest are associated with a host of negative emotions such as shame, anger, fear, and depression. At the same time, social movement research demonstrates that developing solidarity with others almost inevitably elicits positive or 'vitalizing' emotions such as pride and joy in connection with the group's new positive collective self-definition.[56]

Societal treatment of non-normative identities as shameful, stigmatized, and deviant (if not mentally ill) can give rise to shame, guilt, and fear. People whose identities do not match cultural norms often feel "crazy" when their experiences do not match the reality structure of surrounding society. These emotions can provoke a search for new self-definitions. Movements create alternative emotional cultures. Taylor gives the example of the post-partum self-help movement, which reinterprets women's feelings of inadequacy and depression after delivering a child, questioning idealized norms of the maternal role.[57]

Emotion work is central to social movements. Emotions connect the macro-politics of a movement to the micro-politics of consciousness and identity. Emotionally-charged public events constitute a movement's collective identity with regard to its opponents and the general public. Emotions are key to the sustainability—and decline—of social movements.[57]

In the micro-practices of social movements, participants may be pulled into commitment through emotional contagion, the tendency to mimic another person's emotional experience such that one begins to feel the same emotions.[58] Embodiment of shared principles, for example in a protest march and other rituals, taps participants' feelings in productive ways.[59] James Jasper identifies the five kinds of emotions that galvanize participants in social movements: urges (bodily needs), reflex emotions (quick automatic responses like anger, joy, shock, or disgust), moods (feelings persisting across settings; can be energizing or de-energizing), loyalties, and moral emotions (feelings of approval or disapproval).[60] In addition, protest is pleasurable when "bodies fall into rhythm with each other," when the "close presence of others triggers many feeling-thinking processes." Crowds are sites of enthusiasm and solidarity.[61]

The political dimensions of emotion came to the fore in the radical feminist movement, whose rhetoric expressed the rage and grief of women who had suffered from misogynistic abuse. As the Radicalesbians' "Woman-Identified-Woman" puts it, "What is a lesbian? A lesbian is the rage of all women condensed to the point of explosion. ... The turmoil she experiences ... eventually drives her to question and analyze what the rest of her society more or less accepts."[62]

Emotion has its basis in pre- or extra-cognitive bodily experience, or **affect**. Rhetoric brings those feelings to the fore and interprets and mobilizes them in social settings.[63] People in movements and other collective settings perform emotion. Emotion is core to human consciousness, knowledge, and identity.[64] In collectivities, a phenomenon

FIGURE 3.6 Three Black women singing and walking in a street in the Capitol Hill neighborhood, the day of the Million Man March in Washington, DC, in 1995.

known as entrainment engages physiological dimensions of experience in order to "share" feelings among members of a group.[65] Specifically, shame, indignation, and joy are emotions common to movements.[66] John Protevi calls the collective brought into being in the process of evoking and expressing emotion a "body politic." In the body politic, people make sense of their situations, establish shared values and collective identities, and adopt an orientation to their collective action while "acting in concert"[67] and "ideas move together with their embodiment."[68] In these ways, emotional communication creates common identity among participants in social movements. Music is an important component in this process.

Social movement scholars identify **music** as key to this process in social movements. When people literally move together—in singing, marching, demonstrating, chanting, or dancing—they are brought together around a shared sense of purpose. Music is a key element of this process of bringing self-conscious collectives into being.[69] Engaging in rhythmic experience with others generates a "collective feeling of unusual energy, power, and solidarity." Rhetoric scholar Erin Rand describes this process as it happened in an LGBTQ organization. She calls the process "choiric communication" that constitutes a collective and orients them to a cause.[70]

Emotion and music contribute to the process of identity framing. But what happens when the identity frames produced and by movements conflict with the hegemonic frames for social reality? Movements must establish a degree of frame alignment with target audiences. In other words, public common sense often perceives social reality differently from movement activists, especially when movements mobilize justice frames that hold others in mainstream society responsible for injustice, suffering, and harm.[71] Frame misalignment, when movement frames depart from hegemonic ones, results in a struggle among contesting frames, during which groups responding to movement charges attempt to reframe the issues in their favor. Snow and Corrigall-Brown give the example of white supremacists' response to anti-racist movements. Against civil rights' injustice frames, the New Racist White Separatist movement reframed their identities in terms of "love and preservation, rather than hatred and destruction."[72] In addition to frame misalignment, frame co-optation happens when a contending group usurps a movement's attempts to frame its activity, thus disabling the movement's public voice and image. Mary Burke and Mary Bernstein describe how this happened when conservative anti-LGBTQ forces co-opted marriage-equality discourses in the movement for same-sex marriage.[73]

In the process of identity framing, it matters how large of an audience a movement is addressing and which members of society are expected to resonate with movement frames. Often, movements are not trying to win everyone in society over; rather, they focus on groups with particular experiences that could align with those framing the cause. For example, radical feminism did not seek to win the approval of mainstream society or win over men. The women reached by the movement shared enough common experience to resonate with the frames put forward in the critique of patriarchy, domesticity, and objectification.

Even when movements are not seeking universal appeal, however, the commercial mass media have a great deal of influence in shaping public perceptions of social movements in the phenomenon known as "media frames."

Media Frames

The self-constructions of movement frames interact with mass media, who employ it to shape public perception of movements. Todd Gitlin's book *The Whole World is Watching* is a study of how the commercial mass media, and particularly news media, defined the social movement of the 1960s through strategic framing. Gitlin defines **media frames** as

> persistent patterns of cognition, interpretation, and presentation, of selection, emphasis, and exclusion, by which symbol-handlers routinely organize discourse, whether verbal or visual.[74]

In other words, the commercial news media routinely presented and interpreted social movement activity—usually in derogatory ways. Gitlin discovered a number of frames that the media used to discredit and trivialize student movements, anti-war movements:

- Trivialization (making light of movement language, dress, age, style, and goals)
- Polarization (emphasizing counterdemonstrations and creating a false sense of balance between justice movements and the ultra-right-wing, giving considerable attention to right-wing opposition)
- Emphasis on internal dissension (conflict in the movement)
- Marginalization (treating protesters as deviant)
- Disparagement by numbers (undercounting of participants in movement events)
- Disparagement of the movement's effectiveness
- Reliance on statements of government officials and other authorities
- Emphasis on the presence of communists
- Emphasis on violence in demonstrations

As a result, the media created celebrity-leaders whose images substituted for the movements, inflated accounts of militancy (extremism and danger) in movements, privileged moderate alternatives over radical change, and decontextualized events (for example, the situation of injustice that prompted movements). All of these had damaging results for the movement. Subsequent popular accounts of that era, particularly framings in popular film, encourage audiences to remember that time as what Kristen Hoerl names, "the bad Sixties."[75] Since the 1980s, media have distorted the events of the decade by portraying movements as immature, irrational, angry, and dangerous. Likewise, commercial mass media framed the radical feminist movement in disparaging ways, labeling feminists as crazy man-haters and traitors to their traditional roles.

Have today's digital and social media, along with the proliferation of media technologies, changed the media landscape, giving ordinary people more agency to control framing of issues and movements? This question is taken up at length in Chapter 6. For now, I will note that there is a great deal more "bottom-up" production and circulation of narratives of experience, of news reflecting diverse realities, of rationales for protest, and for disruption of master frames. For example, public awareness of police murders of Black people across the country was fostered by video recordings on the telephones of witnesses to these events. Movements like the Movement for Black Lives organized primarily online and through social media. The circulation of knowledge from below challenged dominant representations of the policing in the United States such that the master framing of the role of police as "to protect and serve" was displaced by critiques of the institution of policing itself. The framing of Black people (and especially Black men) as inherently criminal gave way to humanizing representations of families victimized by the police. Police organizations throughout the United States responded by reorganizing themselves, replacing leaders and enacting new policies that were steps toward reform.

At the same time, in the mainstream media and on online platforms, a right-wing backlash, couched in a rhetoric against "Critical Race Theory" has taken hold in a dispute over whose stories are told at universities and in the media. There is a struggle for hegemony in the domains of culture and politics that remains unresolved.

Conclusion: What Do Movements Achieve?

It is out of such struggle that we see the achievements of social movements. Movements for social justice have accomplished a great deal across history. These accomplishments are of three kinds: reforms, which refer to adjustment in hegemonic institutions, policies, and habits; revolutions, which are wholesale disruption and replacement of these structures and the replacement of established systems of power; and ideological and cultural change. Reforms are generally the result of significant popular pressure. For example the reforms of the

New Deal made by President Franklin Roosevelt were made under extreme pressure by labor and other people's movements from below. Movements do sometimes make gains through electoral action, lobbying, and court cases. A case in point is how the LGBTQ movement has won supportive legislation and a number of court cases including the 2015 *Obergefell v. Hodges*, which legalized marriage equality across the country.[76] Such gains are often the result of combined moderate "insider" work and pressure from the outside.

While revolutions are rare in the United States (although we must recall the War for Independence and, in some sense, the Civil War as revolutionary accomplishments), around the world they are more common.[77] Tilly has argued that a revolutionary situation is one in which there is more than one social bloc attempting to exercise control over state power. A revolution is the displacement of one set of power holders by another, usually on the heels of the escalation and radicalization of a movement. Often, but not always, such displacement generates and even requires violence.[78] Far from being spontaneous and irrational, violence is an expression of politics. Governments sometimes concentrate the means of social control through coercion, and those pushing for democratic and economic change must also assert some threat. Sometimes revolutions are undermined by counter-revolutions, in which threatened powers re-establish their hegemony. As in the American Revolution, the French Revolution, and many others, revolutions can have progressive and democratizing effects, empowering ordinary people and introducing new language and practices of rights and freedoms.[79]

The achievements of social movements are the results of interaction between structures and frames of culture and identity. Often, shifts in cultural beliefs and practices result from organized challenges to established ways of thinking, and reforms are often made in response to revolutionary threats. For this reason, we cannot separate out the processes of revolution, reform, and cultural shift. The acceptance of new frames and claims grows out of contentious politics.[80]

For example, feminist movements radically shifted dominant ideas about gender, women's roles, the family, and sexuality. Before the first wave, the ideas of the "Cult of True Womanhood," according to which (white) women were urged to be pious, pure, domestic, and obedient held sway. The suffrage movement led not only to the right to vote, but to cultural changes in the definition of womanhood. One interesting example is the invention of pants for women—"bloomers"—by Amelia Bloomer. Freedom in attire, athletics, and physical mobility was an outgrowth of new political ideas and institutional reform. In the second wave, feminists likewise radicalized society's views of women and their roles. For example, the birth control pill, which came into being in 1965, increasingly gave women direct control over reproduction. Feminists began to demand consideration in their erotic lives. In popular culture, images of career women, single women, and different ways of imagining the family came into being as a result of the women's movements. There are many such examples resulting from all movements for social change.

Globalization, or the spread of one economic system (capitalism) around the world, made dominant institutions and interests stronger. Beginning in the post-Second-World-War period and intensifying into the later part of the 20th century, hegemonic elites in society solidified their control over ordinary people during recurring economic crises. The ideology emerging out of this situation is known as "*neoliberalism*," or the philosophy of austerity and the privatization of social responsibility (the burden of the private family).

Tarrow has called our attention to transnational activism in the context of the globalization of the economic system, political ideas, and cultural expression (enabled by electronic media and the currency of English and other dominant languages).[81] Internationalism is both a constraint on human agency and an opportunity structure for activists who are questioning global inequality. With global capitalism, the ideas of a smaller social welfare system, crackdowns on immigration, conventional gender norms, and the policing of minorities secured a hold on institutions and popular consciousness.[82] International struggle against capitalism grew in size and complexity through the 1990s, culminating in the large 1999 Seattle protest against the World Trade Organization, and the militant protest at the Genoa (Italy) Summit of the G8 countries in 2001. The bombings of the World Trade Center towers in New York City and the subsequent wars in Afghanistan and Iraq stifled this internationalism, however.

In this context, sociologists and other scholars began to emphasize the identity and cultural achievement of social movements. In **new social movements**, they argued, claims about identity and representation in culture came to the fore.[83] There was pessimism about the capacity of ordinary people to unite *en masse* on the basis of shared common interests. The collapse of Soviet power in Russia and the Eastern Bloc fueled skepticism about any claims to collective authority. In the "information age," challenging codes becomes a core task of movements.

In other words, the study of movements, along with movements themselves, began to emphasize the war of position over the war of maneuver.[84] (See Chapter 2.) It was not as if reform and revolution were no longer possible, nor did structural and organizational dimensions of movements become irrelevant. Nancy Fraser has argued that struggles for recognition operate alongside struggles for institutional change and the redistribution of resources.[85] It was just that culture and identity work, in which people struggling under oppression and exploitation focused on developing their identities and working for greater representation in popular discourse, were regarded as more in the domain of the possible in a time of social and political stability.

As we will see in the next chapter, this orientation resonated with rhetorical perspectives on social movements. Sociological research initially dominated rhetorical studies of movements. However, in the 1980s, rhetoricians increasingly challenged sociological models in favor of a focus on the strategic production of ideas and the processes of meaning-making in social movements.

Suggestions for Further Reading

Charles Tilly and Sidney Tarrow, *Contentious Politics*, 2nd Edition (Oxford: Oxford University Press, 2015).

David A. Snow, Sarah A. Soule, Hanspeter Kriesi, and Holly J. McCammon, *The Wiley Blackwell Companion to Social Movements*, 2nd Edition (Hoboken, NJ: Wiley Blackwell, 2019).

Alice Echols, *Daring to Be Bad* (Minneapolis: University of Minnesota Press, 1989).

Jeff Goodwin and James M. Jasper, Eds., *Social Movements Reader: Cases and Concepts* (Malden, MA: Wiley Blackwell, 2015).

Questions for Discussion

1. Identify a movement happening around you today. Find a news story about that movement and describe how it frames the movement's participants and activities.
2. Discuss the differences between the resources mobilization tradition in social movement studies and the cultural turn. How can we use the concepts all together to describe social movements?
3. In what ways is the personal political for you? In other words, what about your personal life is affected by issues of institutional and cultural definition and power? (Do not feel obligated to share anything you are uncomfortable sharing.)

Credits

Fig. 3.2: Fred Hess & Son, "Miss America," https://commons.wikimedia.org/wiki/File:Miss_America_1953_swimsuit_competition.jpg, 1953.

Fig. 3.3: Copyright © by Pax Ahimsa Gethen (CC BY-SA 4.0) at https://commons.wikimedia.org/wiki/File:Protest_against_Dakota_Access_and_Keystone_XL_Pipelines_20170126-1441.jpg.

Fig. 3.4: Copyright © by Ivan Radic (CC BY 2.0) at https://commons.wikimedia.org/wiki/File:Woman_with_headscarf_at_Pride_parade_holding_colorful_sign_with_text_%22Sorry_Jesus_I%27m_GAY%22_(51261603807).jpg.

Fig. 3.5: Zoe Nicholson, https://commons.wikimedia.org/wiki/File:Women_Hunger_for_Justice_activists_meeting_with_the_Grassroots_Group_of_Second_Class_Citizens_in_support_of_the_Equal_Rights_Amendment_in_1982.jpg, 1982.

Fig. 3.6: Duncan Spencer, https://commons.wikimedia.org/wiki/File:Three_African_American_women_singing_and_walking_in_a_street_in_the_Capitol_Hill_neighborhood,_the_day_of_the_Million_Man_March_in_Washington,_D.C..jpg, 1995.

4

Rhetorical Traditions in the Study of Social Movements

KEY TERMS

instrumentality
stages of social movements
body rhetoric
rhetoric of the streets
rhetoric of confrontation
constitutive rhetoric

In the previous chapter, we saw that the field of sociology took a "cultural turn" toward the end of the 20th Century, increasingly emphasizing matters of identity, media, affect, and the constitution of communities. Sociologists also accounted for narratives, emotions, and other discursive phenomena in later work on social movements. These emphases dovetailed with the primary concerns of rhetoric: attention to the language, symbolism, and narratives of social movement participants and groups. Rhetoricians were as excited as sociologists to witness the eruption of social protest at the end of the 1960s, which was sustained into the 1970s.[1]

As the world erupted in protest, rhetoricians asked: How were they to study these events, people, and rhetoric? What concepts and methods should they use? What should the stance of rhetoricians be toward embodied, militant protest that deployed not only words and other symbols but also physical pressure? Two general answers to these questions emerged. One group of rhetoricians, represented by Herbert Simons and John Waite Bowers, Donovan Ochs, Richard Jensen, and David Shulz, found the sociological tradition valuable and brought some of its insights and perspectives into rhetorical studies in models stressing resources, organization, leadership, and "stages" of social movements. In other words, the sociologically-inclined scholars have focused on the instrumental—practical, institutional, and change-oriented—aspects of movements. A second group of scholars, represented by Michael McGee, urged colleagues to focus not on organizations, resources, and instrumental power but on identities, discourse, and meaning. In other words, these scholars have focused on the constitutive—community-, identity- and meaning-creating and sustaining aspects of movements.

Overview of Rhetorical Traditions

Rhetorical studies of social movements emerged in the 1960s and 1970s with work largely based on the sociological tradition in its emphasis on organizations, leaders, requirements, problems, and strategies.[2] This work is called *functionalist* because it emphasizes the intentional, strategic character of movements whose activities serve concrete functions; *instrumentalist* because it focuses on how movements exert pressure upon established institutions toward certain instrumental ends. We can also understand this approach as *modernist* in its emphasis on movements as causal agents with direct effects on society.

The functionalist approach was challenged in 1980 when rhetoricians began focusing on the identities and meanings communicated in efforts toward social change, efforts much more loosely conceived as existing outside of or beyond formal organizations or leadership. This constitutive turn, which coincided with the cultural turn in sociology, gave license to rhetoric scholars interested in the myriad forms of "what moves the social,"[3] rather than social movements as identifiable, discrete, phenomenal objects. The dichotomy between the functionalist-instrumentalist (social movement as phenomenon) approach and the constitutive (movement as meaning) approach has structured rhetorical studies' engagement with social movement discourse over the last several decades.

After 1980, rhetorical scholarship on movements developed new sets of specific concepts (like hybridity, subjectivity, and globality) to describe social change rhetoric. It challenged any clear distinction between agitators and establishment, noting that many social change discourses do not target the state or other powerful institutions; they may seek shifts in consciousness and meaning in specific populations or networks. The Occupy Movement of 2011 is a case in point of a movement that did not make instrumental demands on the system; its main effects were the circulation of new identities and meanings, for example, the articulation of a distinction between the 99 percent of the world's population and the one percent who own and control the world's resources and populations. Moreover, sometimes instances of social change rhetoric are aimed at other movements rather than at an easily identifiable "establishment."[4]

During this period, rhetoric largely let go of the language of the social movement and expanded the domain of phenomena to be described beyond traditional protest: embodiment, place, relationship to space, memory work, and performance. Scholars attended to one effort at a time in specific case studies that did not seek to theorize the rhetoric of social movements in general or reframed social movements in terms of counterpublics, defined more fully in later chapters.

As we move forward in this chapter, I will summarize the foundations of the rhetorical study of social movements, including the study of the stages of social movements, the problem of confrontation (and its employment of body rhetoric and rhetoric of the streets), and the distinction between constitutive and instrumental rhetorics. Throughout the chapter, I will refer to the movement of activists demanding access to information about and treatment of HIV-AIDS in the 1980s. I will primarily focus on the rhetoric and action of the AIDS Coalition to Unleash Power, or ACT UP.

Case in Point: ACT UP

ACT UP was founded in 1987 by gay men and their allies from diverse backgrounds to respond to the devastating impact of the HIV-AIDS virus. In the mid-1980s, gay men began to die by the thousands in New York and other cities in what activist and historian Sarah Schulman labeled "a mass death event."[5] (To this day, more than thirty-six million people have died as a result of the virus.) Many of the suffering and dead were gay men, whose friends, families, and lovers watched those around them sicken and die. Outrage grew against the broader society, its leaders, and its medical institutions—most of whom were ignoring the virus and stigmatizing its victims.

Gay people faced enormous stigmatization and discrimination in politics, culture, and daily life. As a result, the political, religious, cultural, and medical establishments initially dismissed the significance of the epidemic. When scientists finally began to study the disease (when it began to impact people outside the gay community), they failed to engage the majority of the people who had acquired and were dying as a result of the virus. Research was slow and dependent upon long, blind clinical trials, which meant that half of the people seeking treatment were given a placebo even as HIV-AIDS ravaged communities across the country.

FIGURE 4.1 An ACT UP demonstration in New York City in 1990.

In response, members of communities affected by AIDS came together and eventually formed the group Aids Coalition to Unleash Power, or ACT UP, which began in New York City and spread to cities across the United States. ACT UP's goals were to challenge a conservative society and its political, religious, and health care institutions, to bring the struggle into public awareness, and to demand that the sick and dying had access to information and care. Through continual meetings and demonstrations, the group did achieve its goals. AIDS awareness led to safe-sex education and broader cultural change. Eventually, government scientists expanded and sped up drug trials, making medicine available to hundreds of thousands of suffering people.[6] Since the 1990s, effective anti-viral treatments have been able to reduce the risk of AIDS and to enable sufferers to survive in the long term. How might we understand this movement in terms of early foundational work about social movements in the rhetorical tradition?

Early Rhetorical Approaches and the Debate Over Confrontation

One of the earliest rhetorical studies of social movements is Leland Griffin's "The Rhetoric of Historical Movements," written in 1952, before the uprisings of the 1960s. Griffin had three key insights. First, he argued that rhetorical studies should extend the concept of rhetoric beyond the individual orator. Collectives, he argued, can be rhetors when groups of people joined together with a common strategically employ language and other symbols (including sounds and images) to persuade others to accept their goals. Scholars of rhetoric can discover "the configuration of discourse, the physiognomy of persuasion, particular to the movement."[7] Second, Griffin described how we can analyze movements in terms of their political orientation ("pro" and "anti" movements) and in terms of the stage of their development, from inception and crisis, through consummation. Inception refers to the emergence of public discourse seeking to influence society. A rhetorical crisis occurs when a movement disturbs existing opinion and social relations in rhetoric that clashes with other interests and groups. Consummation happens when a movement succeeds or fails.

For example, the inception of the Movement for Black Lives was a response to the crisis created by the exposure of increasing numbers police murders of Black people. Activists by the thousands crafted both "pro" and "anti" frames—arguing against the police's use of force and against systemic racism and for the validity of Black lives. The movement waned after its peak of 2020, reaching a point of consummation as police and other institutions made reforms and protests subsided. Since that time, we have seen an organized backlash against Black movements and knowledge in the form of attacks on critical race education and diversity initiatives at universities and in government institutions. In the case of ACT UP, the mass death caused by the virus propelled the inception of the movement, which provoked a crisis by disturbing opinion and social relations in clashes with established institutions and leaders. The consummation of the movement lay in its success.

In addition to urging those studying movements to conduct a chronological analysis of these stages, Griffin lays out criteria by which to evaluate a movement: effectiveness and responsiveness to the public opinion and political climate of the agitators' historical moment. Most importantly, Griffin argued that for a movement to be rhetorical, it must be undertaken in persuasion rather than coercion or force. Rhetoricians should be concerned with the movement's discursive strategies, and with historical movements that have relied primarily on persuasion to achieve their ends.

Sociology's Influence: Instrumental Rhetoric

In the 1970s, some rhetoric scholars incorporated elements of the sociological tradition into their theories. For example, Herbert Simons argued for a "requirements, problems, and strategies" approach to the rhetorical study of social movements.[8] In this "leader-centered" conception, movements face rhetorical requirements, rhetorical problems, and rhetorical opportunities and therefore need rhetorical strategies. The rhetorical requirements include attracting, maintaining, and molding followers into an organized unit; persuading larger power structures to adopt demanded changes, and reacting to resistance from established powers. Social movement leadership is complex, as organizations balance these requirements and address the problems of binding together activists in common cause and to formulate ideology boldly, coherently, and powerfully while maintaining structures of participatory decision-making.

In its employment of identity-based rhetoric that brought people together in shared cause, its targeting of vulnerable constellations of established institutions, and its democratic organization, ACT UP is an example of a movement that we can describe using Simons' model. Leaders of social movements navigate multiple audiences—constituencies internal to the movement, sympathetic outsiders, and recalcitrant authorities. Sociology's approach came to define conceptions of social movements in terms of their **instrumentality**, or how a movement functions to achieve practical ends through organized, concerted, collective action.

Simons identified rhetorical strategies common to social movements and described how moderation, militancy, and intermediate combinations of these poles adapted to various rhetorical situations. Although Simons favored moderation, it is the one-two punch of modest claims and militant presence that often wins the day, and this was the case in ACT UP, who used an inside/outside strategy that placed activists inside pharmaceutical, medical, and political organizations while also pressuring these organizations from outside in militant direct action. Simons' framework might overstate the significance of individual leaders, as many social movements—including ACT UP—are characterized by less hierarchical decision-making structures and broad collective participation.

Also influenced by sociology, Charles Stewart (and co-authors Craig Allen Smith and Robert E. Denton, Jr.) adopted a functionalist approach that understands rhetoric as the primary agency enabling movements to meet opposition and bring about change.[9] They defined the social movement as a unique phenomenon, refining Stewart's functions to include *transforming perceptions of reality (past, present, and future), altering self-perceptions of protestors, legitimizing the movement, prescribing courses of action, mobilizing for action, and sustaining the social movement*. Social movement participants employ language fostering identification and polarization, slogans, obscenity and ridicule, music, arguments, stories, and threats and harassment (coercive persuasion) to serve these functions. They must also react to the strategies of control, which include surveillance, harassment, incarceration, and violence enacted by the establishment. All of these functions happen in stages of a movement's life cycle, from genesis, through unrest and mobilization, to maintenance and termination.

The Movement for Black Lives transformed perceptions of reality by circulating images of police violence against Black people, showing how policing represents structural racism. Mass demonstrations of protesters increasingly recognized as leaders mobilized outraged masses of people to act in defense of Black lives and against police aggression, which the movement framed as a product of systemic racism. The language of Black Lives Matter fostered identification among supporters and polarization against the police and racists who denigrated Black life and experience. Appearing on signs and social media, the slogan defined the movement. In the wake of that movement, perceptions of reality were profoundly shifted even as the anti-racist awareness promoted by the movement came under attack from the right in politics, culture, and the law.

This work on stages of social movements follows sociological thought in its focus on organization, strategy, instrumental goals, and the stages of movement evolution. Another foundational text in this category is *The Rhetoric of Agitation and Control*, by John Waite Bowers, Donovan Ochs, and David Shulz.[10] Like Stewart, Smith, and Denton's work, Bowers and his coauthors guide readers through moments or **stages of social movement development**: *petition* (when agitators ask establishment representatives for change), *promulgation* (when, failing to succeed in those requests, movement organizations reach out to spread the word about the cause and to recruit others), and *polarization* (another moment of escalation in which movement representatives criticize society in terms of an "us" and a "them"). It is at this point when the forces of control (corporations, the state, police, or other authorities) most assertively engage in attempts to suppress or contain the movement. Establishment violence often provokes the next step in movements, what the authors call the "*Gandhi vs. Guerilla*" stage (a split in the movement between moderates and militants, the latter of whom become frustrated with resistance to change and invested in self-defense against establishment violence). Further escalation is characteristic of revolutionary movements. However, at any moment in this process, various combinations of movement gains and establishment reaction can lead to the decline and end of the movement.

ACT UP's Instrumental Rhetoric

In ACT UP, participants sought to transform perceptions of the realities of gay life and the trauma of the HIV-AIDS virus; importantly, coming together to form an agentive collective altered the self-perceptions of the protesters as they moved from grieving and suffering victims to agents of historical change. The group prescribed courses of action for government and corporate agencies, who were called upon to make research public and inclusive and to provide medication and resources for care. In the process, ACT UP polarized the public while also shifting public perception of and winning identification with gay people, who were increasingly coming out into public view. Slogans like "ACT UP, Fight Back, Fight AIDS!" united activists and challenged the public to see the affected communities in a new way. They used every resource of the protest cycle to win their demands.

Regarded through these instrumentalist models, how did ACT UP achieve its goals in a hostile climate with an activist core suffering massive levels of sickness, death, and loss? What were their rhetorical strategies? In Griffin's terms, ACT UP's inception or genesis was sparked by the suffering and outrage of gay men and others who realized that it would take a collective effort to win awareness and resources. Over a period of years, the group provoked a broad social crisis by challenging dominant institutions and cultural norms. One particularly effective moment occurred when the collective, led by David Barr, Gregg Bordowitz, Michelangelo Signorile, and Ann Northrop, occupied the Food and Drug Administration in 1988 to demand immediate release of drugs, the abolition of double-blind studies, and public education about the virus.[11] Another key moment was a 1989 demonstration—taking the form of a "*die-in*"—during a mass at New York's St. Patrick's Cathedral, an iconic symbol of the power of the Catholic Church in the city.[12] The movement's consummation stretched over a decade, during which culture, policy, and science shifted in response to the movement's efforts. One can argue that the movement was both effective and responsive to its context, successfully challenging an entrenched anti-gay society. Griffin's framework does not tell us exactly how to identify the particular rhetorical strategies—the language, narratives, and images—deployed by ACT UP.

Leadership was crucial in ACT UP, but it was also decentralized. Sarah Schulman's oral history of ACT UP documents some of the voices of leaders who developed messages and tactics in the movement. ACT UP used what came to be called an affinity-group model, in which specific action groups and their leaders take on distinct and interconnected projects, including education and treatment committees and grassroots direct action planning groups. This structure generated multiple leaders. Some of the prominent voices were Larry Kramer, David Barr, Michelangelo Signorile, Maxine Wolfe, Mark Harrington, and Ann Northrop. As media professionals, Signorile and Northrop led media strategy for the organization. The St. Patrick's Cathedral "Stop the Church" action gave rise to a new layer of leaders. It also brought transwomen and feminists seeking reproductive justice into its ranks. Schulman writes, "ACT UP had no singular *leader*, although we had many *leaders*."[13]

According to Stewart's model, ACT UP succeeded in transforming perceptions of reality; it was profoundly effective in altering self-perceptions of protestors, people who had been isolated, marginalized, and stigmatized. Over a short period of time, those suffering reconstituted themselves as collective, confident, and expert agents of transformation. ACT UP succeeded in legitimizing the movement and demanded courses of action that were eventually undertaken by establishment leaders. ACT UP's members trained its members and mobilized them for action.

FIGURE 4.2 The pink triangle with the slogan "Silence=Death" became an iconic piece of ACT UP's visual rhetoric.

In the process, ACT UP developed new language defining its members. One key strategy was to develop messages and actions uniting gay men, lesbians, drug users, the poor, and women on the basis of shared experience. One example was when ACT UP held a demonstration specifically demanding treatment for women with HIV-AIDS, using the slogan "Women don't get AIDS; they just die from it."[14] Activists shared arguments and stories to create and convey their new sense of identity. ACT UP's slogans and images used obscenity, polarization, and ridicule. A regular chant was, "ACT UP, fight back, fight AIDS!" The movement invented slogans and signs with lasting power, for example, the statement "SILENCE=DEATH."

The group did exhibit movement through stages, from promulgation as the group spread its message both in mainstream culture and targeting specific experts and institutions—to polarization and greater militancy when the system did not move quickly enough to stave off suffering. These moments of struggle did not happen in a linear sequence. They occurred simultaneously as movement affinity groups moved back and forth among audiences and tactics.

The Problem of Confrontation

However, for those privileging movements relying on civil symbolic action, ACT UP poses something of a challenge. In addition to writing articles and speeches, creating artwork and other community-centered cultural texts, holding rallies, and meeting with officials, ACT UP engaged in direct action, using members' bodies to disrupt business as usual at political sites, religious spaces, and in popular culture. At the FDA protest, activists pressed their bodies against the fence as workers looked on from office building windows. During a 1992 action, activists emptied the ashes of their loved ones onto the White House lawn.[15] In St. Patrick's Cathedral, some interrupted mass by lying down on the cathedral floor as if dead—and some jumped up on pews to shout "Stop Killing Us!"—while others demonstrated outside. In these and other settings, they went beyond speech in their militancy. Does that make ACT UP something other than a rhetorical movement? How should we regard the repertoire of speech and action developed and deployed by members of this organization?

Griffin offers one answer to this question in a discussion of what he called **body rhetoric**, defined as a mode of protest in which activists interrupt or disrupt spaces (like streets and buildings) and the routines of powerful institutions and elites with their bodies. Griffin condemned such confrontations as coercive and contrary to the rhetorical valorization of persuasion.[16] However, other early rhetorical studies of social movements assessed militancy in more positive terms. Drawing on observations of the civil rights movement, Frank Haiman coined the phrase **rhetoric of the streets** to describe civil disobedience, law-breaking, property damage, and other militant actions.[17] Haiman argued against Griffin and other anti-militancy rhetoricians, who argued that civil disobedience bred anarchy, violated conventions of time, place, and manner, and exceeded rational discourse. In contrast, Haiman noted that the rhetoric of the streets had often been effective. Moreover, Haiman argued, there is an ethical imperative to challenge the *status quo* through confrontational action when basic human rights and lives are at stake and regular channels of reasoned discourse are closed. To condemn the rhetoric of the streets, Haiman stated, one must close one's eyes to the realities of the world. In this conclusion we can see how the dramatic confrontations of the civil rights movement against racist violence and discrimination inspired Haiman and led him to the conclusion that confrontation "in the streets" was an ethical imperative. ACT UP's protest at the FDA, where participants released the ashes of their loved ones on the steps, is a poignant example of body rhetoric—where the bodies in question are of the deceased—and the rhetoric of the streets. Hunger striking is a particularly powerful form of body rhetoric, as it endangers people's health and lives as a statement of protest that ironically mobilizes the weakening body as an expression of powerful agency.[18]

Recently we have seen other examples of body rhetoric in the streets in the movement against Israel's war on Gaza, which began when Palestinian insurgents attacked a number of Iraeli targets (including civilians) in October, 2023. Israel's response was intense and catastrophic for Gazans. As of the time of this writing, more than 34,000 Palestinians are dead, the majority of them women and children.[19] In the United States and around the world, masses of people have demonstrated in the street. University students at Columbia, Yale, and the University of Southern California have occupied campus spaces and built encampments, even as their administrations have attempted to suppress their activity through expulsions, lockouts, and arrests. They have protested these arrests, in one case surrounding and climbing on top of a police car, resulting in a detained student being released. These activists are engaged in the rhetoric of confrontation, putting their bodies in the streets and on the university malls against the war and for Palestinian self-determination. They also have been confrontational, igniting controversy over whether the demonstrations are criticizing the state of Israel or whether they constitute an antisemitic threat.

FIGURE 4.3 The California State University, Los Angeles, Palestine Solidarity Encampment in June 2024.

In 1969, Robert L. Scott and Donald K. Smith named the **rhetoric of confrontation**: a social drama in the clash of "us" versus "them," the "haves" versus the "have-nots."[20] They observed that advocates of confrontation rhetorically create a sense of radical division between agitators and their targets. In movements like the Black Power Movement and the New Left, movement participants engage a symbolic "rite of the kill" by harassing, embarrassing, and disarming identified oppressors.

Scott and Smith described confrontation as a "totalistic strategy" characterized by a rhetoric of death and rebirth and by appeals to the constancy, fortitude, and unity of the forces of opposition. The totalistic strategy of confrontation is constitutive of the ideological core of a movement. One could argue that ACT UP's strategy of confrontation was totalistic: The movement was literally about death and survival, which were at the movement's core. Scott acknowledges that civility and decorum might be "masks for the preservation of injustice" in a fundamentally unjust society. Movements scholar Robert S. Cathcart also notices that confrontation not only challenges establishment power but also creates shared identities and meaning.[21] That process of building identification among activists, he says, is necessary to social movements, especially in movements seeking significant change rather than simply adjusting to existing society. Confrontation, in Cathcart's view, is a defining and necessary feature of social movements.

Returning, then, to the militancy of the movement organization ACT UP: Members engaged in the rhetoric of the streets, body rhetoric, incivility, appropriate and necessary moral inversion, and robust social drama in their efforts for change. In every possible setting, participants demanded attention to their suffering and dignity. Confrontation was both a local tactic and a totalistic strategy in ACT UP, as the group formed itself around radical demands. Footage from organizing meetings of ACT UP shows how in-group conversation about their antagonism toward oppressive institutions created a common bond of solidarity and identity. In a non-hierarchical organization that enabled smaller groups of members to engage in independent action, the movement members motivated each other on the basis of life-and-death struggle. The group's slogans communicated militancy and defined passive U.S. citizens as complicit with mass death.

ACT UP's members employed diatribes, defined by Theodore Otto Windt, Jr. as a bitter, vituperative, counter-moral rhetoric that turned the norms of society on their head.[22] Far from serving the ego-function derided by rhetorician Richard Gregg, the movement's rhetoric was not about allowing activists suffering from mere feelings of inadequacy to feel better about themselves.[23] In redefining gay Americans as agentive human beings deserving of recognition and care and relocating social responsibility from the private sphere to the public interest, ACT UP succeeded in winning reforms necessary to the survival and flourishing of people with AIDS, and, by extension, the recognition of LGBTQ communities as a political force.

At this point we have described how the rhetorical study of social movements accounts for the instrumental—practical, organized, system-focused, and change-oriented—dimensions of movements. Other rhetoric scholars have rejected this focus in favor of attending to how movements appear as inchoate developments in meanings and identities: the constitutive rhetorical elements of rhetorical change.

Social Movements as Meaning: Constitutive Rhetoric

In response to the instrumentalist accounts of movements coming from Griffin; Simons; Stewart, Smith, and Denton; Bowers, Ochs, Jensen, and Shulz; and Cathcart, other rhetoricians rejected what they saw as a blunt account of movement organizations' means and ends. They preferred to focus on social movements as happening primarily as evolutions in meaning and language. That difference is captured in the distinction between instrumentality and constitution in social movements. Instrumentality refers to the deployment of organizations and resources to win demands from established institutions and groups. An instrumentalist perspective focuses on how movements achieve their goals with external audiences. On the other hand, an emphasis on **constitutive rhetoric** focuses on the emergence of identities and meaning instead of organizations and public confrontation. Thus, rhetorical scholars of movements carved out an identity for itself distinct from sociology. Rather than seeing social change as a series of demands and confrontations, such scholars regarded social change as a process of shift in cultural meanings.[24]

Many "new social movements" promoting the recognition of diverse identities are meaning-centered rather than instrumental. These movements focus on changes in identity, lifestyle, and culture—as Melucci puts it, they challenge "codes" rather than seeking economic and political change at the institutional level.[25] Although some identity-based movements, including the movement to raise awareness and promote institutional change around HIV-AIDS are significantly instrumental in their orientation and tightly organized, some parts of the gay rights movement fall into the category of new social movements. Today, environmental movements—tied to anti-racist and Indigenous movements—are loosely networked and emphasize changes in cultural meanings as much as they do instrumental action. But such movements as the one to stop "Cop City" in Atlanta clearly challenge institutions of policing and city governance and face systemic repression by institutional forces.[26] However, in this book I am stressing that we cannot cleanly separate the meaning- and identity-making (constitutive) moments of social movements from their instrumental goals and actions. However, rhetoricians found the aspects of social movements dedicated to meaning-making most interesting, given the field's emphasis on language and other symbol use.

Michael McGee rejected the idea of "the movement," arguing that every instance of what we might call a movement is an interpretation of phenomenal data. In general, social movements order social and historical facts to "maintain the illusion of 'morality,' 'purpose,' and 'destiny' in largely self-aggrandizing collective behavior."[27] As a shift in

FIGURE 4.4 ACT UP meeting in 1988.

public consciousness, a movement is not a discrete thing for McGee: "I see no phenomenon at all but only a series of worlds and meanings to be discovered and verified."[28]

Illustrating this principle, in ACT UP, every meeting and action generated new meanings, ideas, and perceptions among members, whose identities shifted from sufferers and outsiders to empowered activists and experts. The grief and fear among those living with and dying from AIDS were channeled into anger and outrage and a sense that those fighting for change had little to nothing to lose. In addition, as ACT UP dovetailed with anti-racist movements, feminist movements, and queer movements, the movement's collective identity became more solidaristic and its targets broader. These developments did not come about as a result of rhetoric exclusively aimed internally, but out of the interaction of public contestation and transformation channeled back into the processes of identity and meaning formation—and back out again.

Conclusion: Dialectic of Instrumentality and Constitution

When one exclusively emphasizes structure, organization, and resources, what is particularly *rhetorical* about social movements is left behind. When one defines all movement as either a self-aggrandizing ordering of facts, a series of worlds or meanings, or something that is discernable not as an actual phenomenon, but only perceived by the critic, everything that makes a social movement effective—everything *instrumental* becomes easily missed. The idea of social movements as meanings discernable only by critics negates the fact that there are groups who are actually oppressed and exploited, whose experience is not the same as that of elites in society, and interests and consciousness therefore flow from another, more critical basis. When these groups come together to engage in agitation for both culture change and institutional change, they engage in orchestrated, purposeful contentious collective action. At the same time, a rhetorical perspective usefully calls our attention to how consciousness and group identity do not flow automatically from experience. Rhetorical work is necessary to consciousness-raising, a process where new identities and perceptions of reality can arise, giving shape to a movement's purpose.

The present book regards the instrumental and constitutive dimensions of social movements as *dialectical*. To say something is dialectical is to call attention to how a concrete situation—relations of the state, politics, culture, and economics—is connected to and partially determines the rhetorical strategies of any collectivity seeking the transformation of society. Existing social relations, values, norms, beliefs, perceptions of reality, alongside social institutions, economic constraints the state, and instruments of power, all constitute what Lloyd Bitzer called a "rhetorical situation": an imperfection in society marked by urgency, in which rhetors may make a difference by engaging in communicative action by addressing audiences with purposes in mind.[29] Rhetorical action always takes place in a setting of constraints that make some ideas, strategies, and tactics effective and others less publicly intelligible.

Social structures include institutions, organized collective identities, and relationships such as class, gender, sexuality, race, and so on. The nation-state is a key part of the structure, one of particular importance, since most states control the armed forces of the establishment. Police and other coercive authorities are also part of the structure that constrains social movement development, and action. Cultural beliefs, attitudes, and values—and prevailing conceptions of what is real, true, justified, and good—also make up a set of constraints. Existing belief systems—for example, the belief that capitalism is the economic system of democracy, that racial and gender differences are real bases upon which social roles and goods may be distributed, that the nation-state is the primary site of social belonging, and so on—constrain what messages from movements will make sense and which ones will not with broader, unconvinced audiences.

In this chapter, we have reviewed traditional rhetorical approaches to social movements. Out of the scholarly literature on social movement organizations, meanings, and stages, I have argued that we should regard movements dialectically—as processes within which constitutive, internal strategies of consciousness-raising and meaning-creating are interdependent with public, external, instrumental movement work. The next chapter turns to specific rhetorical repertoires of contemporary social movements as they engage both "internal" (within the movement) and "external" (broader public) audiences.

Suggestions for Further Reading

John Waite Bowers, Donovan J. Ochs, Richard J. Jensen, and David P. Schulz, *The Rhetoric of Agitation and Control* (Long Grove, IL: Waveland, 2010).

Christina R. Foust, Amy Pason, and Katie Zittlow Rogness, *What Democracy Looks Like: The Rhetoric of Social Movements and Counterpublics* (Tuscaloosa: University of Alabama Press, 2017).

Charles E. Morris, III and Stephen Howard Browne, *Readings on the Rhetoric of Social Protest*, 2nd edition (State College, PA: Strata, 2006).

Sarah Schulman, *Let the Record Show: A Political History of ACT UP New York, 1987–1993* (New York: Farrar, Strauss, & Giroux, 2021).

Nathan Crick, ed., *The Rhetoric of Social Movements: Networks, Power, and New Media* (New York: Routledge, 2021).

Suggested Viewing

Jim Hubbard, *United in Anger* (Bronx Documentary Project, 2012). https://www.unitedinanger.com/.

Questions for Discussion

1. Describe the difference between instrumental and constitutive approaches to the rhetoric of social movements.
2. Think about a movement happening around you today. Would you describe it as instrumental or constitutive, meaning- and identity-centered or instrumental? How so?
3. What do you think about social movements' use of confrontational strategies, with reference to your own experience or to the strategies of ACT UP?

Credits

Fig. 4.1: Copyright © by MACMILLAN (CC BY-SA 4.0) at https://commons.wikimedia.org/wiki/File:Gay_act_up_nyc_manhattan.jpg.

Fig. 4.2: ACT-UP, The AIDS Coalition To Unleash Power, "Silence = Death," https://commons.wikimedia.org/wiki/File:A_pink_triangle_against_a_black_backdrop_with_the_words_%27Silence%3DDeath%27_representing_an_advertisement_for_The_Silence_%3D_Death_Project_used_by_permission_by_ACT-UP,_The_AIDS_Coalition_To_Unleash_Power._Wellco. Copyright © 1987 by ACTUP New York, Inc.

Fig. 4.4: Copyright © by Chuck Stallard. Reprinted with permission.

5

Contemporary Rhetorics of Social Movements

KEY TERMS

worldmaking
undercommons
argument
narrative
visual rhetoric
violence
silence
internal audiences
consciousness-raising
external audiences
militancy
radicalism
flanking
radical flank effect

This chapter turns to the rhetorical repertoire of social movements and its uses in the different rhetorical situations, facing internal and external audiences. I then describe how movement rhetoric appeals to the broader public or to specific publics, and how movement rhetoric constitutes counterpublics that both sustain themselves as enclaves and/or attempt to influence broader public opinion and the state, its policies, laws, structures, and leaders. The chapter then distinguishes between the elements of radicalism—the extent of ideological beliefs and goals (for example, whether to reform existing society or to mount a broad critique of dominant systems and elites)—and tactics—degree of militancy (for example, whether to employ confrontation and bodily disruption), arguing that we ought not conflate the two axes. One can employ militant tactics in the service of modest reforms, or employ moderate, less confrontational tactics toward overarching systemic change, and engage in any other combination of these elements in various formulations over time. Following those basic frameworks, I will describe specific rhetorical strategies—parts of the rhetorical repertoire—common to most social movements: affect/emotion, bodies, narratives, arguments, images, slogans, and music. This chapter carries on with the central case study of ACT UP, with reference to other examples along the way.

Early rhetoric scholars of movements were preoccupied with the problem of confrontation and debated whether social movements were "phenomena" or "meaning"—or whether that binary even makes sense.[1]

Recent Work on Social Movement Rhetoric

This perspective is informed by the dramatism of Kenneth Burke, who argued that rhetoric is at the core of identification, division, and meaning-making. Rhetoricians have focused on issues of culture and symbolic production, the articulation of identities, and smaller-scale movement tactics and communication networks, including digital networks.[2] Movement scholars are expanding their view to recognize enactment of resistance by oppressed communities who, denied the usual means of public expression, mobilize bodies and spaces to demand change.[3]

The Occupy Movement of 2011 is a good example of this emphasis. The prefigurative politics ("be the change you want to see in the world") of the Occupy movement resulted in multiple innovations in social movement repertoires, including the mass-democratic public meeting and the use of computers and phones to live-stream their content. The Movement for Black Lives employed the dissemination of images of police brutality via cell phone video over social networks.[4] The #MeToo movement, as the hashtag suggests, became a viral phenomenon on social media.[5] Recent work has also described movements' use of media, including conventional forms like documentary film and video and emerging digital platforms.[6] Queer organizing has generated new articulations of gender identity and expression and created spaces for self-definition and self-defense, with specific attention to transgender liberation and the production of transgender and gender non-binary or non-conforming identities in struggle. Attention to subjectivity (the social production of identities) and affect, or emotion, in the practices of emancipation is among the more recent emphases in our field's work on the processes of social change.[7] Similarly, we are paying more careful attention to culture—mass media, music, literature, dance, theater, and other forms of expression—as context, target, and emergent product of movements.

FIGURE 5.1 An Occupy Wall Street demonstration on October 17, 2011.

Intersectionality

One crucial development in our understanding of movements for social justice is the concept of intersectionality or, as explained in the Introduction, the idea that no oppression happens along a single axis.[8] Therefore, scholarship on movements must trace these intersections, for example, between queer identity and immigrant movements, labor and race, feminism and gender identity, climate injustice and ableism, and so on in new ways that are accountable to the complexity of experience and the struggles of people who do not lead "single-issue" lives. The intersections of identities and oppressions operate in complicated ways, for example, when queer Latine migrants at the U.S./Mexico border must navigate homophobia on the one hand and the experience of detention and deportation on the other.[9] Another example is the idea of racial capitalism, an economic system of exploitation that rests upon racial oppression manifested in the institutions of prison and policing.[10] Other scholars have also used the term colonial racial capitalism to describe how capitalism has always depended upon Indigenous dispossession and systemic racism to function, for example, through the theft of land and resources to a reliance on devalued racialized labor.[11]

An intersectional perspective allows us to see how rhetorics of resistance are simultaneously conditioned by race and gender. For example, Amani Husain studies letters of detained migrant women on a hunger strike to discover how their "feminist archive of resistance" intersects their identities and trauma as immigrants.[12] Likewise, Stacy Sowards' work on the rhetoric of United Farm Workers leader Dolores Huerta reveal's Huerta's navigation of the roles of mother and labor leader.[13]

Worldmaking

A body of work in rhetorical studies has focused on the worldmaking dimensions of all are examples among many of the studies of the rhetoric of movements for social change, representing a constitutive approach to movements.[14] **Worldmaking** refers to how communicators, especially those who have been less powerful in society, co-create their identities, goals, and communities through rhetorical effort. Feminist philosopher María Lugones cultivated fertile ground with her concept of "world-traveling." We travel among worlds of actual society and its construction of the relationships of class, gender, and race; or our own communities and movements where people in oppressed groups can be at ease, mutually understood, and conceptually as well as physically safe; we also "travel" between the worlds of movements focused on one identity to those of others. The goal is to traverse these worlds with love, humility, and solidarity.[15]

Work in rhetorical studies has attended with love and solidarity to the diverse worlds crafted in rhetoric by subordinated groups. These studies fall under constitutive approaches in their attention to how communities engage in worldmaking to craft identities and engage in the creative production of cultural texts and practices specific to them.[16]

Worldmaking operates in tandem with the public, collective organizing and institutional achievements of identifiable movement organizations and leaders. The authors mentioned here are just a few among dozens of rhetoric scholars attending to the role of rhetoric by communities forging not only organized public movements but also communities of identity crafting and performance and mutual care. A related concept to worldmaking focuses on how oppressed communities—with particular emphasis on Black, Indigenous, queer, and poor peoples—create knowledge, meaning, and resistance from below: the **undercommons**.[17] While some studies of social movements focus on how groups mobilize in the public spheres of mainstream culture and politics or state-oriented counterpublic spheres, an emphasis on the spaces of local, subversive, self-determination, identity, and consciousness characterize theories of the undercommons.[18] A total review of contemporary rhetorical studies of social movements is not possible here, but these are some good starting points.

Rhetorical Repertoires

At this point, it is useful to recall a concept about social movements from the sociological tradition: the idea that social movement participants and organizations—like musicians or theater troupes—deploy repertoires, sets of standard and practiced actions effective with different audiences in diverse situations. Now we can refine the idea of repertoires in a specifically rhetorical way, by identifying the particular rhetorical strategies of social movements. These include argument, narrative, image, emotion, music, and embodiment up to and including confrontation and violence.

Arguments

An **argument** is a proposition supported by evidence and reasoning. Arguments can be about information (advancing a claim of information or fact), judgments (advancing claims of value/evaluation), and/or future action (advancing deliberative claims). Often, these kinds of arguments nest within each other. For example, ACT UP argued that national health institutes and pharmaceutical companies were delaying research and treatment and ignoring the interests of those suffering from HIV-AIDS. That is a claim of information aimed at changing beliefs. Then, they argued that these practices were wrong. That is a claim of judgment or evaluation aimed at challenging the audience's values. Finally, they argued that the institutions in questions should change, aiming at changes in action. That is a deliberative claim.

In order for a communicative act to be regarded as an argument, it must be supported by evidence. Evidence can take the form of examples, statistics, stories, and testimony (or expert opinion). ACT UP developed the expertise of its own members so that they could challenge doctors, policymakers, and others when told that the process could not go more quickly or be more inclusive. ACT UP members could discuss medical data and biological processes confidently, providing citations from studies, examples, and testimony from their own experience. An evaluative claim depends upon shared values, so that an ACT UP member could appeal to others' alleged commitment to healing, equity, and an end to suffering—and call them out when they did not honor those values. A policy claim depends upon establishing both the factual and the evaluative claims in order to make a recommendation for action. The drug approval process is too lengthy and discriminatory. This fact harms us. Treating us like this and allowing us to suffer is wrong and contradictions your stated values. Therefore, you should speed up the trials, expand the testing, and make the medicines that we do have freely available.

Narratives

Much human influence takes place by sharing stories about experience and using elements of a story as reasons for changing one's beliefs, values, and actions.[19] A **narrative** is simply a story: a recounting of a process in which something happens; in a story, there is usually a beginning, a middle, and an end, if the story is to be coherent. Stories are based on shared experiences and values and affirm community in the process of shaping belief, values, and action. Stories work by asking a listener or audience member to identify with a protagonist (sometimes a hero; individual or collective), whose actions (often against an antagonist) and their consequences convey some sort of lesson. In identifying with the character, audiences are moved to accept the lesson and any change in outlook or behavior that such a lesson entails.

Stories were core to the formation and influence of ACT UP. At organizing meetings, people would tell their stories: how they got sick or how a loved one became ill or died. Activists told stories about demonstrations, about how their experience engaged in public action changed their self-concept and confidence. Stories are crucial to internal, constitutive rhetoric, since stories powerfully convey shared meanings and identities, invite audience identification, and build collective identity and solidarity. Narratives, organized around shared values and compelling accounts of experience, are also important to persuasion with audiences external to movement organizations.

Narratives organize a sense of our past, both individual and shared. With regard to HIV-AIDS, the AIDS Quilt project stands out as collection of powerful narratives. The project began in 1985, spearheaded by activist Cleve Jones, as a commemoration of mounting AIDS deaths

FIGURE 5.2 The NAMES Project AIDS memorial quilt on display on the National Mall in 1996.

and honoring the lives of previously stigmatized sufferers.[20] Each of the 105,000 squares of the quilt, which now weighs 50 tons, marks a person's life story. In just a few words and images, each constitutes a story about a person who lived and who is mourned. The lesson of each panel's story is about registering the impact of the disease and recognizing those who have died as human beings. One reads: "My name is Duane Kearns Puryear. I was born on December 20, 1964. I was diagnosed with AIDS on September 7, 1987 at 4:45 p.m. Sometimes it makes me very sad. I made this panel myself. If you are reading it, I am dead."[21] In this story, the protagonist is Duane Kearns Puryear, who undertakes the creation of his panel. We thus learn that he lived for 23 years and died a young man who was perhaps alone (having to make his panel himself) or possessed of an urge toward creative agency.

Another panel reads, "Leonard P. Matlovich, a gay Vietnam veteran. They gave me a medal for killing two men and a discharge for loving one," under the banner of two pink triangles and the words "Never again—never forget."[22] And so in two lines we have a story about Leonard Matlovich, a man who served the nation in war. There is an implicit values argument in the panel as well: The country betrayed the ideals for which I fought.

Images

The use of pink triangles by the LGBTQ liberation movement starting with ACT UP is an example of visual rhetoric. **Visual rhetoric** is the communication of ideas (including arguments and narratives) using images (moving or still), which can be icons (realistic representations) or symbols (an image standing in for another object, idea, or event).[23] The pink triangles are references to Nazi Germany, which persecuted and murdered gay people alongside Jews, Roma people, Catholics, and the disabled. The Nazis made gay people mark themselves with pink triangles. In reclaiming that symbol, LGBTQ movements communicate both an identity—we are gay, we are here—and a critical argument by analogy: to persecute gay people is to be like Nazi Germany. Scholars of visual rhetoric have noted that images have the capacity to make arguments, to evoke emotion, to offer points of view on events and other people, and to condense time and meaning into a compressed instantaneous message.

Scholars of visual rhetoric argue that images can tell a story in a more immediate way than verbal narration. Photographs, often regarded as icons because of their resemblance to the objects or events they attempt to represent, possess an especially powerful capability: to appear to reflect reality and therefore to serve, in themselves, as proof that something happened the way that the photographer perceived it to happen.[24] However, photographs always convey a perspective, and editing, lighting, color, framing, and other features serve a persuasive function. No image is rhetorically innocent or free from persuasive influence. In Kenneth Burke's terms, images, in their attempt to "reflect" reality, must "select" certain features of that reality and therefore "deflect" other elements.[25]

The AIDS Quilt's visual rhetoric exemplifies a number of these rhetorical strategies. As noted above, each panel condenses a narrative about the person who died; each panel and the Quilt as a whole make an argument that the scale and human cost of the epidemic were monumental and deserving of public recognition. The panels also assert the humanity of each person represented. The massive quilt as social movement rhetoric also establishes the public memory of the HIV-AIDS academic and conveys lessons for public values and action today.

Affect and Emotion

The Quilt also has a profound emotional impact on those who experience it. The invocation and deployment of emotion is another rhetorical strategy of social movements. Emotions arise from what psychoanalytic communication scholars call affect—a pre-emotional state of intense feeling without clear meaning or labels.[26] Erotic desire (not necessarily expressly sexual) is part of the landscape of affect. Affect undergirds experience in an inchoate way. In social movements, members are moved by affect to seek identification with others who might help to interpret and give name to individual and collective feelings. ACT UP activists and historians have noted, for example, how coming together in weekly activist meetings provided not only the intellectual and political experience of organizing, but also the social experience and frisson of connection to others. ACT UP meetings had an erotic charge that amplified collective commitment, belong, and confidence.[27] In movements (and other social groups), people strive to put names on their feelings and interpret their meaning in frames that make sense of experience. An emotion is a socially named, intelligible, and powerful feeling. Emotional appeals constitute, name, tap, and deploy those feelings toward particular ends. When so named and invested with meaning, affects become identifiable emotions, for example, anger, grief, and desire. These three emotions were core shared experiences of ACT UP participants. Collective sharing of stories and experience fit emotions into frames of understanding; that sense-making process then contributes to the crafting of collective identity framing and new interpretations of reality. Another good example is Amani Husain's study of 27 hunger strikers at an immigrant detention center in Taylor, Texas. Husain analyzes the letters of the detainees and finds "powerful testaments to trauma, anguish, and ultimately solidarity through defiance."[28]

Body Rhetoric and Music

Affect is first experienced in the body as a set of sensations of intensity. When emerging into intelligibility as emotion, such feelings are expressed in words and bodily action. Interpersonally, those actions may involve physical touch, dancing, or other movement. Collectively, movement participants embody their emotions in ways conducive of togetherness, collective goals, and collective action. I have noted above how rhetoric scholars have identified body rhetoric as a key component of a social movement's repertoire, especially when activists engage in physical confrontation or disruption. Protests and marches are manifestations of affect-driven, emotional "body rhetoric" in which moving together creates a powerful force. ACT UP's Saint Patrick's Cathedral die-in is a poignant example.

Another event in which body rhetoric was especially powerful was the 2013 sit-in in support of abortion rights at the Texas Capitol during a summer legislative session during which legislators attempted to push through draconian restrictions on abortion access. Sparked by a filibuster by Representative Wendy Davis, thousands of people—women, men, gender nonbinary, transgender, youth, students, professionals, educators, politicians, and social movement organizations—occupied the Capitol over a period of two days in a massive demonstration of common cause.[29] The massing of so many bodies together unified diverse groups into what conservatives lambasted as an "unruly mob."

Proponents of the anti-abortion legislation attempted to ban people from the legislative chambers and banned even the possession of feminine hygiene supplies (like tampons and pads), fearing that women would use these items as projectiles against legislators. Activists and reporters took advantage of this invocation of the body by flaunting and wearing tampons and ridiculing the ban and the people who demanded it.

As the midnight deadline for passage of the legislation neared, Capitol occupiers began to roar in chants, songs, and shouts, carrying on continuously over a period of hours. The pressure of sound waves connected people together physically. The roar became so loud that the legislature could not hear each other, even through heavy doors, to pass the legislation. One reporter commented that the demonstrators had "shouted the bill to death." In this way, social movement activists mobilized their bodies in a monumental way to disrupt business-as-usual in the Texas legislature. The congress passed the legislation in a second, hastily-called second special session after the protest dissipated. We cannot know whether a continued occupation of the Capitol would have prevented it—but certainly the absence of bodily pressure enabled the legislature to finish their work.

That event involved chanting, dancing, and singing. Social movement scholars have identified music and song as powerful strategies of social movements. As many sociologists have recognized, music and song are compelling components of every social movement. Singing in movements literally bonds participants to each other, and the rehearsal of shared music and lyrics serves a unifying and empowering

FIGURE 5.3 The mass demonstration for reproductive rights in the Texas Capitol on June 25, 2013.

function for both internal and external audiences of movements.[30] Rand describes what she labels "choric communication" in an LGBTQ movement training camp. The civil rights movement was united around protest songs, some either hymns or derived from hymns (like "We Shall Overcome"); other songs were invented in the movement, so that youth being arrested and carted away in Southern cities sang "Ain't Gonna Let Nobody Turn Me Around." Folk performers like Joan Baez and Bob Dylan organized student and anti-war movements around songs, and the impetus of movements drove changes in popular music, including soul and hip-hop, over a period of decades.

On Violence

You will recall that early rhetorical scholars of social movements often excluded confrontation from the range of rhetorical strategies of movements, arguing that coercion is neither rhetorical nor ethical. Confrontational movements are often accused of violence. However, for our purposes, "**violence**" refers only to actions that harm or kill other human beings and is more often a tactic of control than of agitation.

There are three exceptions. One exception is in cases of self-defense. The members of the Black Panther Party for Self-Defense armed themselves but did not use their weapons to assault others. On the contrary, the FBI and other policing agencies surveilled the Panthers, employed informers, and wounded and murdered Party members.

The second exception regards agitators on the far right of the political spectrum. As the assault of right-wing protesters on January 6, 2021 on the U.S. Capitol demonstrated, right-wing agitators are willing to employ physical violence to assert control and silence their opponents. The murder of protesters at a demonstration in 2017 by a right-wing activist who drove a car deliberately through a protest is another example. In the wake of the Civil War, vigilante lynching campaigns represented efforts to discipline free Black people using extreme and graphic violence.

A third exception pertains to revolutionary situations, which are rare (and haven't happened in the U.S. since the War for Independence), when insurgents have mobilized sufficient forces to threaten the nation-state itself, along with its beneficiaries and leaders. Such revolutionary situations often take the form of open war.

Activists for social justice have, however, engaged in the destruction of property and vandalism (for example in the 1999 Seattle anti-globalization protest). Looting often accompanies insurgencies. Sometimes property destruction and looting are expressions of anger against capitalism as a system and a claim to society's resources. We can disapprove of these actions without labeling them as violence. We must also be mindful that there are forms of symbolic harm, including hate speech, that, for some, constitute violence.

Movements often employ nonviolent forms of coercion, however. For example, blockading a street, jail, government building, and other spaces forces the regular use of those spaces to cease. In direct action, activists collectively impede the functioning of important institutions. When ACT UP staged a die-in at Saint Patrick's Cathedral, or when members of that group blocked the entrance to the National Institutes of Health, they engaged in a form of coercive pressure alongside their symbolic efforts. In the labor movement, strikes deploy the economic power of workers who, when they stop working, threaten employers' profits by halting the production and delivery of commodities. A broader strike wave can challenge the capitalist economic system. When such a wave occurred during the Great Depression, President Frankly Delano Roosevelt was compelled to make economic reforms, legalizing the right to organize and strike, increasing employment, and creating social safety nets. One could say, then, that a strike is coercive—it relies not only on persuasion to organize workers and build public support but also on bodily and economic clout. However, neither direct action nor strikes in themselves constitute acts of violence.

Silence is a strategic response to violence against oppressed people. For example, Black textile workers in the South in 1934 refrained from engaging the massive uprising for social justice that unionists had mounted. When asked about their roles in the movement, Black workers communicated indirectly that they had remained silent for fear of state and vigilante (Ku Klux Klan) retribution. In their brief allusions to this violence, they conveyed a message about their being silenced but also using silence as a form of agency and survival.[31] Muted group theory is one way to understand how silence is related to injustice and struggles for justice, focusing on how marginalized groups are muted and excluded via the use of language. Either muted groups must remain silent, or they must adapt to the dominant language used by others to communicate, losing cultural specificity, the ability to communicate ideas, and the emphasis on injustice in the process.[32]

Women's voices are structurally muted in Western society "so that their experiences are not fully recognized in language." Muted group theory calls our attention to the epistemic injustice (see Chapter 1) faced by oppressed groups; recovering the language from the standpoint of oppression is necessary to confront the controlling function of silence.[33]

It is the perspective of this book that when we are discussing movements for social change, we should reserve the word "violence" for instances of actual physical harm to another person or people. This reservation is important because, too often, establishment leaders and media label any militancy and confrontation as violence in order to discredit movements whose success depends on their capacity for militancy. Discrediting confrontational protest is a mechanism of control, when the most common perpetrators of violence are state authorities and conservative vigilantes. Appeals to civility can work to delegitimize critics of established social institutions, including universities, corporate power, and the government. Framing social movements for violence is a common practice of powerful institutions, representatives of which are the actual proponents of violence.[34]

For the most part, social movements do not employ violence to achieve their ends. In this chapter, we have covered the rhetorical strategies common to movement participants: argument, narrative, image, emotion, embodiment, and song—operated for both internal and external audiences of ACT UP. Communication with fellow activists inside developing movements requires rhetorical forms that differ from the ways in which activists address broader publics.

Using the Repertoire With Internal Audiences: Preaching to the Choir

You may have heard detractors of social movements complain that, in advocating controversial worldviews and change, social movement agitators are only "preaching to the choir." You may have heard something like, "Those people are espousing such radical ideas they have no chance in persuading people in power and mainstream citizens." Or, "You have to be reasonable and start where people already are." In response to such charges, we can answer, "Yes and no." Anyone who has ever attempted to put on a choral (or any other) concert knows that, before the choir can reach its audiences, the musicians must organize themselves, select repertoire, decide upon their purposes and audiences, and rehearse their pieces. They may need to recruit additional members to the choir and integrate newcomers into their organization and process. Engaging in that coordinated meaning-making and rehearsal is necessary and is itself a rhetorical process. In other words, of course, movements "preach to the choir." Movements need the choir. They need to find and integrate members with shared ideas, identities, skills, and practices. They need to build up their collective confidence in addition to coming to shared understandings of the tasks ahead. Before and alongside any strategic engagement with broader publics, movements engage in constitutive rhetoric that builds the number, coherence, persuasiveness, and overall strength of agitational groups.

Rhetoric scholars have described the strategies undertaken by movement participants to build their knowledge, connection, analysis, and confidence in rhetoric aimed at organizing **internal audiences**—themselves and others joining the ranks of the movement.[35] In the next chapter, I will call this process the moment of *formation*. For now, we can review what other rhetoricians have identified as mechanisms of drawing together movement participants internally to the movement. In the essay "Tactics of Internal Audiences," Morris and Browne write, "The success of any movement depends on the allegiance of its members—the enduring strength of their commitment and personal investment. Under certain circumstances, creating and maintaining that allegiance may well be the most pressing challenge that movements confront. … [T]he very possibility of joining a movement presupposes a sense of identity that may not initially exist."[36]

In other words, the experience of oppression and exploitation does not automatically translate into consciousness and identity. Rhetoric can have a "consummatory function" that deploys communal resources to generate internal documents like statements of principle or manifestoes. Sometimes a movement's rhetoric evolves to address the need to change the identity, beliefs, values, and practices of a group of people as a goal of the movement itself. For example, the gay rights movement took on the task of self-education in practices of safe-sex and new norms of intimate behavior. The group's very survival depended on changes brought about through internally-directed discourse.

Karma Chávez stresses that we cannot regard rhetoric focused on building the identities and skills of communities as simple, isolated enclaves. Not only does such a description make an unhelpful binary distinction between instrumental and constitutive rhetoric; it also recognizes that separate enclaved groups use externally-based rhetoric to build coalition with other groups. In Chávez's study, queer rights and migrant rights organizations "intra-group" rhetoric was also "inter-group," facilitating a combined public face when the movements turned to public audiences.[37]

A major rhetorical strategy for drawing out critical consciousness and framing coherent movement identities for internal audiences is **consciousness-raising**. Consciousness-raising is a collective practice in which groups of people share their experiences with one another in conversation, including stories.[38] These people will have come to a movement space seeking some explanation of why things are the way they are. Connecting to others who also have the sense that something is very wrong with society provides a sense of confidence and solidarity. In consciousness-raising, participants develop critical analysis and theory—ideas about how an oppressive system works and for whom. In addition to identifying establishment forces, the conversations generate ideas about how to enact social change.

The label "consciousness-raising" came out of the feminist movements of the 1960s and 1970s to describe how women came together to share experience, recognize their common grievances, and recognize that there was a system in place (sometimes called patriarchy) that affected them collectively. On the basis of their raised consciousness—analysis of society and plans for action—they emerged as a group, along with all of the other movements of the day, to demand change.

It is the swelling of a movement's ranks and self-concept that enables change agents to introduce radical ideas in broader contexts and to effectively pressure establishment forces. come together to share experience, come to collective identity and consciousness, develop confidence and feelings of belonging and solidarity, and practice the communicative and embodied skills necessary to exert public pressure. Participants in social movements usually gather because they share experiences in common. For example, ACT UP was composed of people, mostly LGBTQ people, who were in the middle of the "mass death event" that was the emergence of HIV-AIDS in their communities. They shared stigma, suffering, and pride. On such a basis, leaders and participants in movements can use communication based on those realities, and, in the process, more and more critical and radical ideas begin to make sense in the act of consciousness-raising. Members of ACT UP could rely on the fact that other participants in the movement regarded gay people and sufferers of AIDS (themselves and their allies) as human beings with rights. People in the movement could assume that everyone in the room was seeking significant change, and believe that certain demands upon the establishment—resources for research, access to care—were legitimate and achievable. Upon shared experience, participants developed their identities as radical change agents and shapers of history.

An example of internally-oriented rhetoric was a speech by ACT UP leader Vito Russo. His famous 1987 speech "Why We Fight" was delivered at a rally at the U.S. Department of Health and Human Services in Washington, DC.[39] The major theme of this speech is the indictment of bystanders for ignoring the epidemic and its toll. In his critique of politicians, media, government officials, the health care industry, and a willfully-ignorant public, Russo unites those who are not ignorant, who are suffering, and who are making demands upon the powerful. He constructs a strong sense of an "us" and a "them."

FIGURE 5.4 Vito Russo, 1946–1990.

First, Russo connects his personal experience with structural oppression, inviting audiences to identify with him and, on that basis, see the reason of his broader critique. Russo had AIDS. He tells a story about being on an airplane and told that if he had AIDS, he would be home dying. Then he says, "If I'm dying from anything, I'm dying from homophobia. If I'm dying from anything, I'm dying from racism. If I'm dying from anything, it's from indifference and red tape." He goes on to indict Senator Jesse Helms, and the President of the United States, and public indifference to the suffering and dying.

> Living with AIDS is like living through a war which is only happening for those people who happen to be in the trenches. Every time a shell explodes, you look around and you discover that you've lost more of your friends, but nobody else notices. It isn't happening to them. They're walking the streets as though we weren't living through some sort of nightmare. And only you can hear the screams of the people who are dying and their cries for help.

Russo goes on the insist that the sick and the dying are dismissed by the media as "disposable populations of fags and junkies who deserve what they get." Russo challenges establishment forces to explain why research funds and advertising are spent exclusively on white heterosexuals, why media coverage of AIDS focuses on white, heterosexual families, and why homosexual identity and issues do not appear in schools or on billboards.

The speech takes a turn on this note: Every public mention of AIDS is silent with regard to its victims, "gay men and IV drug users." If these are the people at risk, he says, "then *we* have a right to demand that education and prevention be targeted specifically to these people. ... We are being allowed to die, while low risk populations are being panicked ... into believing that we deserve to die."

Then the speech addresses those gathered in the movement: "Why are we here today? We're here because it is happening to us, and we do give a shit. ... When future generations ask what we did in this crisis, we're going to have to tell them that we were out here today. And we will have to leave the legacy to those generations of people who will come after us." In a task crucial to the strength of the movement, Russo delivers a message of confidence to his audience: "Someday the AIDS crisis will be over. Remember that. And when that day comes—when that day has come and gone—gay people and straight people, men and women, black and white, will hear the story that once there was a terrible disease in this country and all over the world, and that a brave group of people stood up and fought, and, in some cases, gave their lives, so that other people might live and be free."

Russo ends with a call that activists commit themselves to strategize, plan, and "kick the shit out of this disease. We're all going to be alive to kick the shit out of this system so that this never happens again." Paradoxically, this message, designed to unite and build confidence among fellow sufferers of AIDS and activists in the movement, has had a profound effect over time with audiences far beyond that initial gathering. The speech stands as challenge to who would stand by and allow suffering and death to plague an oppressed group of people.

Using the Rhetorical Repertoire With External Audiences: Persuasion and Pressure

Morris and Browne contrast studies of movement-building (internal) rhetoric and tactics for **external audiences** "in which movement activists adapt strategically to the situations they confront, and examine how rhetoric is directed from a movement outward [and] negotiate relationships with their audiences, opponents, and publics."[40] Tactics for external audiences include engagement with and adaptation to opponents' arguments, engagement of controversy in the public sphere, and the employment of familiar persuasive styles and genres to make radical ideas more palatable. Public movement tactics also can involve moral challenges, the interruption of normalcy, spectacle and image events, the calling-out of establishment representatives and publics on their hypocrisy, confrontation, and coercive tactics like direct action and strikes.[41]

Public rhetorical strategies and embodied collective actions designed to reach broad audiences and to pressure established institutions face a dilemma common to social movement rhetoric. One basic idea of rhetorical theory is that rhetors must meet audiences on common ground as the foundation for persuasion. Bringing existing beliefs, attitudes, and values into movement discourse establishes bridges with audiences who might be skeptical, passive, or hostile. However, movements frequently demand change, including shifts in beliefs, attitudes, and values. Bowers, Ochs, Jensen, and Shulz describe how movements both use and critique existing societal values in the terms "*vertical deviance*" and "*lateral deviance*." Vertical deviance occurs "when the agitators accept the value system of the establishment but dispute the distribution of benefits or power within that value system." Lateral deviance refers to when agitators dispute the entire value system itself and aim to replace existing social commitments with new ones.[42]

Vertical deviance has the advantage of using existing social beliefs and values as common ground with external audiences. But how does a movement make a deep critique of societal institutions and norms while reaching people entrenched in those institutions and norms? Lateral deviance is likely to be effective in the midst of a broader social crisis during which many people are questioning established institutions and norms. For example, during the Great Depression, radical ideas about the righteousness of working-class power (when Americans had not been used to talking about social class in this way) became influential because millions of people had been thrown into joblessness or poverty. That experience became the basis for altered consciousness and a crisis of legitimacy and credibility of the establishment. Lateral deviance is also compelling if agitators have large numbers and significant material resources with which to challenge elites in corporations and the state.

While internally, movement actors focus on the rhetorical tasks of identity constitution and the organizational tasks of mobilization, external communication is strategically oriented to public audiences. Such audiences are either a) ignorant of or unfamiliar with the situation, b) undecided or ostensibly neutral toward the goals of the movement, or c) actively opposed to or hostile to movement aims (or any combination or all of the above). The category of hostile audiences generally includes establishment forces of whom the movement is demanding resources and reform. With each group, the rhetorical task is unique. Uninformed people require messages providing basic information about the situation, people, and struggle; people who have no existing point of view on the crisis require persuasion that takes into account their current beliefs, attitudes, and values. For example, with church, school, and political groups, ACT UP rhetors stressed the humanity of sufferers of AIDS and tapped public belief in equal rights. Such efforts extended the base of the movement's efforts and expanded the organization's circles of support.

Establishment representatives' beliefs, attitudes, and values are usually less malleable in movement contexts than that of other audiences. Their recalcitrance is a product of their material (economic or institutional) investments in the *status quo* and interests in maintaining wealth, power, and social stability. Often, the aims of movement actors are threats to those interests when activists seek the redistribution of resources and power, the removal of society's leaders, and changes in the structures and practices of cherished institutions. For these audiences, the rhetoric and practice of confrontation become necessary tools in the movement's symbolic and physical repertoires to, in the words of Martin Luther King, Jr., "dramatize a shameful condition" by provoking the powers-that-be to reveal their investment in oppression and willingness to resort to violence. Militant tactics evolve in this way to pressure entrenched establishment forces.

One interesting dimension of militant action is that it draws the audiences of the uniformed and unpersuaded in as witnesses to confrontation. When the state or other institutions reveal themselves to be backward, coercive, and violent, the unpersuaded can be pulled into identification with the causes of agitators for social change. Confrontation with powerful opponents often relies upon coercive tactics (but not necessarily violence) like bodily disruption or strikes. For example, ACT UP's disruption of mass at St. Patrick's Cathedral and blockades of government agencies like the FDA are examples of confrontational and militant tactics. At any point in this process, establishment forces may engage in tactics of control such as evasion, adjustment, or suppression.

Rarely do established powers capitulate entirely. Historically, they have been more likely to engage in various forms of control: avoidance of movement messages, demands, and challenges; the maintenance of secrecy that protects the powerful; denying access of movements to resources, including funds, members, and media; and suppression (including purgation, armed struggle, murder, and other forms of silencing). It is the prerogative of the nation-state—simply for being an established power with all of the resources of control available to it—to employ violence—the causing of bodily harm or death to other individuals and groups using physical force. Movements for social justice do not have the media, the military, the police, the law, or other crucial resources in their pockets. For this reason, movements for change rely upon the resources of numbers of people and persuasion. Rhetorical approaches to social movements make a virtue of this necessity, privileging tactics that are civil, non-confrontational, and nonviolent.

However, when the forces of control use violence to crack down on movements (for example, in the civil rights struggle), increasing numbers of activists move toward greater radicalism and militancy. Realizing at moments when government is not on the side of justice can lead to a critique of the state and the system as a whole. Facing armed resistance to even modest social movement goals can lead to a reevaluation of movement tactics and a shift toward self-defense (as in the Black Panther Party for Self-Defense and the Black Power Movement that split from the mainstream movement's pacifism).

The degree to which the establishment gives in to movement demands depends, in part, on how arms of the movement—more moderate groups and more militant ones—work together in conjoined pressure.

Militancy, Radicalism, and Flanking

Militancy—the intention and enactment of disruptive confrontation in service of movement aims—emerges at a crisis point in movements when the establishment resorts to suppression and/or when more modest tactics have failed. During the Black freedom struggles of the 1950s and 1960s, the call for Black Power put out by the Black Panther Party for Self-Defense and the Nation of Islam corresponded to new, militant tactics, including armed self-defense. Those organizations also reformulated Black identity as both powerful and separate from white society, whereas earlier civil rights movement leaders embraced integration. The ideology of Black separatism corresponded to the tactical militancy of armed self-defense.

Militancy and Radicalism

It is important to distinguish between militancy and radicalism. **Radicalism** refers to the degree to which a movement, or a particular sector of a movement, challenges the beliefs, attitudes, values, institutions, elites, and their practices of established rule. Radicalism's spectrum features inclusion and reformism (seeking to reform, not replace, existing social relations) on one end and revolutionary critique (seeking to replace existing social relations) on the other. Militancy measures the degree to which movements engage in confrontation, disruption, destruction, or violence. Violence is at one end of that spectrum; at the other are moderate methods of engaging elites, such as petitioning, letter-writing, meetings, speeches, lobbying, and so on. Importantly, however, militancy does not equal violence. There are a range of militant tactics—including direct action (in which a group challenges establishment representatives and spaces in a bodily way) and striking (when a workforce refuses to labor, threatening economic power of corporations and ultimately society as a whole)—that are well short of doing others physical harm.

Moreover, militancy does not necessarily correspond to ideological radicalism. One can use confrontational tactics to achieve relatively modest reforms within existing institutions. ACT UP is a case in point. Demanding reforms in pharmaceutical research and medical care, the group mobilized members' bodies to block the entrance to the FDA and to halt mass at St. Patrick's Cathedral. Less frequently, advocates of radical change shun militant confrontation. One could argue that the Black civil rights movement began on the basis of inclusion in society as it existed, but it became evident that integration and equal rights were truly revolutionary concepts, especially in the U.S. South. To argue for inclusion and protection in a white supremacist society was to assert significant lateral deviance. Nonviolent civil-disobedience (sit-ins, marches, occupations, other disruptions, and the willingness to be embarrassed) shamed U.S. society and the politicians and police in the South. When Martin Luther King, Jr. and others in the SCLC were demanding that the nation demonstrate consistency with its own values, they attempted vertical deviance—the employment of dominant values and meaning frames. Soon, however, it became clear that the civil rights project was much more radical in its vision of a transformed society. Its tactics remained nonviolent (although confrontational) even as the movement's ideological commitments shifted. New organizations in the Black Power movement then split with the established movement in both ideology and tactics.

In short, movement scholars and activists ought not reduce movements to the single axis of tactical militancy, especially if doing so leads to the denigration of the movement. We cannot describe movements as simply "moderate" or "militant," when the movement's participants are also revolutionary or reformist to various degrees independently of their tactical repertoire. Various parts of a movement (of what sociologists call a social movement industry or sector) may be engaging in a whole range of tactics from the moderate to the militant in different situations. Moreover, any movement's resort to confrontation emerges out of a particular set of variables making up a rhetorical situation in which previous strategies have failed and the establishment has revealed itself to be set against the goals of agitators to the point of violent suppression.

Below is the two-axis model of the rhetoric of social movements, with the spectrum of moderation to militancy on one axis and the spectrum of reformism to radicalism on the other. You can locate a particular movement, organization, agitator, part of a movement, action, or document in a quadrant: A *moderate reformist* movement does not employ militant tactics but rather works within the system or uses arguments and non-confrontational persuasion to press for reforms—changes to the system that leaves the system intact; a *moderate radical* movement uses non-confrontational tactics but argues for a wholesale transformation of the system; a *militant reformist movement* uses confrontational and coercive (not necessarily violent but disruptive and threatening to profits and business as usual) tactics to win modest reforms; a *militant radical* movement uses confrontational and coercive (which might include labor strikes) tactics to press for revolutionary change. When we avoid confusing questions of tactics and ideology, a more complex account of a movement becomes possible.

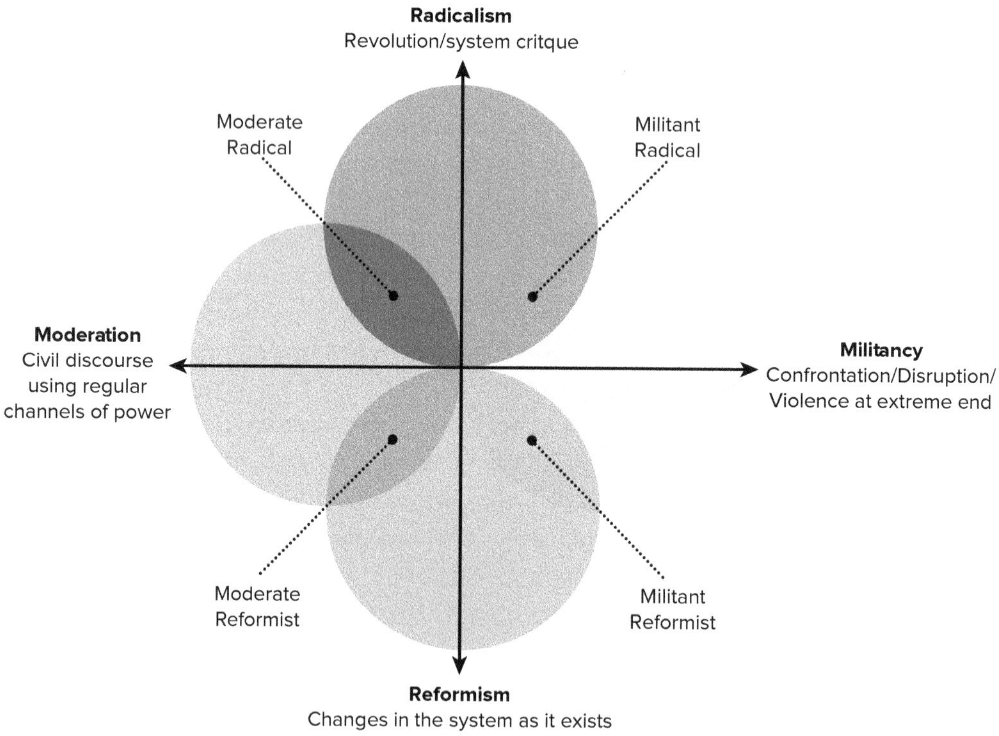

FIGURE 5.5 Two-axis model of the rhetoric of social movements.

You can see that we have four quadrants, one a combination of reformism and moderation (blue + yellow = green), a second a combination of reformism and militancy (blue + red = purple), a third a combination of moderation and radicalism (yellow + red = orange), and the fourth a combination of militancy and radicalism (red + red = red). An example of a moderate reformist movement is the organization NARAL Pro-Choice America, a group that works to expand reproductive rights and freedoms, including the right to abortion, through lobbying and legal action. An example of a moderate radical movement is the Southern Christian Leadership Conference (SCLC), the civil rights organization led by Martin Luther King, Jr. Committed to nonviolent and and peaceful action, the group advocated a wholesale change in the institutions, laws, and culture of the South.

On the other hand, nonviolent civil disobedience can be extremely confrontational, complicating this placement. In April, 1963, King was jailed during an act of civil disobedience. (This was a few weeks before the march and demonstration of young people in Birmingham, during which police set upon young demonstrators with fire hoses and dogs. From jail, he crafted the "Letter from a Birmingham Jail," in which he made an historic case for the practice of nonviolent civil disobedience alongside a ringing indictment of institutions of white supremacy in the South; he justified civil disobedience as a form of disruption undertaken when more moderate actions like negotiation had been rebuffed. He wrote, "My friends, I must say to you that we have not made a single gain in civil rights without legal and nonviolent pressure."[43]

An example of a militant reformist movement was the LGBTQ organization GetEQUAL, which advocated the inclusion of LGBTQ people in the military and marriage equality with tactics that included disruption, direct confrontation, heckling, activists' chaining themselves to the White House Fence, and other militant tactics.[44] An example of a militant radical movement is the Black Power movement, which advocated armed self-defense and had a revolutionary perspective to overthrow capitalism and white supremacy.

Complicating this model are two facts: First, organizations and people can move around the quadrants over time, adjusting toward militancy and radicalism from a starting point of moderation and reformism, for example. This is what happened to Martin Luther King Jr. as his politics evolved from basic civil rights to opposition to the Vietnam War and a critique of capitalism. Second, the different parts of any particular movement can be located in different places at the same time. With regard to ACT UP, for example, their insider strategy sought reforms from inside the FDA and the pharmaceutical industry, while the outsider strategy pressed for full liberation with the tactics of confrontational direct action.

ACT UP, like many other movement organizations, held weekly membership meetings which engaged in all of the tasks of internal persuasion. The organizing process enabled members to plan and enact pressure on external audiences and institutions, some quietly, and some outrageously. Multiple groups and organizations can be working with, "ahead of" or "behind" others. Different expressions of the establishment, for example the courts as opposed to the pharmacy giants, draw different forms of pressure from movements. In ACT UP, some members who were lawyers worked to educate and advocate for others in those settings, while others were demonstrating in the streets. Meanwhile, other organizations entirely, like Gay Men's Health Crisis and the proliferation of gay pride and queer liberation organizations, are cycling in and through the same historical moments of formation and pressure.

Flanking and the Radical Flank Effect

People and groups who become militant and/or radicalized in social movements are often charged with detracting from the moderates' credibility with the mainstream public and powerful elites. However, research on social movements has found that in many cases, the availability of a visible militant challenge to the establishment works to make the demands of the moderates seem even more reasonable and credible. Increased militancy sometimes also entails a direct threat to the spaces, institutions, and persons of the establishment, which motivates leaders to acquiesce to demands that may have once seemed radical, but now appear to be quite reasonable. In a hypothetical example, in ACT UP, some members might be involving doctors in letter writing campaigns to expand inclusion in research protocols, others demanding federal research funding at the steps of the Health Department, while others are demanding the overthrow of pharmaceutical companies. When a movement cycle comes to this point, the double punch of militancy and moderation gives elites both motivations to act and also practical avenues for doing so.[45] Alongside the creation of movement experts on research and treatment, other activists planned "zap" actions on Wall Street and against pharmaceutical giant Burroughs Wellcome in North Carolina.

FIGURE 5.6 A photo of the Stop the Church protest, a 1989 protest organized by ACT UP in response to the Catholic Church's homophobic and dismissive attitudes towards the AIDs crisis. Stop the Church garnered widespread media coverage due to the confrontational tactics of the protestors opposing one of the dominant cultural institutions of the time. One protestor is seen reaching through a line of police officers to gesture sharply at the cathedral while others hold signs directly attacking Cardinal O'Connor, the face of St. Patrick's Cathedral. Some protestors interrupted services and chained themselves to pews. While Stop the Church was questioned by moderate members of the movement, it did demonstrate that ACT UP and related LGBTQ and feminist organizations were willing to take direct action as needed. It proves the efficacy of direct action, as this action combined with the overall work of ACT UP successfully challenged both social norms and institutional practices.

This process, following sociologist Herbert Haines, is called **flanking**.[46] Flanking is a military metaphor that describes how one part of a military force will move to the side of another to come at an opponent from another direction. In social movements, flanking refers to how parts of a movement shift in a more radical and/or more militant direction, giving the moderates and reformists credibility while orienting toward the establishment in a different, more militant way. Often, there is a **radical flank effect**, in which a movement is benefited by militancy even when some people and organizations in the movement are hostile to the militants and radicals. Sometimes movement events show how militant and more moderate organizations and leaders enact a cooperative flanking process. For example, in the 1965 voting rights march from Selma to Montgomery, Alabama, Martin Luther King, Jr. and John Lewis, whose organization SNCC had broken with King, walked side-by-side.[47] That march was initially brutally suppressed by the police, twice. On the third attempt, SNCC's Stokely Carmichael joined King even as Carmichael and other SNCC members pressed for Black Power. It was the building pressure in Selma that pressed President Johnson to utter, for the first time in a national address, the words, "We shall overcome."

In one scene in the civil rights documentary series *Eyes on the Prize*, actor and activist Ossie Davis describes perfectly how flanking works.

> Martin and the regular civil rights leaders were presenting to America our best face, our nonviolent face, our desire to be included into American society and we wanted to show the world that we had no evil intentions against anybody, we just wanted to be included. But they also understood that America, in spite of our reassurances, would be frightened and hesitant to open the door to black folks. So Malcolm as the outsider, as the man they thought represented the possibilities of violence was the counter that they could use. They would say to the powers that be, "Look, here's Martin Luther King and all these guys, we are nonviolent. Now outside the door, if you don't deal with us, is the other brother, and he ain't like us."[48]

Regardless of whether moderate and militant groups approve of each other's tactics, and however much organizations argue among each other over the proper course of action, Haines' analysis shows that often, militant pressure makes moderate demands much more likely to succeed. This dynamic also operated in ACT UP.

For each action, ACT UP designated Insider and Outsider roles. While some members negotiated with establishment representatives face-to-face, others were demonstrating in the streets.[49] Some of those "Insider" actions were meetings between ACT UP Members and scientists at the NIH, including Anthony Fauci, whose leadership during the COVID-19 pandemic is well known. Approaching experts with new information while disrupting business as usual from the outside exemplified the flanking process. Under such pressure, mayors, police chiefs, governors, legislators, employers, business owners, and other representatives of the establishment are likely to adjust in keeping with the movement's demands. Haines calls this process the development and mobilization of militants and radicals in a "radical flank effect." This idea is a military metaphor: When troops amass against contending forces, some wings of the battalion spread out to catch opponents from the side. These flanks deviate from the main arena of battle and pressure opposing armies to retreat.

Conclusion: Repertoires of Radicalism and Militancy

In both contexts, activists mobilize basic rhetorical strategies argument, narrative, image, bodies, emotion, and sound/music to reach constitute their identities and collective solidarity, on the one hand, and appealing to broader audiences external to movement organizations, on the other. We can distinguish between the elements of ideological radicalism and tactical militancy and recognize how various movements combine those features in an evolving and complex way, and in ways that use militant flank effects to press the establishment for change.

In the next chapter, I will lay out a model for understanding the rhetoric of social movements that integrates all of the material introduced so far, including hegemony theory, sociological traditions, and rhetorical approaches to social movements. This model is called the "Hegemony-Formation-Pressure" model. It takes the form of a cyclical flow chart, the steps of which orient our observations of social movements and explain how movements work in a sequence of goals and situations common to movements operating in democratic societies, where there is public space for contestation, voice, and transformation.

Suggestions for Further Reading

Jonathan Alexander, Susan C. Jarratt, and Nancy Welch, Eds., *Unruly Rhetorics: Protest, Persuasion, and Publics* (Pittsburgh: University of Pittsburgh, 2018).

Nathan Crick, Ed., *The Rhetoric of Social Movements: Networks, Power, and New Media* (New York: Routledge, 2021).

Sarah Schulman, *Let the Record Show: A Political History of ACT UP New York, 1987–1993* (New York: Farrar, Straus, and Giroux, 2021).

Questions for Discussion

1. Describe how the two-axis model of militancy and radicalism works. Where would you put ACT UP on that model—which quadrant, and why?
2. What is the radical flank effect? Give an example.
3. Watch the documentary *United in Anger* and give examples of arguments, narratives, images, emotion, body rhetoric, and music as parts of ACT UP's rhetorical repertoire.
4. After reading this chapter, do you understand why movement organizations and activists need to "preach to the choir"?
5. Where do you personally see the line being between confrontation and violence?

Credits

Fig. 5.1: Copyright © by Boris D. Leak (CC BY-SA 4.0) at https://commons.wikimedia.org/wiki/File:Occupy_Wall_Street.jpg.

Fig. 5.2: Copyright © by Elvis Barnes (CC BY-SA 2.0) at https://commons.wikimedia.org/wiki/File:04.04.AIDS.Quilt.WDC.11October1996.jpg.

Fig. 5.3: Copyright © by Blackbird Film Co. (CC by 2.0) at https://www.flickr.com/photos/laurengerson/9142576226.

Fig. 5.4: Copyright © by Massimo Consoli (CC BY-SA 2.5) at https://commons.wikimedia.org/wiki/File:%C2%A7Russo_Vito_(1946-1990)_-_foto_di_Massimo_Consoli_28-VI-1989,_NY.jpg.

Fig. 5.6: Ellen B. Nelpris, "Stop the Church Protest," https://www.rferl.org/a/before-pussy-riot-act-up-confronted-church-and-won/24668230.html. Copyright © 1989 by Ellen B. Nelpris.

III

The Hegemony-Formation-Pressure Cycle

6

The Formation Cycle

KEY TERMS

Hegemony-Formation-Pressure cycle
hegemony frame
formation cycle (experience, feeling, consciousness, identity, agency, organization)
rhetorical repertoires of formation cycle (experience, feeling, bodies, affect, consciousness-raising, identity, identity frames, agency, meaning formation, slogans, narrative, myth, song)
organization (leadership, resources, training)
recursivity and nonlinearity of the model

Up to this point, this book has covered two schools of thought regarding communication and social movements: the sociological tradition and the rhetorical tradition. The sociological tradition primarily explores how groups engage in contentious collective politics (social movements), taking advantage of resources, social crises, and other opportunities in the social structure in order to achieve either reform-oriented or revolutionary social change. Sociologists bring other important concepts to the table. Repertoires of contention are those bodies of practiced discourse and action that movements employ in cycles of contention. Participants in social movements form organizations; often efforts spread across multiple organizations in a "social movement industry."

The cultural turn in sociological studies of social movements brought scholars' attention to how movements employ narratives and meaning frames to craft shared identities, motivations, and social analysis—often in contention with establishment meaning and media frames. Sociologists also explored the role of music and emotion in galvanizing members of social movements and solidifying their commitment to the cause. The cultural turn dovetailed with the second tradition we have explored so far, the rhetorical tradition.

Inspired by the movements of the 1960s and 1970s, scholars of rhetoric —persuasive public communication—described and analyzed the rhetoric of social movement adherents as a core component of how change is made. Drawing from the sociological tradition, some rhetoricians emphasized the collective, organized, and instrumental elements of social movements. These scholars described how social movement rhetoric was strategic and purposeful, evolving as movement organizations proceeded through a number of stages in their formation, evolution, and devolution. A particularly useful concept from sociology in connection with rhetorical studies is that of movement repertoires. Rhetorical repertoires include the emotional appeals, arguments, narratives, images, bodily expression, and music that activists practice and use to achieve their aims.

A major question that arose in this early work in rhetoric on social movements was the value and validity of confrontation—both verbal and physical—in the rhetoric of social movements. Detractors of confrontation argued that it was by definition outside the bounds of the rhetorical because it violated norms of persuasion that depended upon building common ground between persuader and audience. Other scholars noted that when established systems of power are recalcitrant, tyrannical, and oppressive, confrontation becomes necessary to expose malignant power and to challenge the stability of prevailing regimes.

In contrast to the scholars stressing the instrumental rhetoric of social movements, a camp of rhetoricians argued that we should see social movement as a complex of social meanings and identities. The purpose of the theorist and critic of movements, on this view, is to chart shifts in culture and language as signs of change. The emphasis in this work is on the constitutive functions of language, or how it creates collective identity and produces meaning in society at large.

In the previous chapter, I argued that we should regard the instrumental and constitutive moments of social movements as dialectically related, in other words, interdependent, mutually influential, and reinforcing of each other. The crafting of identities leads not only to meaning shifts but also to self-identified, intentional groups of people who organize themselves in processes of social change. The public pressure on established institutions and the outcomes of that pressure can lead to shifts in meaning and identity among movement participants and to shifts in feelings. Defeats and crises can threaten confidence and unity; successes embolden those senses and bring others into the processes by which identities and meanings are formed. There is no reason to decide whether a movement is a phenomenon *or* a set of meanings. The making of social change always requires and generates both. The goal of this chapter is to integrate sociological and rhetorical perspectives in a new model demonstrating the rhetorical processes of social movements: the Hegemony-Formation-Pressure (HFP) Model.

Introduction to the HFP Model

This model is a visualization of the conjoined modes of constitutive and instrumental rhetorical action and their corresponding repertoires; altogether, these make up the **Hegemony-Formation-Pressure cycle**. Although it is indebted to them, this model differs from previous "stages" models of social movements in bringing the constitutive moments together with the instrumental in dialectical—mutually determining and influencing—ways. It details the rhetorical repertoire of the formation cycle (constitutive) in detail and explains the relationship between those moments in a struggle to the pressure cycle.

The basic model appears in the figure below. You can see how the rhetoric of social movements engages both constitutive processes—the formation and organization of identities—and instrumental pressure—the public, organized mobilization designed to influence structures and systems of power.

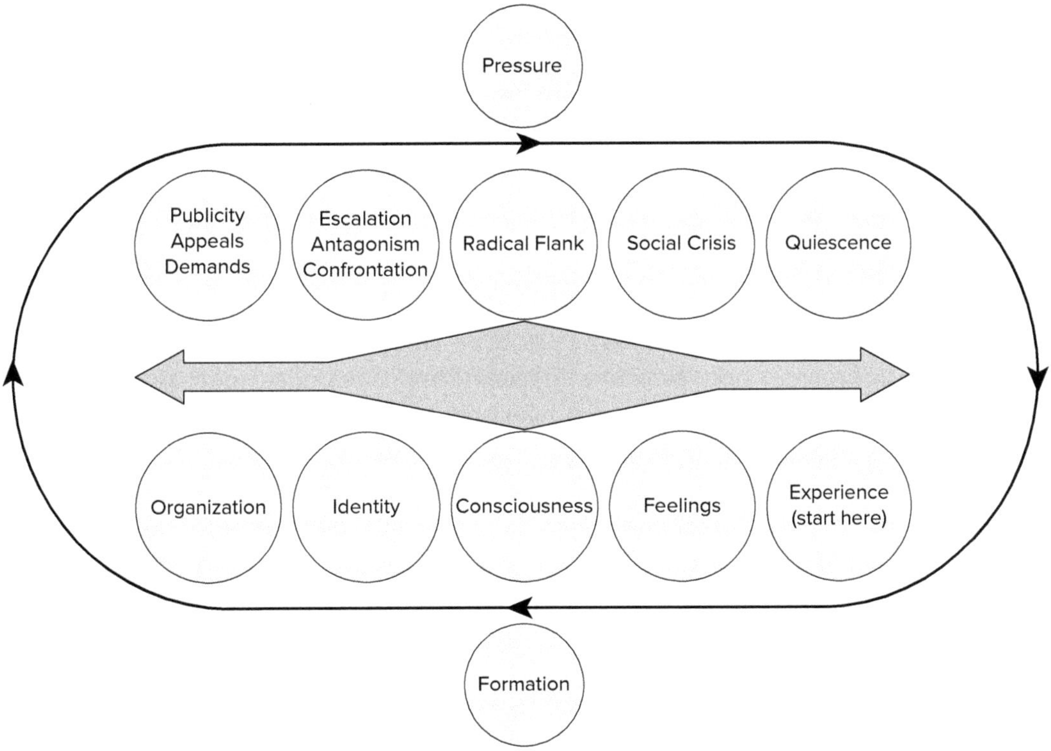

FIGURE 6.1 Hegemony-Formation-Pressure Cycle.

The two cycles overlap in a process in which the internally oriented constitutive rhetorical work of constituting identities for movement participants feeds into the instrumental, externally oriented rhetoric designed to put pressure on existing systems and structures of power. Each cycle features particular moments and repertories in the process of building and mobilizing movements. The outer "box" for these cycles stands for existing hegemonic social relations—legal, economic, political, and cultural systems that will be challenged by movements for social justice. Hegemony is the frame and the basic rhetorical situation of any social movement.

Hegemony as Totalizing Frame

Now it is time to set the concepts from sociological and rhetorical traditions into the basics with which this book began: the contestation over hegemony in a society characterized by multiple kinds of injustice. You will recall that hegemony is the balance of economic, political, and cultural power in a given society at a given moment in time. When social relations are unjust, as we noted in Chapter 2, hegemony describes how an oppressive and exploitative system maintains its power. Hegemony is never neutral: We must always ask, *whose* hegemony is it and *whom* does it benefit? Although, as explained in Chapter 2, hegemony does not refer only to domination and control, most social movement participants would describe the hegemony they challenge as oppressive and unjust and those holding hegemony as undemocratic at best and brutal at worst. We regard the dominant idea systems, in Marx's terms, as the ideas of a ruling class whose hegemony is maintained, in part, through ideological justifications of its power. Thus, when scholars of rhetoric and culture today use the word, "hegemony," it seems to mean "dominance," or "dominant ideology."

However, hegemony is neither positive nor negative, neither oppressive nor liberatory. "Hegemony" does not mean "dominant ideology" or "oppressive power." Hegemony simply is always there. All societies by definition involve complexes of economic, coercive, political, and cultural influence, no matter who is in charge and no matter what social priorities and practices they maintain. If the majority of a population governed itself on democratic and egalitarian principles, that leadership would exert hegemonic power in ways that activists today might regard as more just or liberating. It would still be hegemony.

Viewed in this way, hegemony is the ever-present frame for all contestation over social relations. The **hegemony frame** is the context for social movements through all of their constitutive and instrumental efforts, which put pressure on the existing hegemonic order and attempt to shift or replace it. Replacing a hegemonic order requires revolutions, but even when movements (most often) seek reforms and cultural change, the aim is to change the shape of hegemony.

For a moment, imagine yourself trapped with hundreds of other people trapped in a room. It is not a particularly pleasant room. No one has enough space or food. Everyone suffers from extremes of heat and cold. The room is dark, dirty, and smelly. It is a situation in which people are prone to fight among themselves through no fault of their own. Periodically, entertaining images, videos, and music are projected onto the walls.

The floor, walls, and ceiling of that room are akin to a hegemonic structure whose boundaries, limits, and rules govern the lives of all who live there. Much of the time, the media provided justify the situation: this room is all there is; it is the best you can hope for; you are in there for your own good; you are being taken care of. If you are unhappy, maybe it is the fault of those other inhabitants who look or sound different from you; you cannot count on them to be on your side. The problem certainly is not the room itself. If you are miserable, why don't you enjoy some comedic entertainment? You start to take the terms of your existence in this room for granted.

However, at some point, you and a few others start to question reality. You tell others that, certainly, this room is not all there is or all that is possible. While the walls are preaching division, you discover in talking with your companions that you have more in common than you thought. You decide that you don't like the messages that the walls provide. Together, you start to make your own art and writing and cover the walls in graffiti. You tell your stories about how you came to be in that room. You share your food and water with the most in need. Then, some folks start to wonder whether there is a way out of the room. The door is solid and locked. There are no windows. But you start to explore, assigning one team of people to begin digging through a soft spot in the wall, another team's members to stand on each other's shoulders to try to open the ceiling vent. Others are tasked with using mechanical tools to solve the lock, and still others have pooled their electronic technology to see if they can work on communicating with the outside. Finally, a group sets to making as much noise as possible by singing, stomping, and banging on the walls. People are giving speeches, writing treatises, singing and making music, dancing, and rehearsing skills that might be needed when they get out.

At this point you've built the rudiments of a social movement inside hegemony's walls. You are mounting a counter hegemonic struggle. Freedom is not guaranteed—some representative of the powers that be could come and enact violence upon you. The wall may be too thick to dig out. But it is possible that in working together, you all can get the vent open and help each other to escape. At that point, you and your compatriots could help to free others. You could find and confront whoever locked you in that room. Collectively, you could replace the existing order with one that is freer and more prosperous than your previous existence. Then, you all will hold hegemony, producing governmental structures, economic systems, and cultural products that serve your people's interests.

It should be said that, while I am using this example allegorically, this thought experiment does actually correspond to the realities of those literally imprisoned,[1] as was hegemony theorist Antonio Gramsci, who organized fellow inmates and smuggled out analyses and proposals for liberation. More broadly, though, activists for social justice see society itself as imprisoning and manipulating people's bodies and minds. They come together, raise their collective consciousness, produce culture, art, and political analyses and strategize ways to increase freedom and decrease suffering. Hegemony as it stands now becomes the structural frame and baseline rhetorical situation of movements challenging established powers.

Image 6.1

Such a situation involves numerous constraints, including dominant ideas, beliefs, attitudes, values, identities, norms, and aspirations. In any more or less stable society, people identify with the prevailing system. Any advocate of change must work within those constraints to reach audiences with messages that could galvanize efforts to resolve the exigence. We all also face hard constraints: limited access to resources like money, people, mobility, and media; the capacity of established interests to suppress movement efforts with violence; and so on. Still, as history has shown us over and over again, people make meaningful, lasting change in spite of all of those constraints.

Position and Maneuver

What movements are able to accomplish is partially dependent upon the configuration of all of those variables taken together. Gramsci (and other theorists of hegemony since his time) noted that sometimes ordinary people can mount an effort against systemic interests, taking on employers and the government. The "war of maneuver" is facilitated by broader material crises in economic stability and political legitimacy. Movements can provoke such a crisis under some circumstances. For example, the U.S. war in Vietnam was protracted and unpopular. Moreover, the U.S. was losing the war to the North Vietnamese, taking heavy losses. Exhausted and terrified, conscripted (drafted, not volunteer) troops rebelled and deserted in large numbers. The news media in the United States publicized casualties and exposed a series of atrocities against civilians, including a massacre in the village of My Lai. (After this war, the U.S. forbade media from independent coverage of wars.) President Richard Nixon inherited this unpopular war, and his administration was rocked by the Watergate scandal (in which, it was revealed, Nixon committed espionage and other crimes against electoral opponents). In this context, the anti-war movement in the United States produced enough pressure to influence the end of the conflict.

In contrast, the "war of position" comes to the fore when the established hegemony is relatively stable and enjoys popular support. Gramsci noted that (unlike under fascism), capitalist nation-states with elected governments (like the U.S.) maintain their authority by winning the "hearts and minds" of the people to the *status quo*. In periods of conservative reaction (for example, the 1950s and the 1980s), it is very difficult to mount a broad challenge to the rule of established economic and political elites. In this situation, advocates for change may be only loosely organized or disorganized against a social system that seems to be invulnerable. Groups of people who may have been involved in past movements and newly disaffected groups often employ tactics of cultural resistance. For example, punk music and hip-hop were both responses to entrenched, racist capitalism. Graffiti and other street art, music, independent media production, intellectual innovation, music and cultural festivals, and other communication practices sustain oppositional consciousness and identities through hard times. British cultural studies scholar Stuart Hall argued that it was this situation that necessitated the "war of position" after the rise of neoliberal capitalism after the Second World War, a regime dominated by the politics of Ronald Reagan in the U.S. and Margaret Thatcher in Great Britain.

Counterhegemony, Reform, and Revolution

Gramsci scholar Peter Thomas has argued that the war of position can be preparatory for a war of maneuver, and that any war of maneuver will of course involve cultural, intellectual, political—rhetorical—work.[2] Sometimes massive instrumental movement activity—like the women's liberation movement of the late 1960s—can lead not only to legal and political reform (like abortion rights) but also to lasting changes in cultural norms and values. After the 1960s, sexism was still serious, but women entered careers and education in unprecedented numbers and the norms of family life were transformed.

Although Gramsci never used the term "counterhegemony" (or "counter-hegemony"), other scholars in communication and other disciplines have adopted the term to describe social movement efforts to challenge hegemonic rule. A counterhegemonic struggle may seek reform, revolution, or both. In the war of position, the aim may be to sustain identities, protect alternative cultural spaces and practices, and shift cultural meanings. Reforms include any adjustments in a hegemonic system that leave the system itself relatively stable and unchallenged. A revolution supplants a hegemonic order and replaces old hegemonic forces with new ones. The American revolution defeated the hegemony of British colonialism and aristocracy, installing a new ruling class of merchants and traders (who would become industrialists and bankers). The Russian Revolution of 1917 overthrew Russian nobility, temporarily in favor of workers' control (which was curtailed by Stalinism.) Ostensibly, other revolutions undertaken by ordinary people could lead to a new hegemonic system. Even a socialist or radically democratic order, if stable, would be called a "hegemony."

The next figure illustrates the basic elements of the hegemony frame—any existing state and economic system, and attendant politics and culture—that form the basic context for any rhetorical social movement action. In this way, we can regard hegemony as the basic rhetorical situation of social movements. A rhetorical situation includes every feature of social reality that might operate as an opportunity for, a constraint on, or barrier to communicative action. In the case of the hegemonic establishment, the elements of that situation include economic, legal (including the courts, police, and jails), political, educational, and cultural domains where established elites have control. Social movements originate in civil society in democratic societies, the space of deliberation, dialogue, debate, controversy, organization, the development of leadership, the education of activists, and so on. Civil society is also where the people work to construct identities and narratives in culture, both mass-popular and community-local. From the position of civil society, it is the goal of movements to put pressure on the other dimensions of hegemonic control so as to change the

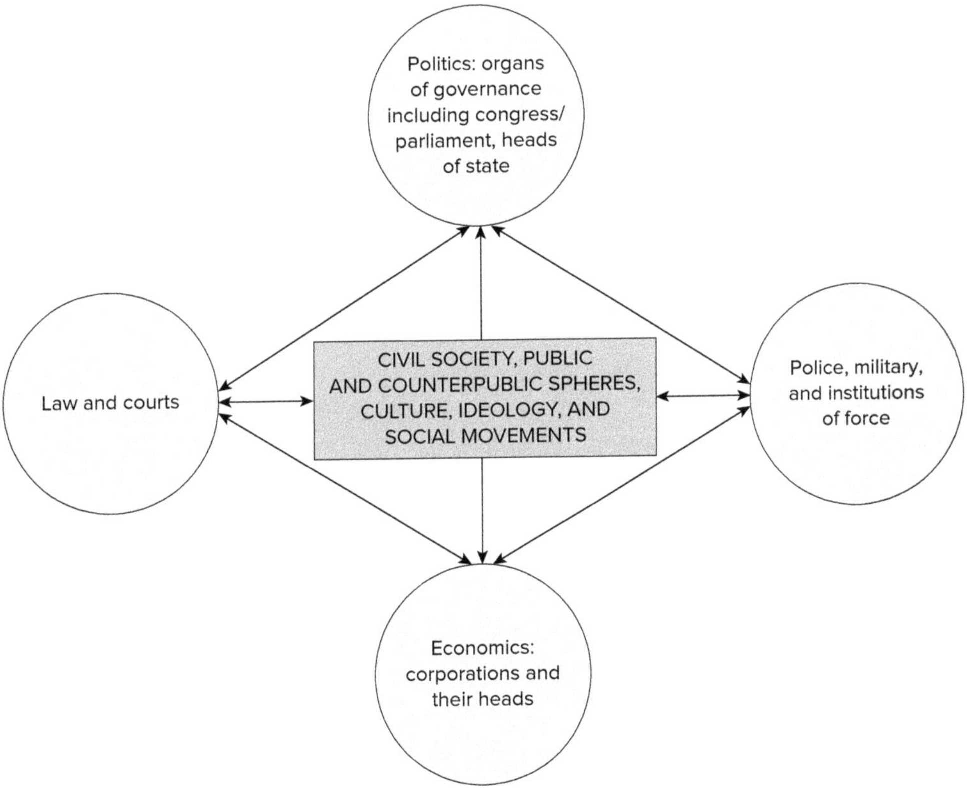

FIGURE 6.2 Hegemony frame for rhetorical social movement action.

configuration of hegemony. The establishment is also working in civil society, producing their own education and cultural narratives and attempting to spread them as common sense at the same time. The war of position is the contestation over common sense in civil society and the creation of cultures out of which our identities and stories emerge.

At any particular moment, different sectors of the hegemonic establishment may be vulnerable to challenges from social movements, and movement participants conduct analysis as to where the pressure points are. In addition, different sectors of the hegemonic establishment may be at odds with one another, which likewise opens up opportunities for pressure. (Coups happen when the military is at odds with the head of state and there is mass popular support for regime change, for example.) Alternatively, the sectors could be operating in a unified and collaborative way with the support of the police and armed forces. This is a situation of vulnerability for movements. Every situation requires an assessment of opportunities and constraints, which movement adherents can take up in the formation cycle as they develop and deepen a political analysis.

Social movements attempt to shift the hegemonic frame—with varying emphases on which sector of the establishment in two cycles: the formation cycle and the pressure cycle. Each cycle consists of a number of moments, themselves characterized by particular repertoires of rhetorical action.

The U.S. Civil Rights and Black Power Movements

The examples that I will use to exemplify the rhetorical work of both cycles are the U.S. Civil Rights and Black Power Movements. I recommend that you watch the award-winning PBS documentary series *Eyes on the Prize* (available on multiple streaming platforms).[3] That series provides an unparalleled audio-visual overview of these movements. The episodes provide examples of many of the processes covered as we proceed, and I will make some references to the series. A brief history of the movements here will provide a common frame of reference.

Although this movement occurred during the middle of the 20th century, and although there have been a number anti-racist movements since then, the *Black freedom struggle* of the 20th century models every step of the formation and pressure cycle. As I noted in the Introduction, movements of the 21st century have often been loosely organized, networked, identity- and culture-focused, and not oriented toward making instrumental gains against institutions and laws. Such movements cannot exemplify all of the aspects of both the formation and pressure cycles to the degree that the 20th century Black freedom struggle does. There are exceptions, including the Marriage Equality Movement, and I will use such examples as we go forward.

Primarily, we will focus on the period between 1954, the year of the historic *Brown v. Board of Education* Supreme Court decision, and 1969, the year that the FBI murdered Fred Hampton, a leading member of the Black Panther Party for Self-Defense. The politics of "Jim Crow"—a set of racist laws and norms—dominated the South after the Civil War and the end of slavery. Between *Brown* and the decline of the Black Panthers, the civil rights and Black Power movements challenged racism in the domains of law, politics, economics, and culture. The period immediately after *Brown* witnessed the struggle to integrate Southern schools and the fight against segregation in public places. The latter was expressed powerfully in the *Montgomery Bus Boycott* of 1955. Then the movement exerted efforts toward voting rights, including civil disobedience, protest marches, and other direct action. Many, but not all, of these were led by Martin Luther King, Jr., his organization the *Southern Christian Leadership Conference*, the *NAACP*, and others committed to the goals of inclusion and the methods of nonviolence. These campaigns culminated in the 1963 *March on Washington for Jobs and Freedom* and in the 1965 Voting Rights Act. A herald moment was when *Fannie Lou Hamer* led members of the independent *Mississippi Freedom Democratic Party* onto the floor of the 1964 Democratic National Convention demanding seats at the table.[4] Their disruption called the Party on its exclusionary racism and hypocrisy and made the routine exclusion of Black people from electoral politics strikingly visible.

Ongoing discrimination and violence in both the South and the North—including the denial of the vote to thousands of Black Southerners—prompted militants and radicals to split from the mainstream civil rights movement. After repeated police and military attacks, as well as vigilante violence by Southern whites, the calls for nonviolence and nonconfrontation became less reasonable to budding militants. The Black Power movement took the form of the *Black Panther Party for Self-Defense*, the *Student Nonviolent Coordinating Committee*, and *Congress of Racial Equality*. In the North, Black militants joined the *Nation of Islam*, whose most prominent figure was *Malcolm X*.

The late 1960s and early 1970s saw a number of victories for anti-racist movements, including desegregation (at least in the law), voting rights, housing and education reforms, and the increasing influence of Black Americans in mainstream politics. None of these achievements would have been realized without the continual and increasingly militant pressure of anti-racist movements.

Of course, this story is much more complicated. Leaders, organizations, membership, and tactics crisscrossed the movement, which evolved in complexity, sophistication, and power. And, of course, in every organization and at every moment in the contentious politics that made up the Civil Rights and Black Power movements, there were people—people who came into struggle as communities of new activists sharing experiences, developing their consciousness and identities, and training themselves up for public engagement, all the while creating, expanding, and innovating upon their repertoires for rhetorical action. They demanded and won change. They challenged hegemonic social practices and changed the basic shape of society. This example will be useful as we proceed to describe the two cycles of the rhetoric of social movements: the formation cycle and the pressure cycle.

The Formation Cycle

Taking the hegemony frame as the basic "container" or situation for social movement rhetoric, we can explore how, "inside" of that frame, social movements go through two interrelated rhetorical cycles: the formation cycle and the pressure cycle. Briefly, the **formation cycle** is the process through which people come together on the basis of shared experience, foster connection among those people, cultivate emotional commitment, create shared identities, and form organizations. Those organizations engage in training and leadership in repertoires of contention. In the formation cycle, consciousness-raising generates awareness of common identities and interests among participants. When the establishment fails to respond to movement demands, activists become aware that they are working against a system and structure.

Including all of these moments, the formation cycle prepares collectives of activists for entry into public contestation, which is the arena of the pressure cycle (covered in Chapters 6 and 7). In other words, the formation cycle is where people sharing the experience of injustice engage in constitutive rhetoric. Scholars in communication studies have referred to the constitutive spaces of groups gathering around a shared cause an "enclave," which, later in the pressure cycle, become "counterpublics."[5]

The Formation Cycle as Site of Constitutive Rhetoric

Let's take a look at a simple model of the formation cycle in Figure 6.3.

The moments of the formation cycle are, from right to left: the experience and feeling of oppression, which, when narrated with others, generates political consciousness, the construction of identity and identity frames, and the formation of organizations. We begin with the experience of oppression.

Experience

At the bottom right, the figure identifies the baseline of every social movement: the experience of injustice. At this moment in the cycle, people experiencing oppression, exclusion, and violence are not yet cohesive under the banner of shared ideas, identities, or organizations. They gather in search of others who share their experiences. For example, people who became activists in ACT UP (described in the previous chapter) arrived at the group's informal meeting space not knowing exactly why they came. In interviews, members recall wandering in and finding connections with others who were also suffering from illness, death, loss, confusion, fear, and anger.

It is the same in the civil rights movement (and every other movement). For example, at the time of the Montgomery Bus Boycott in 1955, most Black people in Alabama suffered poverty, demeaning treatment in near-slavery domestic servitude, segregation and exclusion, routine

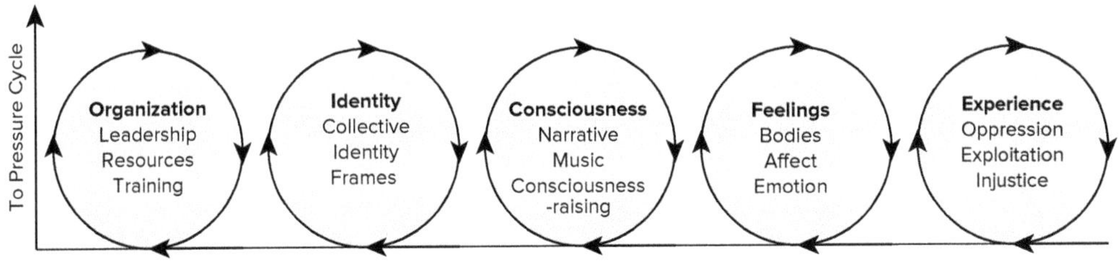

FIGURE 6.3 The Formation Cycle: Meaning-making constitutive rhetoric with internal audiences.

racist vigilante violence, and many other harms. The NAACP was a longstanding organization of people who were farther along in the formation and pressure cycles. It was seeking a test case to challenge segregation in public facilities. They assigned longtime activist Rosa Parks (who did not sit down spontaneously out of fatigue) to take a place in the white part of a metropolitan bus. She refused to give up her seat for a white passenger. The backlash against her action and her arrest galvanized Black citizens of Montgomery. The NAACP's E. D. Nixon took up her legal case as thousands of people whose experience resonated with the dehumanization challenged by Parks gathered in churches and other spaces to talk (and preach, and sing) about what they shared in common.

Feelings

Those gatherings, like most inaugural social movement gatherings, were places where people shared not only their stories but also their emotions. The second step in the formation cycle model is when people's lived experience, bodily feelings, and emotions ring together to form bonds among those gathered. Both sociologists and rhetoricians noticed how movement gatherings brought bodies together in ways that were emotionally charged and even erotic, in the sense of drawing people together based on desires (mostly) not for sex but rather for connection, community, and agency. Being together with others generates intense feelings, the bodily reactions to experience before those feelings are translated as emotions that can be named and expressed as such. As Jeffrey Bennett explains, the AIDS Memorial Quilt was an opportunity for a kind of public emotionality when reasoned mourning was limited and limiting.[6] In the process of building a movement and communication with others in that context, feelings become emotions. Betty Friedan wrote about the second wave of the U.S. women's movement starting with women feeling inchoate dissatisfaction, which Friedan called "the problem that has no name."[7] Social movements are the sites where dissatisfaction can be named as the basis for common cause. In the movement for the right of same-gender people to marry (the marriage equality movement), people came together to share emotional stories about how they had been excluded from marrying their lifelong love, how not being able to do so jeopardized their material security and their relationships with their children, how it felt dehumanizing to be denied a fundamental anchor of what it means to be a person in our society. Out of those feelings, when a crisis emerged in 2008 with the passage of Proposition 8 in California,[8] people grouped together to connect their stories and begin building a movement.

In the civil rights movement, activists drawn together out of shared experience packed Black churches, historically sites of resistance and organizing when society afforded Black people few other spaces and where a spiritual bond buttressed collective resistance. Singing was very important in the movement; in addition to traditional hymns, movement songs (some based on hymns) swelled from the pews. For example, the song "We Shall Overcome" became a refrain of the movement. Video footage of these meetings shows the gathered people in a state of deep feeling and even rapture. People move together to music, and the coordinated movement of embodied feelings creates powerful bonds. Another communication element that taps feelings and brings them together in identifiable emotions is a pattern of speechmaking, common to Black preaching, known as "call-and-response." In this pattern, called *anaphora*, a speaker will use repeated words or phrases to bring audiences into sync with the message and with those around them. Martin Luther King, Jr. was brilliant in this regard with his refrains "I have a dream," and "Let freedom ring." With every repetition, audience involvement builds in intensity as people start to expect repetition and feel satisfaction when it comes. Taken all together, the mobilization of embodied feelings through speech, music, and movement becomes a vehicle for collective identification and shared consciousness.

Consciousness

As we move leftward along the formation cycle, we arrive at consciousness. From an inarticulate set of experiences and feelings, groups of people gathered to challenge injustice build a shared analysis of society, the need for change, and their roles in the process. In the previous chapter, I identified consciousness-raising as a strategy of identification and theory-building. As Karlyn Kohrs Campbell explained in her work about the rhetoric of the U.S. women's movement, people tell their stories to each other, and, in the process, discover that experiences and feelings they thought were unique to themselves are, in fact, shared with others. And if experiences are not only subjective, but also are features of collectively-felt realities, the fact of shared suffering points to there being a source of injustice beyond the individual and beyond small groups. In telling stories in the process of consciousness-raising, emerging movement participants establish common knowledge and built theories on the basis of stories.[9]

Stories of consciousness-raising are of three kinds, as identified by media scholar George Gerbner: stories about how things are; stories about why things are the way they are; and stories about what should be done about how things are.[10] With regard to the civil rights movement, activists argued: Black people are denied the promised goods of society and are subject to arbitrary racist violence. (That's how the world is.) Participants variously explained their analysis of why this situation existed. Was the government simply inactive? Was there an absence of appropriate laws or failure to enforce those laws? Or is there a structural system that promotes racism to benefit elites? Discussion of what to do about a situation depends on stories about why the world is the way it is. The movement developed plans to pressure the government, change the laws, and, in the wake of state violence, to confront broader structures. In combination, these narratives build systematic insights about participants' shared experiences.

These stories, told repeatedly by people about their lives, start to explain social reality and generate plans of action. In the feminist movement, stories about the burdens of domestic labor (and the double shift of work outside the home and work in the home), work and economic discrimination, sexual violence and abuse, demeaning media representations, and the dehumanization of being treated as sex objects revealed that there was (and remains) a system in place that affected many women similarly and structurally. The "rap groups" of second-wave feminism were sites of consciousness-raising. No one's experience and feelings are automatically translated into shared knowledge, theory, and action. When people organize feelings and experiences in narratives, consciousness is "raised" from the disorganized and atomized life experiences of individuals. Consciousness is a group phenomenon.

At this point, it is important to note, as I will throughout the discussion below, that the moments or elements of the formation cycle do not move in a linear way. Feelings and experiences don't automatically lead to shared consciousness. Consciousness also develops in the pressure cycle as activists come up against the recalcitrance of the establishment and develop a critique of the system. Organizations and activists who have already established themselves can intervene in this process and motivate and accelerate it, and raised consciousness can produce new feelings and experiences that then become the basic for further awareness and action. Consciousness-raising can happen intentionally in small groups, but it also happens in what I will identify as the "pressure cycle." When people are engaged in public action, the lessons from those experiences feed back into the process of consciousness and theory-building.

For example, recently at my university the administration suddenly and unilaterally shut down and defunded the campus Women's Center, which had been an important place for support for students who identified as women (and for exactly the purpose of consciousness-raising). The university fired Center staff and gutted the physical space where it had stood within the space of a month. Scholars from across the campus—particularly professors of women's and gender studies—got together to talk about the situation. Initial plans focused on meetings with administrators, petitions, and academic senate resolutions. However, the administration would not budge; they would not even meet with the faculty involved. At that point, one of the faculty members wrote to the whole email list, saying: "I'm so disappointed in them. *My whole worldview has changed*." It was the experience of being denied and stonewalled that transformed consciousness. In this way, the pressure cycle can feed back into the formation cycle.

Another example of this principle comes from the civil rights and Black power movements. Over the course of the years from 1955 to 1965, the emphasis of the movement was on nonviolent civil disobedience focused on desegregation and inclusion in the American Dream. However, during the march from Selma to Montgomery in 1965, activists were attacked by police, first during the initial attempt to cross the Edmund Pettus Bridge, and again during the course of the march, when the National Guard tear-gassed activists while they slept. That event was emblematic of the role of policing and suppression thwarting the movement. For some time, young activists had been thinking about breaking off from the SCLC and forming a more militant wing of the movement. Ella Baker encouraged students to form the Student Nonviolent Coordinating Committee (SNCC), which, although still nonviolent, was interested in escalating the struggle through confrontation and a radical analysis of the role of policing in the perpetuation of racism (among other things).[11] Other activists were thinking about calling for Black Power. At the start of the Montgomery March, *Stokely Carmichael* walked alongside King while also talking with Black people living along the route about the idea of Black Power. At the end of the march, King's speech echoed, "I have a dream." Carmichael led another group in a song with the lyrics, "Freedom's got a shotgun. Freedom's gonna use it." The experience of being brutalized by police generated the opportunity for shifts in awareness of the need for antagonism against the State. So consciousness-can start with stories of the lived experience of injustice, but activists tell stories constantly throughout the building of a movement, and new experiences of the struggle feed back into the process of consciousness-raising.

Another way to explain this process is to say that it is **recursive**. This means that the process is non-linear—not step A, then step B, then step C, etc. "Recursive" also means that the moments of struggle return back on themselves continually. The moments of movement

FIGURE 6.4 This image shows, from left to right, Martin Luther King, Jr., Floyd McKissick, and Stokely Carmichael marching arm-in-arm during the 1966 March Against Fear. This display of solidarity reinforced public perception of the Civil Rights Movement as a cohesive pursuit of equality and liberty for Black Americans. All three activists publically held differing perspectives on racial justice and how to achieve it. King was well-known for organizing non-violent demonstrations while Carmichael and McKissick both advocated for the use of force or violent resistance when necessary. Further, both McKissick and Carmichael were known proponents of Black Power and resistant to collaboration with white activists and organizations. Nevertheless, King, McKissick and Carmichael presented a figurative and literal united front during the March, and this cooperation strengthened the movement as a whole. In presenting a united front, this march demonstrates the principle of the radical flank; more militant perspectives do not detract but operate in solidarity with more moderate ones.

cycles are all always happening at once with participants engaged in processes at different levels. In the Rosa Parks example, already-organized activists provided information to people new to the struggle. Their information became part of the consciousness-raising process. Emotions, narratives, and analysis work together all the time, so that a church meeting brought new people in, tapped their feelings, encouraged fellow feeling through song and movement, and also featured speakers who provided analysis of the situation in Montgomery and argued for plans for moving forward.

Another aspect of recursivity lies in the "always-already" character of history. No movement is born out of thin air. Before any particular iteration of a movement for social change, there is a history of past efforts and lessons, experience, leaders, and struggles. The civil rights movement of the 1950s emerged out of cultural and political developments in the post-slavery era and the abolition movement. In this context, it is important to note how arts and culture lend themselves to consciousness-raising. For example, the Harlem Renaissance and the Black Arts Movements of the early 20th century laid analytical, emotional, and creative ground. Artists like Aaron Douglass, Poets like Langston Hughes, novelists like Zora Neale Hurston, playwrights like, musicians like Louis Armstrong, Paul Robeson, and Billie Holliday, and social critics like W.E.B. Du Bois had created enduring resources for consciousness and action, messages of Black creativity, pride, experience, and struggle. Debates among Black leaders during this period, for example between Marcus Garvey (who advocated Black Nationalism and led the "Back to Africa" movement), Booker T. Washington (who argued in favor of Black self-reliance rather than collective struggle), and W.E.B. Du Bois (who argued for political action and co-founded the NAACP), set up basic lines of identity, analysis, and direction that were then taken up in the post-war civil rights movement.

We must keep in mind how, in actuality, the moments are condensed, overlapping, and mutually-informing. This recursivity is indicated in the model by the circles showing the revolving flow of movement tasks. When the swell of experience, feeling, and consciousness converges, a sense of cohesive identity can emerge and transform the self-perception of those involved. Identity work is a key moment of the formation cycle, during which identities emerge internal to groups and organizations. The crafting of a collective self-identity is carried out in a number of ways.

Identity

Consciousness, as described above, results from the combination of experience, feeling, and the production of shared narratives about reality. Identity is the product of systematic strategic efforts to craft consciousness into a cohesive message about the identity of a movement and its participants. If we experience grueling oppression, join together with others who share that experience, talk about the shared nature of our experience, and develop an analysis of the source of oppression, the next step is to fashion a set of statements about who "we" are. Debates over movement participants' identity can generate an impetus to diversify organizations to express differences in analysis. Identities are crafted around ideologies and tactics.

In civil rights and Black power movements, some ideological identity frames were the equality frame (stressing the self-identity of movement participants with the goals of existing society and desire for inclusion) vs. a "difference" frame that emphasized the distinctiveness of Black experience and voice and the goal of garnering respect for those differences as part of the movement goals. While Booker T. Washington exemplified the "equality" frame, Marcus Garvey's plan to repatriate African with Black Americans epitomized the "difference" frame. In the post-war movement, the integrationist goals of the mainstream civil rights leaders and organizations were a reiteration of the "equality frame," whereas the Black Power and Black nationalist movements critiqued the demand for integration in a society that would not grant it.[12]

An example from the marriage equality movement happened in 2009 at a thousands-strong march for equality. Organizer (and AIDS Quilt founder) Cleve Jones. At the rally, Jones gave a speech that ended with the refrain, "We are equal! We are equal! We are equal!" This is an example of an identity frame that insists that LGBTQ people not only should be equal, but already *are* equal. The repetition is a prefigurative moment of identity formation.

Tactically, identity frames have to do with what kinds of actions members of movements believe to be necessary and desirable to achieve their goals. The central tension between nonviolence and militancy exhibits different identity frames with regard to tactics. Thus, identity frames can be discovered by identifying a group's statements about who "we" are, what "we" want, and what "we" will do to achieve our goals.

The integrationist, nonviolent identity of the mainstream civil rights movement is summed up in the orations of leaders like Martin Luther

FIGURE 6.5 Cleve Jones speaks during the National Equality March at the Capitol Building on October 11, 2009 in Washington, DC.

King, Jr.: We have a dream that is fundamentally connected to the American Dream. We see ourselves as persons on a par with white citizens and seek equal treatment under the law. We envision a world in which all people are regarded equally as God's children. We are faithful, identified with Christian ideals. We are nonviolent, defined by our participation in direct action that draws out the nature of the establishment and its violence. (Keep in mind, however, that the demand for equal treatment in the context of the Jim Crow South was not a modest demand and that nonviolence involved direct confrontation with the agencies of the state, including the police and military.)[13]

In contrast, the ideological identity frames of the Black Power movement stressed freedom and pride as opposed to simple integration. Out of the experience of state brutality, this wing of the movement developed a militant tactical identity as well. "Say it loud, I'm Black and I'm proud," sang James Brown. "Freedom got a shotgun," sang SNCC activists at the end of the March on Montgomery in 1965. Carmichael and others expressed the desire to break with establishment politics, forming an independent party that became the Black Panther Party for Self-Defense. These expressions show how identities crafted in the formation cycle of social movements give rise to divergent social movement leaders and organizations.

Organization

In the formation cycle, organizations crystalize around shared identities and produce leaders who both express and foster those identities. Recall from Chapter 3 on the sociological tradition that a social movement **organization** is an agitational group that has become concrete and codified around ideology, goals, and tactics—or, institutionalized, involving people, ideas, and governance structures. Organizations have bylaws, identifiable leadership, and regular routines. Social movement organizations operate out of identifiable spaces in a regular way. They promote themselves to recruit new activists into the fold. They raise money and other resources. They engage in logistics and planning. They organize identities and meanings for public consumption.[14]

In most social movements, multiple organizations arise to express movement identity differences when activists move to create vehicles for divergent points of view and to take on leadership of multiple efforts on multiple fronts. For example, activist Ella Baker was a leading member of King's Southern Christian Leadership Conference. However, she identified with the rising militancy of young people in the movement and advised young militants to go their own way. She became a founding member of the Student Non-Violent Coordinating Committee as a result. While the SCLC carried out demonstrations to integrate Southern society and register Black voters, SNCC and other emerging organizations began to focus on self-defense and the expression of pride in difference.

Movement leaders facilitate the framing of identities and issues in movements; they also must frame themselves as legitimate leaders in the process. As in the case of Jewish ghetto uprisings against Nazism, the success of leaders in achieving such authority work is a matter of life and death.[15] Rhetoric scholarship on social movements also identifies the characteristics and roles of social movement leaders. Stewart, Smith, and Denton explain that social movement leaders demonstrate the practical organizational skills necessary to attract people to movements; successful organizers are also decision-makers who play diverse roles, and they serve as symbols identified with their causes. They become the "face" of a social movement for members and the public, responding to the challenge of rendering sometimes radical ideological messages clear and sensible to the broader society. Often sounding a prophetic tone, leaders employ rhetoric that inspires action and commitment, a quality identified as "charisma." Charismatic leaders like Cesar Chavez and Dolores Huerta in the farm workers' movement, Susan B. Anthony in the suffrage movement, Frederick Douglass in the abolition movement, and Stokely Carmichael in the Black Power movement tap into the experience and feelings of movement participants. Often, their authority lies in their willingness to sacrifice and take risks in the service of the cause.[16] However, not all movements have singular charismatic leaders.[17]

Training and education are major functions of social movement organizations. Movement education takes place in both formal and informal settings around shared readings or activities, and includes history, theory, and training. Many movements hold events featuring workshops on various elements of the repertoire of action, from organizational forms to civil disobedience. Training, the process of preparing groups of people to act in coordinated ways around protest repertoires, can likewise be formal or informal; it can happen in events and spaces dedicated to this process or emerge from the experience of struggle.

FIGURE 6.6 Activists at the Highlander Folk School in Tennessee underwent consciousness-raising and training in the tactics of civil rights protest.

In the civil rights movement, for example, the Highlander School in Tennessee gathered hundreds of Black and white activists for civil rights for educational sessions on voting rights and political action, desegregation workshops, and practice in civil disobedience, public speaking and writing, singing, and other coordinated activity. This school, founded in 1934, was formative for activists like Rosa Parks, Martin Luther King, Jr., and Julian Bond.[18] Importantly, the school's programs tapped into participants' experience, emotions, and embodiment, for example in enactments of integration demonstrations in which white activists intentionally bullied and harassed Black activists to prepare for real-world confrontations on schoolhouse steps, on buses, and at lunch counters.

Conclusion: Agency and the Formation Cycle

The formation cycle of the Hegemony-Formation-Pressure cycle model of the rhetoric of social movements describes the process by which activists build upon feelings and experiences to come to consciousness of systemic oppression and create organizational outlets and leadership for the crafting of shared identities, both ideological and tactical. The formation cycle corresponds to the constitutive, internally-oriented rhetorical dimensions of social movements. It is the process by which the metaphorical and literal choir comes together to coordinate meaning and practice. The most significant product of the formation cycle is the sense of shared agency, meaning the commitment and confidence to take action in control of one's destiny.

The major rhetorical repertoires of the formation cycle are narrative and embodied expression of shared belonging in consciousness-raising. The moments of the formation cycle are experience, feeling, consciousness, identity, and organization. These moments do not flow in one direction or necessarily in sequence. While some people begin to explore consciousness and identity, already-established organizations and leaders are training those farther along in the repertoires of identity framing, and education. Those leaders-in-training cycle their attention back to guide newer potential activists. Meanwhile, a whole historical formation built on earlier movement rhetoric, organizations, and culture serves as context and resource for the emergent formation process. Based on differences in ideological perspective and tactical approaches, the formation cycle generates multiple organizations as part of the same movement in a historical process that pre-exists the current movement's incarnations.

In these ways, the formation cycle becomes the site of social movement-as-meaning. The formation cycle can constitute a movement in itself if the goals of participants center on changes in meaning and identity. Some movements rest in the formation cycle. For example, the Occupy Movement of 2011 was instantiated in mass collective meetings and the establishment of communal spaces in which people lived, educated themselves, spoke, sang, and marched. That movement is often criticized for not having clear "demands" on the hegemonic establishment.[19] Such movements are called "prefigurative," in which the practice of the movement models the society envisioned by its activists. Most of the time, however, the generation of the formation cycle prepares movement activists to engage in public protest and systematic political challenges to laws, institutions, and the social order more generally. That kind of challenge happens in the second major social movement cycle, the pressure cycle, which is the subject of the next chapter.

Suggestions for Further Reading

Clayborne Carson, David J. Garrow, Gerald Gill, Vincent Harding, and Darlene Clark Hine, *The Eyes on the Prize Civil Rights Reader* (New York: Penguin, 1991).

W. Stuart Towns, *"We Want our Freedom": Rhetoric of the Civil Rights Movement* (Westport, CT: Praeger, 2002).

Howard Zinn, *SNCC: The New Abolitionists* (Cambridge, MA: South End Press, 1964).

Question for Discussion

1. Recall and describe a situation in which your consciousness has been raised about an issue of social justice. When, where, and with whom did this situation occur? How did communication play a role in explaining your experience? How did communication enable you to connect with others who shared your experience?

Credits

IMG 6.1: Copyright © by Alisdare Hickson (CC BY-SA 4.0) at https://commons.wikimedia.org/wiki/File:Abolish_All_Prisons_Protest_outside_Belmarsh_Prison.jpg.

Fig. 6.4: Copyright © 1966 by High Museum of Art.

Fig. 6.5: Copyright © by Gil Goldstein (CC BY-SA 3.0) at https://commons.wikimedia.org/wiki/File:Cleve_jones_NEM.jpg.

Fig. 6.6: Annemarie Schwarzenbach, "Highlander School," https://commons.wikimedia.org/wiki/File:CH-NB_-_USA,_Monteagle-TN-_Highlander_Folk_School_-_Annemarie_Schwarzenbach_-_SLA-Schwarzenbach-A-5-10-118.jpg, 1938.

7

Pressure Cycle Part 1

Going Public

KEY TERMS

pressure cycle
recruitment
publicity
public sphere
counterpublics
appeal
demand
equality and rights language
slogan
performativity
diminishment

A key insight of the Hegemony-Formation-Pressure model is that all struggles for social change are challenges to hegemonic power, and this struggle is oriented toward shifting economics, politics, culture, and the law. The model posits a dialectical (interdependent) relationship between the internally-oriented rhetoric of consciousness-raising and identity-creating, on the one hand, and the rhetorical strategies of public pressure on society's institutions, on the other. In the process of formation and pressure, movements can galvanize adjustments in hegemonic power relations, lead to revolutionary change (in which a new hegemony is established), meet with both repressive and cultural resistance from hegemonic standpoints, maintain themselves in a holding pattern over time, and/or decline and fail. Chapter 6 covered the first part of the model: the formation cycle. Chapters 7 and 8 continue the development of the Formation-Pressure-Hegemony model with an explanation of the **pressure cycle**, or, the moments and strategies of activists and organizations that pressure established institutions and elites. As a case in point, we will carry on with the example of civil rights and Black power movements in the United States. The figure below summarizes the workings of the pressure cycle.

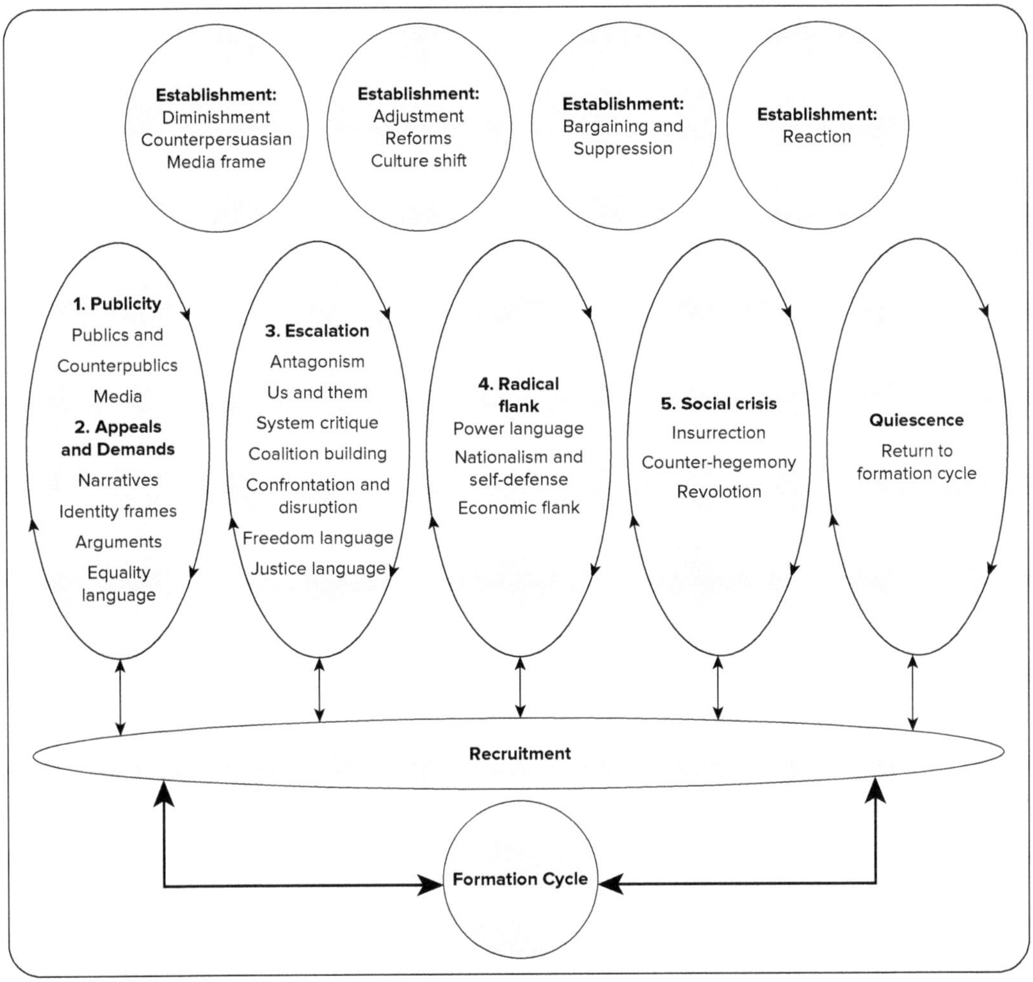

FIGURE 7.1 Pressure Cycle: Instrumental, externally-directed rhetoric and action.

To review, in the formation cycle, which is still ongoing as represented at the bottom of the diagram, activists have come together to share feelings and experiences, which has resulted in shared identity, political consciousness, and analysis of their situation in society. These activists have formed organizations, in which leaders have emerged. They have undertaken the education and training of people who are gathered in common cause. It is at this point that the activists gathered in these spaces and organizations may decide to "go public" with their analysis, messages, and demands. This is where the pressure cycle picks up the process.

Notes on the Model

Before we dive into the next steps in the process, there are a couple of things to remember. First, the model is characterized by *simultaneity.* Although it is easy to talk about the activity of social movements as happening in discrete stages or steps—first A happens, then B happens, etc.—it is important to remember that at any given moment in time, all of the steps can be happening at the same time, with some groups and organizations oriented to one set of tasks while others are devoted to something else. All of the simultaneous activity contributes to the movement's shape and development.

On this point, movements can fold, cease, or decline in activity at any point in the cycle. Movements fold when key demands are met, when they face unbearable suppression from hegemonic forces, or when they lose members and cultural and political influence. Movements can also end when their leaders enter mainstream politics or corporate life to work "inside" the system.

Second, recall that the model is *recursive*. Actions can be intermittent—they can start and stop; activists can and do return to tasks from previous moments in the movement, and that activity cycles into the shape of the movement as a whole. Third, there is constant interaction between the pressure cycle and the formation cycle in the form of recruitment. **Recruitment** is the process by which new members of a social movement are brought into the movement's activity through the persuasive efforts of existing participants. Rhetorics of recruitment must tap the experience and emotion of potential activists in discourse connecting their personal experience to systems and structures of power. Recruitment discourse must also convey a sense of agency: how activists find the capacity for effective response to their situation of exploitation and/or oppression.

Activists engage in persuasion in the pressure cycle that can attract other interested people, at which point people already involved can invite them into the formation cycle. Then, activists undergoing the processes of sharing feelings, emotions, narratives, identities, political consciousness and organization in the formation cycle can move into the pressure cycle. This can happen over and over again, as all active participants must return to their community or organizational home base (the formation cycle) to share insights and plan for upcoming activity.

Activists can meet newcomers at any point in their activity in either the formation or pressure cycle, but as an example, say that you are working in an immigrant rights organization. Your organization holds a public rally (which would be in the pressure cycle). There you meet several people who may be interested in joining your cause. If you are well-organized, you can invite them to the next meeting of your group and give them educational materials. At that point, you will have just invited them into the formation cycle. They will continue to take part in public activities also. You will go to the meeting, maybe to give a talk for new members. They, and you and all other participants, will oscillate between the tasks of formation and pressure over the course of a movement's life.

Lessons learned in the public, pressure-oriented activities of a movement get channeled back to the educational and consciousness-raising processes of the formation cycle as well, moving the entire process forward and advancing participants' knowledge and confidence along the way. In short, while understanding movements in terms of moments or steps is helpful for the purposes of analysis, in actual practice, the scene is more complex, messy, contradictory, and uncertain.

Wars of Position and Maneuver

You may recall from Chapter 2 that the theorist Antonio Gramsci said that there were two kinds of struggle: the war of position and the war of maneuver. The war of position refers to a moment in history when large-scale, system-oriented, instrumental (pressure-oriented) activity is highly constrained. Such periods may involve an entrenched, undemocratic, or authoritarian establishment elite, economic and other kinds of crises, or (paradoxically) economic boom times when conservative and traditional ideas flourish. Instead, the war of position refers to strategies in which activists and reformers hunker down and do identity and culture work, build organizations where there were none, engage in educational activities, and so on. Roughly speaking, this distinction corresponds to the formation-pressure duo, with the war of position being characteristic of the formation cycle and war of maneuver corresponding to the pressure cycle. This separation is not hard and fast, however. Many of the activities in the pressure cycle, including the making and distribution of movement media and culture, belong to both formation and pressure cycles.

As the moments in the pressure cycle escalate, a social movement becomes increasingly engaged in the war of maneuver: challenging political elites, the economic system, and laws with the goal of making significant changes. Let us turn now to the steps of the pressure cycle

Transition from Formation to Pressure

In addition to mapping onto the concepts of war of position and war of maneuver, the difference between the formation and pressure cycles can be understood in terms of how movements orient more toward "internal" audiences—that is, people involved in the movement itself—which corresponds to the formation cycle or more toward "external" audiences, publics at large who may not yet know much about a particular movement. The pressure cycle is where activists meet external audiences.

However, just as with the other dimensions of the model, this distinction is not tidy. At some public protests, a speaker may aim some remarks at their fellow movement activists and some to the broader public; a group of a dozen new people who met at a public event might come to the internal meeting of a social movement organization, at which point, rhetors in the movement have to balance talking to people who have been around a while and know the ropes with addressing the questions and concerns of the newcomers. Many movement communication situations are hybrid in this way, as rhetors are more often than not faced with multiple audiences at the same time. The trick is the adaptation of all of the rhetorical resources—narrative, argument, language, structure, and image, mainly—to succeed at such a complex task.

Take, for example, Martin Luther King, Jr.'s remarks at the March on Washington for Jobs and Freedom in 1963. This speech has come to be known as the "*I Have a Dream*" speech.[1] This speech is more controversial and more complex than many people think. It is an eloquent example of how a speaker advocating social justice adjusts their rhetoric to multiple, diverse audiences, both internal and external. One of these was the 250,000 or so people actually gathered on the Washington Mall at the base of the Lincoln Memorial. These were people of all races, including enormous numbers of Black Americans with some involvement in the civil rights movement up to that point. A growing number of these audience members were becoming impatient with the slow pace of federal action for civil rights. There were sectors of the movement breaking away from the mainstream movement's nonviolent commitments. Millions of people were watching and listening worldwide, also. And the speech would go down in history so that future (or historical) audiences like ourselves would be evaluating the speech's message.

Perhaps King's most important audience was the presidential administration of John F. Kennedy, for it was that administration that had the capacity to take action to secure and defend basic civil rights. So, what did King do? First, he brought in the vast assembled and international audience into his message in a series of metaphors that made the situation that King was describing accessible and concrete. These included metaphors of light, fire, seasons, oceans, and darkness, what Michael Osborn called *"archetypal" metaphors* because they seem to apply universally to the human condition.[2] King also develops an extended metaphor about how the movement had come to the nation's capital to cash a check, a promise made to all people in the Declaration of Independence to the rights of life, liberty, and the pursuit of happiness. In a stern moment, he charges the nation with defaulting on that check, the "bank of justice" having come back with the message: "insufficient funds."

FIGURE 7.2 Martin Luther King, Jr., delivers his famous speech to the March for Jobs and Freedom in 1963.

This challenge to the nation and its current president sustains the speech. There are moments when he addresses other specific audiences, however. When challenging the Kennedy administration, he rejects arguments that the movement should be patient and wait for the slow pace of reforms to unfold. Instead, King asserts the "fierce urgency of now" during which he cannot be satisfied with ongoing injustice. In the passage where King repeats the phrase "Now is the time," he presses again and again that immediate action is needed and expected. He even tells Kennedy, "It would be fatal for the nation to overlook the urgency of the moment." He threatens the administration with a "rude awakening" and "whirlwinds of revolt" if it were to fail to act. (Anyone who thought that this speech was all kindness and love would be wrong.)

Then he shifts to address movement adherents and dissatisfied Black Americans in general: "But there is something I must say to my people." He warns this internal audience not to turn to the cup of bitterness and hatred to slake the thirst for justice and urges listeners to "meet physical force with soul force." In this way, this powerful example of social movement rhetoric shows how movement activists adjust their ideas, language, arguments, and so on—even in a single speech—to both internal and external audiences.

In the civil rights movement, the formation and pressure cycles were always ongoing, all at once, simultaneously reaching new people and educating and leading those already in place. The transition from the formation cycle into the pressure cycle takes place when activists and organizations have crafted a message and a sense of their identity and take action to bring the movement into broader public view. This happens many times even in a single movement in a constant process of developing ideas and taking them on the road. The work of a movement engages at this point in publicity and appeal, at which point the establishment could deny those appeals and attempt to diminish the movement's influence in the media and in public opinion. At this point, a movement might then escalate its efforts, developing a rhetoric of antagonism that polarizes society into an "us" and a "them." At this point, activists, now engaged in multiple organizations and coalitions, wonder why the system won't meet their very reasonable requests; they then ratchet up their analysis of why the systems of power in place won't adjust to become fairer and more equal. What comes out of this question is an account of who has power—they do—and who needs to demand some of that power—we do.

At this point, the establishment might adjust by granting some changes demanded by the growing and influential movement. But dissatisfied wings of the movement may escalate efforts toward disruption, which the establishment then might try to suppress through the police and armed forces. At this point, the state's violent actions cause the movement to intensify in militancy and radicalize, leading to instability in movement coalitions. Ongoing confrontations can generate a broader social crisis and greater repression. The pressure cycle is not only in a dialectical relationship with the formation cycle; it also shapes and is shaped by the actions of establishment institutions and elites as they respond to movement demands.

Alternatively, the establishment might, under such pressure, capitulate or give in to some or all of a movement's demands. Most of the time, at this point a movement will fold (and could do so at any prior point), unless there is a revolutionary situation on the horizon in which a whole new class of people could take power and replace existing elites and institutions. This scenario does not often happen. After achieving a number of its aims through reforms in law, policy, and cultural norms (or else after being impaired or destroyed by establishment forces), a movement can go quiet or take different forms. People seeking redress of injustice in these quiet times may find themselves in the beginnings of a new formation cycle, laying the groundwork for the fire next time.

At every moment in the pressure cycle, activists are assessing opportunities and resources, working together to decide whether to stay on or change the course. The formation cycle spaces and events become very contentious and characterized by debates about the ways forward. Far from being a negative development, such controversy fuels the evolution of movements.

Step 1: Publicity

One can look at the formation cycle as a kind of workshop where identities, ideas, and messages are crafted and practiced. At some point—and oftentimes simultaneously with the formation process—activists take their show on the road: to appeal to public opinion and powerful agencies in society, to make demands, and to leverage whatever resources they have available to them to press their cause. This step is called, simply, **publicity**—not to be understood as the shallow practices of advertisers and public relations firms using media to manipulate public opinion, but rather as the much more profound step of entering the public sphere.

Public and Counterpublic Spheres

The **public sphere** consists of all of the spaces, forums, media, and audiences available to people attempting to shape society.[3] The public sphere is a domain where neither obligations to intimates nor state authority govern what can be said (within some limits). The public sphere is the sphere of mutual communication, debate, and controversy. It is where public opinion is formed in such a way as to influence corporate elites and politicians dependent upon public support. It is the domain of society protected, imperfectly, by the First Amendment.[4] To be public, a message or a movement has to be addressed to an audience of strangers, a group or groups of people not already invested in or knowledgeable about the cause. When social movements go public, they often give rise to **counterpublics**. Counterpublics are spheres of debate and deliberation organized around a particular identity, group, cause, or movement.[5] The public sphere is where controversy, debate, and publicity happen, but because the institutions and media that govern the public sphere are dominated by established powerful interests and hegemonic ideas and frames, people seeking to articulate new ideas and identities and advocate for change gather for conversation and common work.

Counterpublics are sites where people gather to explicitly articulate alternatives to wider publics that exclude their interests.[6] Feminist scholar Nancy Fraser defines counterpublics as "parallel discursive arenas where members of subordinated social groups invent and circulate counterdiscourses to formulate oppositional interpretations of their identities, interests, and needs."[7] One example is the coalition to expose environmental causes of breast cancer described by Phaedra Pezzullo constituted a counterpublic that challenged mainstream public narratives about breast cancer.[8] Counterpublics can be spaces of withdrawal and internally-focused activity (in which case they are called "enclaves"). For example, over the last decade, groups of queer disabled people have formed "communities of care" in which they collaborate to meet each other's material and bodily needs and produce art, writing, film, and other cultural products.[9] Counterpublics also seek to circulate their alternative discourses more broadly. Counterpublics are sites not only of instrumental action for policy change in the public sphere but also of the organizing of subordinated groups in society to challenge the unequal distribution of power and resources.[10] Most, if not all, social movements form counterpublics, although not all counterpublics are social movements.

We could say that ACT UP—and the broader communities mobilized to challenge anti-queer society and, in playful, campy rhetorics, to constitute and celebrate queer identity[11]—created a counterpublic around the issue of HIV-AIDS in the 1980s. Counterpublics often find themselves challenging, and being challenged by, hegemonic mainstream publics and their representatives. However, they can also grow in influence and generate significant energy for a cause. Sometimes "counterpublic" is used as a synonym for "social movement," but it is more accurate to specify "social movement counterpublics," as there are other kinds of communities not focused on social justice who constitute counterpublics. ACT UP is a case in which activists created counterpublics that oscillated between vernacular (or grassroots and bottom-up minority spaces) and official publics.[12] They used an "inside-outside" strategy to put pressure on institutions of government and health care, with militancy pressing from the outside and experts working as insiders with scientists, politicians, and other officials.

Social Movements and Media

Traditional media

Media are important to the work of counterpublics. When entering the public sphere, social movements use the affordances of three kinds of media. First, movements rely on mainstream, commercial mass media to cover events and relay messages about the movement to a broad audience. Reliance on commercial mass media—controlled by corporate elites dedicated to representing the voices and arguments of hegemonic interests in society—comes at a price. Producers, reporters, and writers for these media engage in media routines that consistently have framed movements for social change in pejorative ways. For example, as Todd Gitlin explained in classic account *The Whole World Is Watching*, mainstream news reporting uses techniques like undercounting participants in movements, choosing visuals that minimize the presence and impact of movements, reporting in voice-over rather than allowing movement activists to speak for themselves, asking guiding questions that call into question the legitimacy of a movement, and framing movements in terms of an irrational confrontation between (only) two "sides," in which both are assumed to be equally valid, even if one is involves something like a far-right, white supremacist organization. In mainstream media routines, government officials and corporate representatives are given priority coverage, which allows those elites to frame and counter movement messages in demeaning or dismissive ways.[13]

Radical alternative media—those that are generally small in scale and expressive of alternatives to hegemonic policies, priorities, and perspectives—are pervasive across the history of social movements.[14] So, the second kind of media engaged by social movements is media produced by movements themselves: leaflets, books, newspapers, documentaries, radio broadcasts, and so on.[15] Most social movements in U.S. history have produced such media, which allows them to promulgate their messages directly.[16] Social movement media constitute public spheres that enable people to communicate laterally—that is, with each other, in order to bring people together around a cause. These media include not only traditional media forms like newspapers, books, newscasts, or television. They can be speech, dance, songs, poetry, fashion, graffiti, street theater, performance art, and culture-jamming.[17]

The socialist and communist movements, for example, developed an extensive public sphere of letters, publishing dozens of books,

FIGURE 7.3 Activists—like these socialists at Syracuse University—use in-person literature tables to attract potential recruits.

newspapers, magazines, leaflets, murals, and artworks that were resources for training and outreach.[18] The Detroit Revolutionary Union Movement, a 1960s movement of Black autoworkers, published a regular, influential newspaper.[19] Then a documentary was made about that newspaper, *Finally Got the News*.[20] The Black Panther Party for Self-Defense published a regular newspaper and distributed it along with groceries to Black people in cities where they organized. People got a dose of politics with their breakfast.

Rhetorician and film scholar Angela Aguayo, in her book *Documentary Resistance*, explains how documentary film can both reflect and critique the existing social order:

> The story of documentary and social change in the United States is one of self-determination. People—often of humble means—demanding recognition and dignity for themselves and their communities have used the documentary to find pathways into a better life.[21]

Documentaries are sites of agency and identification for groups seeking to protest injustice and use media to build their movements. In such cases, documentaries are participatory media that can be forces for grassroots change. Like newspapers, documentaries can be organizing agents—sites around which people can gather, discuss, and formulate action. The aural, visual, and affective dimensions of documentary film are powerful tools in orienting people emotionally to a cause.[22]

Aguayo notes a couple of dangers of relying on documentaries as vehicles for social justice, including the tendency of filmmakers to exploit the experience of the oppressed in order to profit from their accounts and the potential for documentaries to position audiences as spectators or tourists to the struggle rather than participants. We should stay focused on how documentary can aid in the struggle for material and cultural justice. Another limitation of these media is their relatively small circulation to movement in-groups. Many of these media are designed to rally adherents to a movement behind the cause and to provide information that fuels activists' arguments and narratives. They also function as sites for recruitment. In this sense, movement media play their most important role in the formation cycle.

Street tapes and similar grassroots documentary are an important category of social movement media. People have long recorded encounters between citizens and an oppressive police force; such recordings enter

> the existing public conversation about police brutality and excessive force ... documenting physical conflicts, reporting on their significance, and providing stories about what these exchanges signify for those who confront state control.[23]

In the Black Lives Matter movement, when ordinary people record police violence, mostly against people of color, and circulate those videos as evidence of the problem of brutally racist policing.[24] The knowledge provided by these videos galvanized hundreds of thousands of people into action. Aguayo shows how street tapes tell alternative histories in which "underrepresented voices gain visibility, circulation and capacity to develop a public voice ... speaking their situated truth with and through the camera."[25]

Social Media

Social and other digital media are often addressed to participants and potential recruits of social movements, but they also are effective conduits of information that ordinary people can control. In the 21st century, movements have increasingly relied upon such media to build numbers and influence public opinion. For example, the Occupy movement of 2011, which brought thousands of people together to occupy public spaces and make arguments against overweening corporate power in society, relied on early versions of live streaming via laptop computers to project its mass meetings and other events to broader audiences.[26]

Social media occupy a special place in the publicity moment, between public and private spheres. They largely address people with whom we are acquainted, not the broader community of strangers that defines the public sphere. They often play a significant role in the formation cycle because they allow networks of friends and acquaintances to share information about ongoing movement efforts and social problems. They can be used to call for and bring people out to both physical and virtual meetings and demonstrations. During Occupy and the revolutionary movements of the Arab Spring in 2011, activists used cell phones and networks to promulgate their messages and let others know where and when events were happening. Social media and the use of cell phone technology can allow activists to avoid the censorship of authorities (until authorities shut down cell networks). In this way, movements can leverage counter-power through the networked society characterized by "multifaceted rebellion" using the communication affordances of the Internet.[27]

Social media carry the promise of forming new spheres of communicative action—through cyber activism—and organizing—the use of social media to draw people together for meetings, protests, and other events; in many cases, social media platforms have supplanted in-person organizational meetings in favor of the looser and timely flow of information and debate. Social movements use the Internet for three purposes: mobilizing social support, managing their network, and creating public spaces for deliberation. A great deal of activism takes place online—in the signing of petitions, culture jamming, and hacktivism. The Internet also has allowed for social movements to go transnational with advocacy campaigns.[28] Online platforms have shifted the repertoire of contention away from the centrality of mass media in a new repertoire of communication that shifts orientation from the collective to the individual.[29]

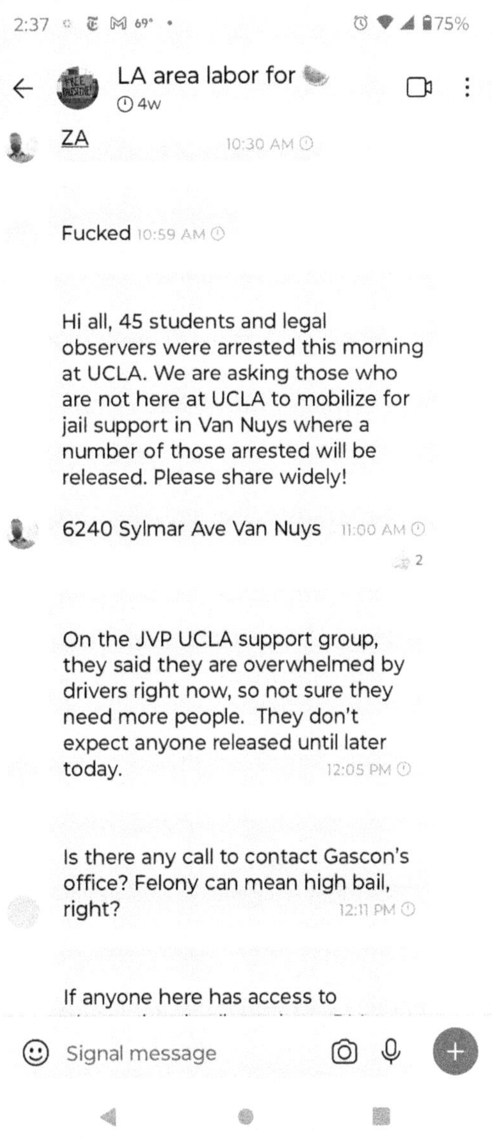

FIGURE 7.4 Activists are increasingly turning to social media channels like Signal to conduct organizing and debate.

Social media platforms have proliferated, as have their uses by social movements. As Jordana George and Dorothy Leidner explain, activists use social media as spectators (clicktivism, metavoicing, assertion), transitional activities (e-funding, digital petitions, and botivism) and gladiatorial activities (data activism, exposure, and hactivism).[30] Social media are thus directly connected to politics and activism for social justice. Blogs and micro-blogs, social networking sites (Facebook, X (formerly Twitter), Instagram, Snapchat, Slack, GroupMe, Signal, and many others), content-sharing sites (YouTube, Flikr, TikTok), social bookmarking sites (Digg, Reddit, Tumblr), and the virtual worlds of gaming are all places where activists can organize, share information, build archives of knowledge, and call people to action.[31] Digital platforms have become essential tools in mobilizing new activists, creating space for networks and coalitions, and shaping public discourse and meaning based on personal meaning frames.[32] Social media activism is connected to corporeal organizing as part of a broader process that can facilitate communicative competence and empowerment and lead to embodied protest. Social media enable activists to share information, stay connected with fellow activists, support protests, and maintain a virtual presence.[33] Social media can function as an information engine that exposes state violence and they can serve organizing functions and combat isolation.

Social media also invoke affect and emotion that bind users together in a technological rendering of the personal as political.[34] For example, in the #MeToo movement, digital platforms generated an "affective public" in which users "lent affective solidarity to survivors through expressions of support, validation of their accounts, and acknowledgment of the systematic nature of sexual violence."[35] Social media also have distinct temporal and visual logics that challenge the linear instrumentalist time norms of conventional organizing and conventional movements' valorization of the verbal.[36] Images condense emotion and invoke playful and metaphorical responses to collective engagement in both traditional media and everyday encounters with social media.[37] Digital activism on platforms like Facebook also do important memory work, for example around the page Justice for Mike Brown.[38]

Memes are a special case illustrating the evolving social media strategies of movements. Memes are units of meaning and imitation" that are passed from user to user across time and space, remixing cultural discourses along the way. Memes possess three parts: content, or ideology; form, or the structural pattern of the argument (often ironic and commonly visual); and stance, or how communicators are related to a particular meme. Memes work to construct and solidify the identities of their creators/circulators/audiences.[39]

Scholars who theorize and describe how social movements use and are enacted in social media call movements of the digital age "Social Movement 2.0," a label for movements at the intersection of social movement and Web 2.0. Social Movement 2.0 operates in a globalized, network, digital society in which the flow of meanings, collective

FIGURE 7.5 A meme created in response to the Columbia University Pro-Palestine protests of 2024 juxtaposes two photographs: one of Columbia students protesting the Vietnam War in 1968 and another of students protesting the Gaza conflict in 2024. Both photos feature a banner reading 'Liberated Zone,' creating rhetorical solidarity between the two groups despite the decades separating them. By identifying with the Vietnam protesters, Pro-Palestine activists highlight the parallels between the 1968 and 2024 demonstrations, both of which were student-led in opposition to U.S. involvement in foreign conflicts. The visual comparison makes an argument for historical continuity among student struggles and the parallel nature of the wars that prompted protest.

identities, and feelings across a fragmented media landscape are at the forefront of what it means, in Foust's terms, "to move the social." Social media "have a powerful capacity to circulate and connect symbols and people."[40] They are sites for the constitution of collective identities, that is, part of the formation cycle. They can also lead to instrumental, embodied pressure on systems and institutions.

There is a debate over the productivity of social media for social movements. On the one hand, social media represent a "fundamental shift in the structure, strategy, governance, and logic of contemporary social movements," in which movements become diversified, transnational, decentralized, and directly democratic.[41] Social media can constitute networked counterpublics in which hashtags organize collective thoughts, ideas, arguments, and experiences outside of elite media spaces.[42] Mattoni explains how "an enlarged conception of media practices allows scholars to explore how even social groups that have no voice in the bourgeois public sphere could elaborate their own mediated representation through the appropriation of media technologies."[43] Sarah Jackson, Moya Bailey, and Brooke Foucault Welles have written about how opinion hubs emerged on Twitter, using hashtags to network people in the Black Lives Matter Movement.[44] They argue in this context, hashtag activism has "forever changed national consciousness."[45] In addition to providing an opportunity for anti-racist organizing, hashtag activism has enabled transgender advocacy and community building.[46]

A number of scholars have called our attention to how networked, transnational, digital counterpublics can serve historically oppressed and marginalized activists and communities. Phaedra Pezzullo describes how affective counterpublics used social media to enable on- and offline activism around plastic pollution.[47] For another example, social media enable the transnational activism of communities in the Global South—regions of the world where people have risen up against historical colonization, subjugation, and dispossession.[48] Indigenous activists, also historically muted, use social media to challenge hegemonic representations and bring indigenous knowledge to the development of Internet communication technologies.[49] For example, digital media work during the fight against the Dakota Access Pipeline in 2016 and 2017. Although the #NoDAPL campaign did not stop the completion of the pipeline, it was an "indigenizing project" that constructed an alternative worldview and value system, disrupting existing colonial systems.[50] Likewise, online technology facilitated information flows and left digital traces of Standing Rock solidarity groups that evolved int lasting activist communities. Digital activism also allows disabled communities to contest definitions of the political that privilege corporeal and public political activism—definitions that are masculinist and ableist.[51]

Thus, digital platforms, including social media, have several affordances for social movements, including the capacity to network counterpublics of the oppressed. On the other hand, reliance on social media can make a movement unstable, highly personalistic, detached from on-the-ground struggles, and difficult to sustain. The Internet lends itself to the self-organizing of movement networks without developing formal organizations at the core of movements. The Internet, and specifically social media, lend themselves to "microparticipation," or the undertaking of small, easy steps (like signing petitions or making donations) in concert with a user's lifestyle and friendship circle ("slacktivism").[52] These activities carry virtually no costs in terms of time and effort for users and therefore can bring new people into movements and advocacy, but in an impulsive and ephemeral way.[53] The rejection of "old" modes of struggle leads digital activists to retreat from the critique of and challenge to capitalism as a system, to become technological determinists, and to de-emphasize political education and leadership development.[54] Wolfson concludes that the new horizontalist modalities of organizing do not have the facility to build power and create real-world change at a system scale.[55]

Social media are also less-than-ideal spaces for organizing for a number of additional reasons. First, social media networks are heavily surveilled by the state and corporate interests, so activists risk exposing themselves to punitive action; corporations routinely monitor social movement media activity on digital platforms. Second, the commercial character of all social media platforms frames potentially political messages with advertising content. Third, social media algorithms funnel carefully curated content to users, limiting and distorting exposure to potentially interesting movement information.[56] Fourth, online environments can be spaces of abuse and violence, particularly gendered violence.[57] Finally, as noted above, social media occupy a liminal space between private and public: Users can engage social media to translate their personal experience into a political cause, but the influence can go the other way, to turn systemic political problems requiring systemic action into matters of lifestyle, emotion, and circumscribed relationships.

Social media contribute to the formation cycle by networking users around shared meanings, identities, and tasks. Because networked social media hubs, organized around hashtags and "likes," emerge as the communication infrastructure of many movements today, they play a role in the pressure cycle as well. Celebrity influencers develop platforms to share influential messages. The non-public character of social media means that many of these messages are aimed at influencing personal, consumer and lifestyle, choices—not

FIGURE 7.6 Police occupy the University of Texas at Austin campus in response to Palestine solidarity protests on April 29, 2024.

political ideas or activism. However, these technologies and platforms represent potentially democratic forums controlled by more-or-less ordinary people, and in this way, contribute to controversies in the public sphere.

In summary, the public sphere is where movements mount their repertoires of contention: their set of activities and messages designed to pressure the government and other elites to make change. Movements use their media practices to create performative public spheres and how digital and mobile media amplify their capacity to do so.[58] As discussed in Chapter 3, these repertoires can include leaflets, treatises, petitions, demonstrations, marches, strikes, boycotts, speeches, music, confrontations, street art, graffiti, performance art, and other kinds of interventions—including social media. We begin with the most basic moment: when a movement asks for what it wants.

Step 2: Appeals and Demands

Appeals and Petitions

An **appeal** is a request or plea for something to change. Making appeals to public officials—bodies of people and institutions tasked with serving the public—is part of the publicity step. **Petitioning**—the act of asking an institution to grant a demand—often launches the publicity step. Petitions include what we think of today as such, statements of demands and explanations followed by long lists of signatures. In *Signatures of Citizenship*, rhetoric scholar Susan Zaeske analyzes women's antislavery petitions of the mid-19th century, arguing that the petition was among the few ways that women could exert political agency and make demands on society.[59]

But to ask, in any form, the powers that be to do something is to petition them. The Black citizens of Montgomery, Alabama asked the city to desegregate city buses. The civil rights movement asked lunch counters and department stores to integrate. Martin Luther King, Jr. (and many others), asked the president to institute and defend the right to vote for Black citizens. The lawyers arguing the *Brown v. Board of Education* case asked the Court to require public schools to integrate and do away with the separate and unequal conditions of education facing Black children in the United States.

It is common to see activists distributing literature in public, making speeches, holding protests, and leading marches through city streets. These are activities where activists share their narratives and arguments and where images are put to powerful use in the service of a cause. In the early civil rights movement, for example, emerging civil rights organizations on U.S. campuses held regular literature tables and rallies to bring people around their messages. It seems like a very simple thing to do—set up a table with some mimeographed copies and distribute these to passersby. The actual momentous character of such activity is revealed when you know that at these universities, for example at the University of California, Berkeley (a hotbed of student radicalism in the 1960s), university officials cracked down on these simple efforts by students to spread the word about civil rights. The repression of public speech there and elsewhere led to the eruption of another social movement, the student free-speech movement, in the early 1960s. A movement was necessary to simply open up space in the public sphere for the narratives and arguments of specific movements to intervene at all.

An appeal becomes a **demand** when social movement participants escalate pressure on an establishment to give ground and when they mount tactics of confrontation and disruption to do so. Often, movements develop a list of demands as part of the process of formation, asking themselves, what do we want? Who can give us what we want? How can we compel them to give us what we want? Under what conditions should this happen? And so on. In the present movement for Palestinian rights and an end to the war in Gaza, protesters have made demands upon their universities, including the demand that the universities divest from—cease investing funds in—companies doing business with the state of Israel, particularly companies that supply arms for the war effort. At the time I am writing, no universities have conceded to this or other demands, and the administrations have engaged mostly in suppression by police of student demonstrations and encampments. (I will take up the concept of suppression in the next chapter.)

In the civil rights movement, early demands included integrated and equal education, the right to vote, the right to enter public spaces and use public facilities, and political representation. Many elements of the rhetorical repertoire of contention (Chapter 5) are deployed in the campaign to win demands, and I review them here.

Narratives

Using media and the repertoires of contention, social movement advocates propagate narratives that challenge existing beliefs, attitudes, values, and norms and assert alternative identity frames. Recall that narratives work by conveying important information, urging identification with the speaker or protagonist of the story using shared norms and values, making situations not personally witnessed come to life in a vivid and concrete way, and establishing lessons where those who identify with the protagonists are to arrive.

One example comes from the Mississippi Freedom Democratic Party (MFDP). The MFDP built a parallel political party and electoral structure to challenge the reign of "Dixiecrats"—Southern Democrats hostile to civil rights. (Interestingly, many leaders in the MFDP were women, which was not the case in many other organizations.) In 1964, the MFDP disrupted the national convention of the Democratic Party in Atlantic City, New Jersey, where MFDP representatives demanded to be seated and recognized as the legitimate delegation from Mississippi.[60]

The proceedings of the credentials committee were televised, and it was during those proceedings that the activist Fannie Lou Hamer employed narrative to compel the body's consideration. It begins, "Mr. Chairman, and the Credentials Committee, my name is Mrs. Fannie Lou Hamer, and I live at 626 East Lafayette Street, Ruleville, Mississippi, Sunflower County, the home of Senator James O. Eastland, and Senator Stennis." Hamer then tells the story of how she and 18 others sought the right to vote in Mississippi to become "first-class citizens." They were arrested and made to pay fines. It is the detail that brings Hamer's story to life:

> We continued on to Ruleville, and Reverend Jeff Sunny carried [drove] me four miles in the rural area where I had worked as a timekeeper and sharecropper for eighteen years. I was met there by my children, who told me that the plantation owner was angry because I had gone down to try to register.[61]

What did the convention delegates learn from this statement? They learned that sharecropping on plantations was the condition of life for Black people in the South, and that Hamer had experienced that life. Also, the brief example shows how the tyrannical rule of plantation owners did not end with slavery. The owner thought that it was his prerogative to prohibit Hamer and other Black people from voting. Hamer's detail about how she got to the plantation and mention of her children makes it easy for listeners to identify with her and her values.

FIGURE 7.7 Fannie Lou Hammer addresses the Democratic National Convention in 1964.

As she goes on, she tells the story of how she and others were shot at for their efforts, and that people had shot into their homes. She tells about how while traveling, the group was not allowed to use public restrooms: "It was a State Highway Patrolman and a chief of police ordered us out." Four, including Hamer, were arrested and beaten.

Another woman in their party was made to use the n-word and was beaten—by Black men (who were forced to do so). When they started to beat Hamer, she recounts,

> I began to work [move in protest] my feet, and the State Highway Patrolman ordered the first Negro who had beat to set on my feet. … I began to scream and one white man got up and began to beat my head and told me to hush. One white man—my dress had worked up high, he walked over and pulled my dress down—and he pulled my dress back, back up.

Here we are called to feel outrage that a mature woman was arrested and beaten and humiliated for simply trying to vote. And we can visualize that humiliation as if it occurred before us. We can imagine fighting off a beating with our legs. We can imagine the shame of the exposure of her body.

Then she flatly states, "I was in jail when Medgar Evers was murdered." This brilliant sentence conveys a great deal of information: Opponents of civil rights are beating her. Far away, others like them killed the activist Medgar Evers. These events are related and lead to a conclusion: The beatings and murder are the product of systematic racist violence. Listeners are invited to feel for Hamer, who was not only arrested and beaten but also prevented from grieving or protesting Evers' death.

Hamer concludes that all of this treatment stemmed from resistance to Black people becoming full citizens (thus returning elegantly to the beginning of the story). In an internationally-broadcast conclusion, she says, "I question America. Is this America, the land of the free and the home of the brave, where we have to sleep with our telephones off of the hooks because our lives be threatened daily because we want to live as decent human beings, in America?" Here the narrative ends with a pronouncement of shared American values. In specific detail, Hamer has conveyed complex information about life in the South and the treatment of the civil rights movement, won the identification of a broad audience with her struggle, and reframed her identity and that of the entire movement in terms of American values. This is the power of narrative.

Identity Frames

Hamer's story is also a compelling example of identity framing. As discussed in Chapter 4, identity framing is the rhetorical process by which rhetors, in this case, participants in social movements, use language and images to craft their identities *as they want to be perceived by audiences.* This process is designed to challenge the received ideas—in this case, racist ideas—held by audiences outside the movement and to influence others to see the activists and the world in new ways—to alter perception and meaning. The process of identity framing applies not only to individuals but also to the movement as a whole.

Hamer employed symbols—including images, words, actions, and objects to construct her public personae (as an educator, truth-teller, and warrior for freedom.[62] Identity work in social movements is how participants create an oppositional stance for themselves as a united collectivity with a strong sense of themselves.[63] Key to this process are the articulations of themes of sameness and difference around which relationships of solidarity can be built (sometimes with difficulty given the intersectionality of race, ethnicity, gender, class, religion, and sexuality) among a diverse membership. Identity frames occur internal to movements when activists arrive at a sense of shared identity and purpose; they are then deployed to external audiences to guide public perception in a strategic way. Sometimes, the identity frames that movements put forward in public emphasize unity and sameness while internally, there is dialogue, debate, difference, and even conflict that might be exploited by the establishment if these were to be on public view.

Gerald Platt and Michael Fraser describe identity framing in the letters of civil rights activists to Martin Luther King, Jr.[64] Writers describe their experiences in the movement, express identification with movement goals, describe the networks and groups that influenced them, and discuss the conduct of the movement. These letters created solidarity and framed the movement in narrative form. They deployed identities of race, gender, and circumstances to construct the meaning of the movement for themselves. They bring their personal experiences to bear just as Fannie Lou Hamer did, contextualizing experience in the broader arguments of the movement itself. They created themselves as active agents of transformation.

Emphasizing how movements shape their identities for public audiences, Jane Rhodes examines the rhetoric of the Black Panther Party for Self-Defense, who presented themselves as committed to Black self-determination, employment, housing, education, and freedom from police brutality. They carried weapons as a symbol of their self-defense agenda. Dominant media frames worked to minimize and contain the meaning of the Panthers by deploying racial ideologies—the idea of Black men as criminal, irrational, violent threats—in the process.[65] Thus we see how identity frames are constructed internal and external to social movement spaces in dialogue with dominant media frames working to constrain public opinion regarding movement participants and goals.

Arguments

Arguments are also important to the success of movement publicity. An argument is a claim backed up by evidence and reasoning. Hamer's argument, like that of much of the civil rights movement, goes something like this: Black people are denied their citizenship rights. (Evidence: beatings and murders when trying to vote.) Being denied these rights is a violation of American values. (Evidence: American values.) Conclusion: It is wrong to deny Black people the rights afforded to white people in American society. Conclusion: Black people should be fully recognized in the electoral process. This, like most arguments, relies on a form of reasoning that Aristotle called *the enthymeme*, one that relies upon appeals to the values shared between rhetor and audience. Hamer's question, "Is this America?" is a powerful example of this principle. If the Democratic National Convention truly stood for the principles of inclusion and representation, the conclusion that Hamer draws, that her delegation should be seated, should be self-evident. When her claim was rejected, it called into question her audience's commitment to its professed principles.

The Language of Equal Rights

Indeed, the language of much of the civil rights movement (and many other movements, including woman suffrage, gay rights, and so on) rests upon the appeal to *equality* and equal rights; the civil rights movement uses **equality and rights language**. (The Black Power movement, however, will turn to the language—as indicated in the name of the movement—of *power*. The evolving movement increasingly relies on the language of *justice*.)

A term like equality is given meaning by those who use and shape it. Moreover, a term like equality can constitute the center of a public sphere dedicated to the principle that it represents. The meaning of such terms changes over time and by situation. Many U.S. social movements, looking to the Declaration of Independence as a statement of equality as a core value, put the language of equality or equal rights at the center of their symbolic efforts. In anti-racist movements, "equality" has been a rhetorical resource to confront the exclusion of Black people from the full rights of citizenship. An argument for full equality challenged the doctrine of separate but equal. Condit and Lucaites argue that the term evolved in the later civil rights movement when equality defined as a matter of opportunity was supplanted by a fuller notion of substantial equality, or equality in fact.[66] We will also see how equality language gives way to justice language and power language as the civil rights movement evolves. This is also a progression common to most U.S. social movements.

Images and Slogans

In addition to narratives and arguments, social movements rely upon visual rhetoric—the persuasive use of images—and slogans. Scholars of visual rhetoric have called our attention to how images are uniquely rhetorical. Their powers are to condense a great deal of information into a single object (the picture), to win identification by providing a point of view, to provoke strong emotion, and, potentially, to bypass the processes of logical reasoning. The result is a moment of persuasion that is immediate and compelling.[67]

One powerful example from the early civil rights movement is the decision of Mamie Till Bradley in 1955 to open the casket of her son Emmett Till, a Black youth brutally murdered, tortured, beaten, and shot to death in Money, Mississippi.[68] In a word, he was lynched, for greeting a white young woman outside of a store. His experience was not unique. Emmett's corpse was gruesomely disfigured. The image appeared not only to the mourners whose strong reactions may have galvanized their commitment to the movement, but also in newspapers and magazines around the world. The nation was made to bear witness to this atrocity. The image conveyed a great deal of information about racist brutality in the South, namely, that it was real and took horrific forms. Till Bradley's exposure of the body asked its audiences to see the young man from a mother's point of view, winning identification with the grief and horror of Emmett's mother. The image provoked strong emotions; the most important of these for the social movement were not just grief but outrage and a desire to commit to the cause of ending such violence. The murder and this image have been credited in popular memory as the beginning of the civil rights movement.[69] All of these tasks are achieved in an instant when visual rhetoric is deployed effectively.

Signs are one kind of visual rhetoric common to most social movements. Protest signs sometimes involve images, often symbols rather than photographs or realistic representations. For example, in the Black Power movement, signs often displayed the image of a raised fist. This symbol is common in protest communication to this day.[70]

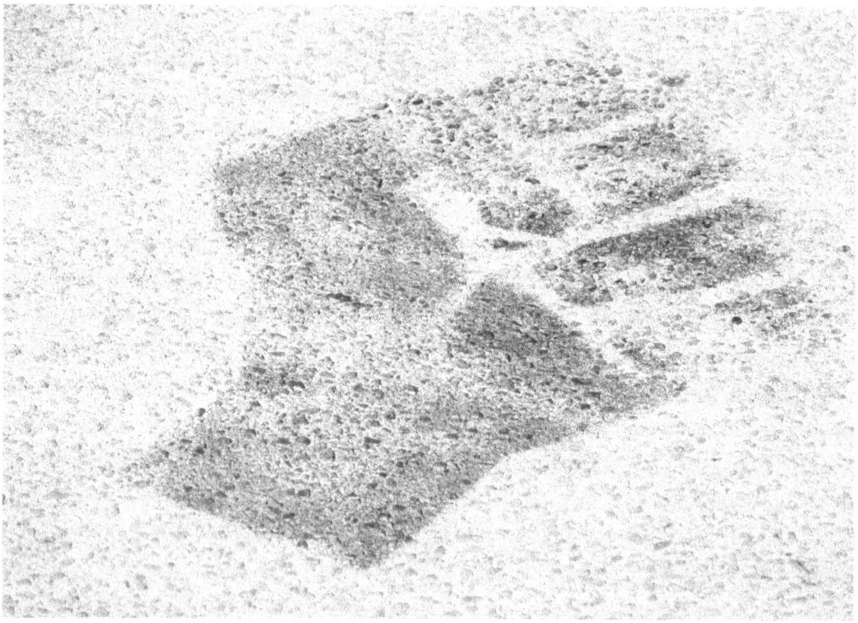

FIGURE 7.8 The image of a clenched fist became the symbol of the Black Power Movement and has been adopted by many social movements since.

The logos or initials of particular organizations often appear on these signs (so that people who like the signs know where to go to take further action). The act of making signs and other protest materials is part of the formation cycle, so slogans come into being and are used in all phases of the movement cycle. Slogans are common in both signage and verbal delivery. A **slogan** is a short phrase or sentence that captures the essence of a movement, calls for a particular action, or announces some clear demand. "Black Lives Matter" is an important slogan of the movement against racist police violence. So is, "No Justice, No Peace." "Defend the Forest," and "Stop Proposition 8." All are examples that make demands for audiences to take an action. In the civil rights movement, common slogans simply asserted the personhood of Black people in the United States. For example, in Memphis in April, 1968, sanitation workers—all Black—went on strike against poverty wages and neglect and abuse. The 1300 strikers were addressed by Martin Luther King, Jr., on the very night before King was assassinated. King told the workers to see the strike through until they won their demands.

Crucial to this strike were the picket signs. They simply read, "I am a man." This was a slogan that conveyed the basic idea, "I am a person."

FIGURE 7.9 The campaign of the Memphis Sanitation Workers in 1968 exemplified an intersectional struggle for both labor and racial justice. Their iconic slogan, "I am a man," condenses an argument about the fundamental humanity of Black workers in a system that routinely dehumanizes them.

This seemingly simple statement was a controversial idea in the racist South, where one legacy of slavery was the perception of Black people as less than fully human. A slogan like this can provoke startling insight. If you were walking past the strikers' picket line and saw that sign, you might say, yes, obviously, you are a person. But racists walking by were confronted with an idea that they would have to refute out loud, admitting the dehumanization of Southern racism. The slogan was a compelling example of both visual rhetoric and language use (the language of equality). Notice how even that basic idea of the full personhood of each striker was something that the establishment felt needed to be challenged with armed confrontation. A dead man is not a person and may be preferable, for some, that way. That's how radical a simple slogan can be.[71]

Publicity and Performativity

A number of scholars have suggested that we regard the public activities of social movements as performative in a particular kind of way. A concept extended by the gender theorist Judith Butler, **performativity** refers not just to the theatricality of public discourse and action, but to the capacity of individuals and groups to use the resources of bodies, media, symbols, and language to engage in a politics of space and space-making based on their embodied experience and knowledge.[72] Butler defines performativity as a form of "acting in concert,"

> an embodied form of calling into question the inchoate and powerful dimensions of reigning notions of the political. The embodied character of this questioning works in at least two ways: on the one hand, contestations are enacted by assemblies, strikes, vigils, and the occupation of public spaces; on the other hand, those bodies are the object of many of the demonstrations that take precarity as their galvanizing condition.[73]

Butler means to highlight how ordinary people's bodies are constructed in dominant terms as precarious—vulnerable, weak, trivial, dangerous, and disposable. At the same time, when people rise up in protest, they challenge the dominant definitions of their bodies and lives. Performativity is the process by which people use the bodies and capacities, defined pejoratively in hegemonic society, to assert new self-definitions both individually and collectively. It is how these evolving self-definitions are demonstrated to broader publics. Social movements are, in this way, performative.

And so, here we are: In the publicity step of the pressure cycle, social movements use narratives, arguments, specific language, images and slogans to enter the public sphere and build counterpublics where they make claims on established elites and work to shape public perception of the identities and meanings of the protesters and the movement itself. Now what? Powerful people and institutions often resist accepting a movement's demands at this stage. At this point, establishment forces will attempt to *diminish* the identity, meaning, and impact of the social movement, its leaders, and its adherents.

Establishment Response: Diminishment

The establishment justifies its saying "no" through a strategy called **diminishment**: the strategy of using counterpersuasion to minimize the size, importance, power, legitimacy, and public perception of a social movement. Diminishment involves the tactics of avoidance: counter-persuasion, evasion, secrecy, and denial of access to resources and institutions. Diminishment can happen when the media undercount participants in a protest. It can take the form of derogatory public statements against a movement or its leaders to deny them credibility and legitimacy. It can also take the form of simply ignoring a movement. When women at the turn of the 20th century asked for the right to vote, opponents published a rash of treatises, articles, political cartoons, and speeches mocking the idea.[73] In the early civil rights movement, white Southern voter registrars simply stated that they would defend segregation now and segregation forever. When the establishment seeks to diminish the perception and efficacy of a social movement, its representatives trivialize the activities and accomplishments of the movement.

In the process, politicians and other leaders may craft public messages that attempt to discredit the movement's own identity and meaning frames and construct counter-frames, using the mass media to influence public opinion and action. Sometimes, movement activists are cast as "outside agitators," implying that the real people of a city or region would not support the movement's aims and encouraging distrust of activists. As noted earlier, the mass media have a long history of reporting about social movements, which results in the trivialization and diminishment of a movement and its leaders, goals, and activities. At this point, officials might give a little ground, but without additional pressure, even modest reforms are remote. The refusal and diminishment typical of established elites prompts movements to escalate.

Hegemonic power is the combination of economic control, political authority, and cultural influence. So, given these investments in the status quo, the most common response by a corporation, politician, or hegemonic institution to even the most basic of a movement's appeals is: "no." When you think about it, it is kind of amazing that when asked "Can we distribute literature?" or "May I vote in this election?" the establishment will engage in denial: the simple refusal to act. They will also engage in avoidance, refusing to meet with movement leaders or delaying access to the halls of power to an unspecified time.

At this point, movement adherents have simply asked for change in a peaceful and nonconfrontational way. Usually, the changes called for are squarely within prevailing social norms and values: equal rights, equal treatment under the law (which is codified in the 14th Amendment), the right to speak out publicly (the 1st Amendment), equal access to public spaces, and equal access to the material resources of society (money and other kinds of power). You might ask yourself, who would be against those goals? We recite the Pledge of Allegiance: equality and justice for all. We abide by the values expressed in the U.S. Constitution. And still, powerful elites often oppose granting reforms to a movement engaged in publicity.

Conclusion: The Light of Day

This chapter has described the move out of the formation cycle into the light of day to conduct publicity using media and other performative actions in support of appeals and demands. They bring to bear many of the skills and practices in the rhetorical repertoire of contention. In these two moments in the pressure cycle, adherents make what seem to be modest demands squarely within the hegemonic values of existing society. However, they run up against opposition in the form of diminishment. When the appeals of the movement are refused, it becomes evident that a) there is potentially a systemic problem that goes beyond mere inclusion and b) it will take more than asking politely to win the movement's goals. The establishment's denial prompts the movement into its next step: escalation.

Suggestions for Further Reading

Angela J. Aguayo, *Documentary Resistance: Social Change and Participatory Media* (New York: Oxford University Press, 2019).

Robert Asen and Daniel C. Brouwer, eds. *Counterpublics and the State* (Albany: State University of New York, 2001).

Brad Duncan, ed., *Finally Got the News: The Printed Legacy of the U.S. Radical Left, 1970–1979* (New York: Common Notions, 2017).

Todd Gitlin, *The Whole World is Watching: Mass Media in the Making and Unmaking of the New Left* (Berkeley: University of California Press, 2003).

Sarah J. Jackson, Moya Bailey, and Brooke Foucault Welles, *#HashtagActivism: Networks of Race and Gender Justice* (Cambridge, MA: MIT Press).

Suggested Viewing

Stewart Bird, Rene Lichtman, and Peter Gesser, with the League of Revolutionary Black Workers, *Finally Got the News* (Icarus Films, 1970/2003), https://icarus-films.com/if-fin#.

Callie Crossley, James A. Devinney, Judith Vecchione, and Orlando Powell, *Eyes on the Prize* episode 5 "Mississippi: Is This America?" (PBS, 1987).

Questions for Discussion

1. What is publicity? What is the public sphere? What are counterpublics?
2. What are three kinds of media social movements employ in their publicity effort? What are advantages and drawbacks of each?
3. Referring back to Chapter 2, why might established authorities refuse to meet the appeals or grant the demands of a social movement?
4. What is the relationship between the formation cycle and the pressure cycle?
5. What do you think the roles are for social and digital media in social movements today? Give examples beyond the ones mentioned in this chapter.
6. What is "equality language"? Find examples in the political rhetoric of social movements active today.

Credits

Fig. 7.2: Rowland Scherman, https://commons.wikimedia.org/wiki/File:Martin_Luther_King_-_March_on_Washington.jpg, 1963.

Fig. 7.6: karmachavez, https://www.instagram.com/p/C6WwIA2p1TL/?utm_source=ig_web_copy_link. Copyright © 2024 by Karma Chavez. Reprinted with permission.

Fig. 7.7: Warren K. Leffler, "Fannie Lou Hamer," https://www.loc.gov/resource/ds.07134/, 1964.

Fig. 7.8: Copyright © by Bart Everson (CC BY-SA 4.0) at https://commons.wikimedia.org/wiki/File:Black_Power_Fist_%28stencil%29.jpg.

Fig. 7.9: Richard L. Copley, https://daily.jstor.org/how-the-memphis-sanitation-strike-changed-history/. Copyright © 1968 by Wayne State University.

8

Pressure Cycle Part 2

Escalation From Antagonism to Revolution

KEY TERMS

escalation
antagonism
system critique
direct action
nonviolent civil disobedience
coalition
solidarity
justice language
freedom language
reform
culture shift
power language
Black nationalism
separatism
strikes
boycotts
buycotts
bargaining
suppression
crowd
rebellion
insurrection
revolution

Step 3: Escalation

When demands for reforms are met with refusal, movements generally escalate in their pressure against established elites and institutions. **Escalation** is the moment in social movement development when activists deepen and radicalize their political analysis of the system and become more militant in their tactics. The political radicalization takes the form of the articulation of antagonisms—a rhetoric of "us" vs. "them"—and of a more pronounced analytical critique of systems that generate oppression and injustice. Increasing militancy involves the emergence of a radical flank in the movement, which takes nationalist and economic forms and involves the rhetoric of self-defense and separation.

Antagonism: Us and Them

In addition to being recursive, the moments in the pressure cycle are also layered or nested. While activists ramp up the impact of their movements, they are still engaged in the basic ongoing work of publicity. After meeting with establishment recalcitrance, movement rhetoric often shifts in such a way as to invoke an **antagonism**: a relationship with the establishment, dividing society into proponents and opponents of change, an "us" and a "them."[1] In speeches, writings, and other media, movement participants call upon audiences to choose sides in the evolving social conflict. This rhetoric is also infused with a sense of urgency. For example, in his "Letter from a Birmingham Jail," Martin Luther King, Jr. (arrested during protest) answers clergy who encouraged him to be more moderate in his demands and more patient with establishment response. Famously, King wrote that he would not wait—because "wait" almost always means "never." "Justice that is too long delayed is justice denied," he said.[2]

Escalating movements engage in increasingly prominent and dramatic public speech and action: rallies, parades, pickets, marches, and various forms of nonviolent civil disobedience. Beginning with the Montgomery Bus Boycott of 1955, the civil rights movement trained its activists and created situations that, as King explained, would dramatize the problems of racism and inequality. King and the Southern Christian Leadership Conference (SCLC) organized movement participants to enter and occupy public spaces to disrupt business as usual. The forces of the establishment—politicians, police, and community—responded to these provocations with vitriol and violence. This rhetoric of enactment is its own proof—that there is a core antagonism between forces of change and forces of reaction.[3]

Birmingham was where, in 1963, police, on the order of City Commisioner T. Eugene "Bull" Connor, trained police dogs and fire hoses on youth and children in images that circulated around the world calling attention to the conditions facing Black people in America. In Birmingham, King was arrested with hundreds of others. In his "Letter from a Birmingham Jail," he argued that the movement had attempted to appeal to leaders, to negotiate in good faith. An escalation to direct action became necessary when even modest promised reforms were not forthcoming. King wrote,

> You may well ask: "Why direct action? Why sit ins, marches and so forth? Isn't negotiation a better path?" You are quite

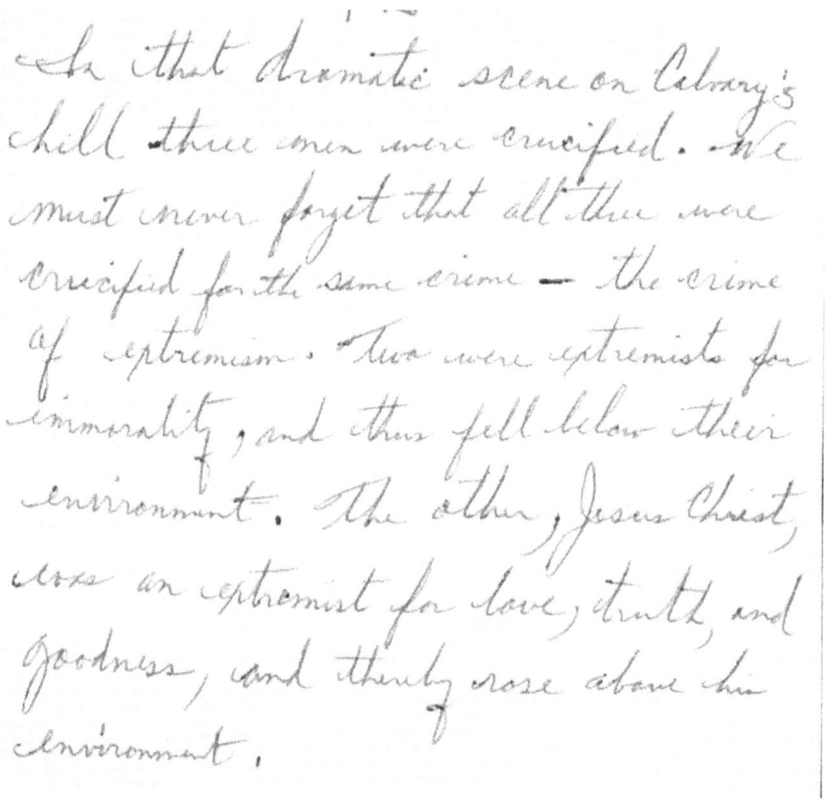
In that dramatic scene on Calvary's hill three men were crucified. We must never forget that all three were crucified for the same crime — the crime of extremism. Two were extremists for immorality, and thus fell below their environment. The other, Jesus Christ, was an extremist for love, truth, and goodness, and thereby rose above his environment.

FIGURE 8.1 Martin Luther King, Jr., crafted the movement's most cogent defense of nonviolent civil disobedience from a jail cell in Birmingham, Alabama in 1963. Outside, police set upon Black youth with fire hoses and police dogs; images of this confrontation circulated worldwide and shamed the racial injustices in the South and in the United States in general.

> right in calling for negotiation. Indeed, this is the very purpose of direct action. Nonviolent direct action seeks to create such a crisis and foster such a tension that a community which has constantly refused to negotiate is forced to confront the issue. It seeks so to dramatize the issue that it can no longer be ignored.

System Critique

Another aspect to this moment of escalation is the development in movement rhetoric of the analysis of establishment motives and **system critique**, a set of explanations of why oppressors behave as they do in terms of a broader social system. In the case of civil rights, activists come to the awareness that it's not a matter of particular racist individuals or ideas. The entire of society is structured in a way that is, in King's words, necessarily ugly and brutal. In this moment, movements become more radical—a word derived from the botanical word for "root." They radicalize, which means to attempt to get to the root of the problem and pull it out.

King makes this point in his letter: "We know through painful experience that freedom is never voluntarily given by the oppressor; it must be demanded by the oppressed." Notice that there is a clear antagonism here between oppressor and oppressed. In addition, the argument that oppressors never give up power voluntarily implies that there is a systematic character to oppression, a set of people and institutions that must be challenged directly. An establishment's refusal to hear a movement's appeals to equality prompts activists to ask, "Why?" Why won't the system give us voting rights or access to colleges and universities? There must be something systematic and organized going on, a set of rules, laws, and forces that works systematically to keep an oppressed group down. At this point in movements, members educate themselves in the workings of the system, naming it—white supremacy, capitalism, patriarchy—and delving into its history and operation.

Confrontation and Disruption

Having identified an antagonism and analyzed the systematic workings of power, a movement is in a place to target the system where it is most powerful and disrupt operations in such a way that the structure of society itself begins to tremble. This task requires movements to assess their resources, constraints, and opportunities. What resources do we have in terms of money, people power, media influence, rhetorical skill, and other goods? What constraints are facing us: hostile publics, inaccessible politicians, lack of access to public space, and other resources? What opportunities can we find to insert a lever of influence?

The Montgomery Bus Boycott is a good example of how after long planning and preparation, activists threatened the profitability of the transportation system and the smooth working order of Montgomery, which relied upon Black workers getting to white households for work. To stop the buses was to use the power of people to confront elites in a realistic but dramatic way. The later actions of the civil rights movement, including the Birmingham sit-ins in 1963, were brilliant in targeting the very institutions seeking to constrain and repress them, using the police and the jails themselves as resources for persuasion and disruptive power. Revealing the brutality of police violence against Black protesters in news media around the globe made the case that, indeed, Black people in the United States faced brutal and systematic racism. Repeatedly filling the jails to capacity with singing and chanting youth impaired the effectiveness of the repressive institution even as it engaged in repression.

As noted in previous chapters, music is a core resource of social movements. Singing and moving in concert literally bonds participants together while also conveying verbal messages and arguments and organizing group movement. The civil rights movement is remarkable in its repertoire of songs like "We Shall Overcome," and "(Ain't Gonna Let Nobody) Turn Me 'Round," the latter of which was the refrain of Birmingham youth as police dragged their resisting bodies into police wagons. Hymns, spirituals, and movement songs blended together to make for a richly sonic movement environment.

There are two major forms of confrontation: direct action and nonviolent civil disobedience. **Direct action** is a transgressive social movement tactic in which activists, often in small groups, target institutions and

FIGURE 8.2 Dan Choi's militancy in pursuit of the right of LGBTQ people to serve in the U.S. military is an example of how militant tactics can operate toward reformist demands, illustrating the significance of the two-axis model of social movements.

public figures for disruption and damage (not violence). Direct action is distinct from the building of a mass, coordinated, instrumental program. Instead, transgression has its roots in anarchist and autonomist traditions and aims to give expression to individual uniqueness and creative power. Transgression, and its tool of direct action, are powerful reinventions of daily life even when they are not tied to organized programs of mass movements.[4] Direct action is unruly, involving bodies engaged in creative disruption.[5] ACT UP's militancy was one example of direct action; the media events staged by the environmental organization Earth First! and Dan Choi's chaining himself to the White House fence for the inclusion of LGBTQ people in the military is another.[6]

When a team of global justice activists destroys the windows of stores in the business part of a city, that is direct action. When groups of people attend political events to call out politicians, CEOs, or other leaders, as ACT UP did frequently, that is direct action. Often, direct action is symbolic in its purpose. In targeting figures and symbols of injustice, direct action dramatizes a movement's analysis and identifies antagonisms. Global capitalism is the source of injustice; targeting store windows and gatherings of global capitalist elites (for example the WTO, World Bank, or IMF) identifies that opposition clearly. Politicians have betrayed their constituents; challenging them directly in public makes that case and draws attention to the movement. Every major social movement in U.S. history has engaged in powerful direct action.

Nonviolent civil disobedience also seeks, in Martin Luther King, Jr.'s words, to dramatize a shameful condition, as well as to point out the brutality of establishment forces by provoking them to engage in such brutality. Nonviolent civil disobedience is a form of direct action on a large scale; it engages in intentional, systematic law-breaking; it organizes, trains, and deploys masses of bodies to disrupt the flow of business as usual in demonstrations, marches, sit-ins, and occupations; and it is designed to draw out establishment forces to reveal themselves for what they are.[7] Martin Luther King, Jr., in "Letter from a Birmingham Jail," defines nonviolent civil disobedience as a response to failed negotiations, broken promises, and "blasted hopes." The purpose of nonviolent direct action is "to create such a crisis and establish such creative tension that a community that has constantly refused to negotiate is forced to confront the issue."[8] Civil rights activists, in concert with anticolonial movements across the globe, turned to civil disobedience as a practice of decolonization in order to emancipate themselves and others, and in the process transform the racial order.[9]

FIGURE 8.3 A Palestine solidarity encampment in 2024 at Columbia University is an example of non-violent civil disobedience.

Typically, nonviolent civil disobedience is carefully planned. Volunteers attend workshops where they learn how best to sit in or lie down in defiance of the police. They are trained not to react with violence when police attack and make arrest; instead, they are to go limp and passively resist being moved. Training also involves a review of the relevant laws that the action intends to break and making connections with lawyers who will defend arrestees when the time comes. There are instructions about what to do when confronted by police: Don't voluntarily show identification and don't strike back. Because police frequently use tear gas and pepper spray, activists are trained in making protective masks and medical aid. In short, nonviolent civil disobedience is carefully planned and orchestrated.[10]

You will notice that neither direct action nor civil disobedience is a form of violence. Even dramatic confrontation and property damage that does not harm other beings are not violent. Labeling direct action and civil disobedience as violent is a way of discrediting the movement and its activists.

In these ways, as movements escalate, they deepen their analysis of the nature of society and its hierarchical and oppressive systems, target the establishment with their demands and actions, call upon publics to take sides in the struggle for equality and justice, and engage in increasingly coordinated and targeted direct action to disrupt the daily functioning of society.

Coalition Building

At this moment, movement coalitions are emerging. A **coalition** is the intentional, structured coordination of activity among multiple movement groups across differences in identities and causes. Coalitions increase the numbers of people in the movement, bringing them in from different communities for the largest possible impact. But coalitions are also challenging and fragile because different groups represented by diverse organizations do not all have equal power and privilege in society. Feminist alliances must form through a politics of relation in which identities and emotions define whose well-being is central and whose survival must be assured. Ethical alliances are faithful to the well-being and survival of all participants.[11] Such alliances are intersectional, organizing people across difference and expressing a political message that honors the complexity of both the communicator and audience.[12]

María Lugones offers a useful conception of coalition-building, asking people seeking justice to relate to different others without falling into "a politics of the same," to relate to the different worlds bridged by coalition from a place of double consciousness and against the grain of power.[13] Karma Chávez also points to the difficulty of creating and sustaining coalitions among groups with differential power. She argues that much coalition-building occurs "behind the scenes" in social movement enclaves, in other words, in what we would call the formation cycle. In such enclaves, activists "invent rhetorical strategies to publicly challenge oppressive rhetoric or to create new imaginaries for the groups and issues they represent and desire to bring into coalition."[14] They interpret public discourse that defines participants and construct alternative identity frames in a way that accounts for the intersectional character of multiple oppressions. For example, Isaac West describes how a coalition of queer and disabled activists came together in coalition around the question of public bathrooms, writing,

> [T]he continued vitality and vibrancy of LGBTQ, queer, and disability politics is dependent largely upon the ability of these advocates to develop forms of coalitional politics that articulate their modalities of discrimination to the interests of other similarly situated groups.[15]

Chávez explores this process in a community challenging both queer and immigrant oppression, where separate groups together analyzed mainstream media, legislation and policy affecting both communities, and developed a shared critique of law enforcement. Coalition was built out of "mutually resonant and interconnected discourses."[16]

Alliance-building is fragile. When more powerful or wealthier organizations in a movement are able to dictate the demands and the direction of the movement, the interests of the less powerful coalition members can get left behind; this often happens when movements coordinate across divides of social class. Identity and cultural differences—of region, age, religion, race, gender, sexuality, national identity, and class—can be impediments to coordinated work when there is not adequate respect for those differences across coalition partners. All social movement organizations are marked by existing oppressive ideas and norms, such that in the civil rights movement, many women were relegated to making flyers and coffee and gay Black leaders like Bayard Rustin could not be open about their sexuality.

It is in the pressure cycle that coalitions appear as forces for change in the public sphere. There were many organizations in the U.S. civil rights movement. These included (and are not limited to) the National Association for the Advancement of Colored People (NAACP, which predates the mid-century movement), the Montgomery Improvement Association, the SCLC, the Congress on Racial Equality (CORE, a Northern-based organization mostly responsible for the freedom rides movement), the Student Nonviolent Coordinating Committee (SNCC), and eventually the groups that represented the Black Power movement, which I cover later in the chapter. Although these organizations represented different approaches to organizing for change, they were all part of the same broader movement. The SCLC, a religiously-guided organization led by prominent Southern ministers like Martin Luther King, Jr., sought reforms through nonviolent direct action. After Montgomery, the SCLC tried to implement the same strategy in different cities across the South, but with some mixed success. In Albany, Georgia, younger, more urban activists wanted some say in how the movement unfolded in their city. In Mississippi, voting rights activists working with sharecroppers wanted to take a more militant approach. On college campuses, students asserted their places in the movement, breaking from the more respectability-oriented and pacifist mainstream organizations.

The tension between the SCLC and SNCC is informative. SNCC came into being in 1960 when what historian Howard Zinn called "young rebels" (including Jim Forman, John Lewis, Charles Sherrod, and Bob Moses) took a "turn away from school, job, family, all the tokens of success in modern America, to take up new lives, hungry and hunted, in the hinterland of the Deep South."[17] Radicalized by participation in the lunch-counter sit-in movement, they did not have established leaders or fixed ideas. They challenged the entrenched civil rights organizations like the NAACP and the SCLC with a new (still nonviolent) militancy. SCLC leader Ella Baker encouraged this formation to be led by a younger generation in alliance with the older organizations. Tensions among the array of civil rights organizations found expression in the lead-up to and the unfolding of the 1963 March on Washington, when SNCC's John Lewis was made to tone down the political content of his speech. Unlike the SCLC leaders, Lewis wanted to challenge the Kennedy administration directly and offered a deep critique of the U.S. government and the Democratic Party. That critique remained muted that day.

Coalitions for civil rights involving white people were both incredibly powerful and incredibly challenging. CORE's mobilization of young people in the North sent hundreds of white youths into the South to stand alongside Black people against brutality and for the right to vote during the "Freedom Summer" of 1964. It was during that summer that the young activists James Chaney, Andrew Goodman, and Michael Schwerner were brutally murdered for their efforts in Mississippi. The Highlander School in Tennessee trained both Black and white activists in nonviolent civil disobedience, with an emphasis on the important role that white allies can play when confronting racist authorities, as they had when escorting children into Little Rock schools in 1957 against white mobs. A basic guiding principle for ethical coalitions is: Whoever faces the greatest oppression and disadvantage in a situation of injustice should have the most say over what gets done about it and how. Another word for this is **solidarity**, consistent organizing and action alongside others in mutal support of each other's goals.

The Language of Freedom and Justice

In the escalation step of the social movement cycle, equality and rights language gives way to **justice language**. The appeal to equal rights is asking for inclusion in society as it exists. The demand for justice calls for radical change to the underlying systems that fuel injustice. In many movements, when you hear calls for "rights," for example "disability rights" or "abortion rights," the activists using that language are calling for reforms achievable in the system as it exists. When you hear calls for "disability justice" or "reproductive justice," chances are that the groups making those slogans are asking for a broader systemic redress of injustice. We can see the shift from equality to justice language in the "Letter From a Birmingham Jail" when King lays out a justification for direct action: There is an unjust system of power that would not negotiate over democratic rights. Justice is the language when illusions about the capacity of an oppressive society to fulfill its democratic promises fall away. Justice language also includes calls for recognition and redress of injustice beyond the legislation of equal rights.

Emerging militant organizations emphasize the critique of injustice and also deploy **freedom language**: the invocation of an ideal of freedom from oppression, violence, and exclusion and the freedom to embrace new identities and take actions challenging existing institutions and norms. In the evolving Black freedom struggle, we recognize such language in the rhetoric of Fannie Lou Hamer. Maegan Parker Brooks examines Hamer's speeches to discover how Hamer extended the idea of citizenship rights to include freedom from hunger, sickness, and substandard education. It includes the freedom to vote. At a speech given in New York, Hamer stated, "If we want America to be a free society we have to stop telling lies, that's all. Because we're not free and you know we're not free." Hamer continually challenged America's image of itself as the "land of the free." In 1965 testimony during a Congressional credentials committee aimed to unseat Mississippi legislators, Hamer asks again, "Can we call this a free country where I am afraid to go to sleep in my own home in Mississippi?"[18]

Establishment Response: Reforms and Culture Shift

The movement has now grown and expanded across organizations; it has developed an ever-deepening analysis of structural injustice; it has called out the forces that have denied even the most basic appeals to democratic rights; and it has engaged in public direct action like nonviolent civil disobedience. It has radicalized and become more militant. What does the establishment do now?

This is a crucial moment at which systems and institutions are most likely to accede to movement demands by enacting some reforms usually located squarely within those systems and institutions. A great deal of disruptive pressure prompts changes in the law, corporate life, and culture. By this point, continual agitation and publicity have brought greater numbers of people into movement organizations and activities. Sit-ins, strikes, pickets, demonstrations, and marches have given the establishment any number of headaches: blocked streets, the cessation of work and profitability, empty buses, packed jails, embarrassing public confrontations like those at lunch counters, and so on. Meanwhile, the ideas of the movement—identity frames and movement frames conveying the identity, purpose, and arguments of the movement (so far focused on and employing the language of equal rights)—have gained traction in the public sphere with voters, consumers, and workers, all of whom established interests would like to keep in their orbit.

Reforms

A **reform** is a change made in the law and other institutions that does not fundamentally alter the activity or nature of that institution. Reforms are often counterposed to revolutions, which make thoroughgoing systemic changes to existing society.[19] Voting rights is a reform that sustains the existing electoral process and representative political system, for example. As movement's escalate into disruptive activity, the system has an opportunity to get rid of these disruptions and maintain the fidelity of voters, workers, and consumers by giving in to some, though usually not all, movement demands. In 1964 and 1965, both civil rights and voting rights acts (respectively) were passed in the wake of numerous acts of dramatic and publicized civil disobedience such as the one in Birmingham and mass demonstrations like the March on Washington where King delivered his famous speech. Those acts awaited vigorous enforcement as organizing continued in both the South and the North, but they were significant gains nonetheless.

A word is in order here about the two-party electoral system and the relationships between movements and the Democratic Party in particular. While the Republican Party prior to the 1930s had been "the party of Lincoln" and the party to whom reformers looked for change, Franklin Roosevelt's New Deal legislation in the 1930s marked a switch such that the Democratic Party became the nominal party of ordinary people. However, a legacy of slavery was that Southern Democrats from city councils and sheriffs to state legislators and governors remained firmly committed to white supremacist race relations and virulently opposed civil rights. Even so, the Kennedy administration from 1960 to 1963 positioned itself as an advocate of civil rights (even though Bobby Kennedy remarked once that he wished that King and his followers would stop all of that "sitting-in shit"). The vice presidency of the Texan Lyndon Johnson was calculated to retain the allegiance of Southern Democrats.

In spite of being what we call a Dixiecrat, Johnson (under intense movement pressure) carried on in that vein after the Kennedy assassinations, although reluctantly; there was no love lost between the Texan Lyndon Johnson and the civil rights movement. Johnson signed both the Civil Rights Act and the Voting Rights Act; during the speech announcing the latter, he echoed a refrain of the movement when he said, "We shall overcome." The historical record has it that a tear ran down the face of Martin Luther King Jr. at that moment. This moment also opened the way for Black politicians to enter public office in growing numbers on the Democratic Party ticket; these politicians, many trained up in the movement, remained committed to reforms.

Culture Shift

Meanwhile political and popular culture shifted dramatically in favor of integration and inclusion in society more broadly. Evidence of such a **culture shift** is when television programs begin to represent oppressed groups in society differently. From *Julia* in the early 1960s to the later *Good Times*, *The Jeffersons*, *and Sanford and Son*, mainstream television took up the identities and stories of empowered Black people in the United States.[20] Shifts in language, for example, to the term "African-American" when before "Negro" (and worse) were dominant, are signs of culture shift. Such shifts (which have accompanied every major social movement in society) should be counted among movement victories.

When the political establishment gives ground on major reforms, significant sectors of the movement might wane and fold, which is common at this point in the movement cycle. Adherents and leaders of even militant movement activity often put their faith in political change, "working within the system," pursuing electoral campaigns and legislative reforms. Mainstream movement organizations devote their time, energy, and money to electing and supporting Democrats. This tendency is why activist Lance Selfa once called the Democratic Party the "graveyard of social movements."[21]

There is a countervailing trajectory taken by the establishment at this time, however. During the escalation moment of social movements, the state resorts increasingly to surveillance, policing, and the deployment of armed forces to suppress social movement activity. Sectors of the movement who have been developing a critique of the system as a whole (rather than seeing the problem as a matter of inclusion in dominant ways of life as they have existed) understandably take suppression as further evidence that the hegemonic order—ultimately expressed in the form of armed violence—is systematically oppressive, further deepening the movement's radicalization. This is the moment of the emergence of the radical flank.

Step 4: Emergence of the Radical Flank

Recall that the radical flank is formed when some parts of a movement adopt more radical ideological positions and more militant tactics, separating themselves out from the mainstream. The movement of disability rights and justice activists moved "from charity to confrontation" when arguments on behalf of the disabled perceived as pitiable "cripples" gave way to organizations demanding deinstitutionalization and respect. The movement moved further toward greater radicalism and militancy when activists took to the streets to demand full access to employment, public spaces, transportation, education, health care, housing, and other resources. Direct confrontation in demonstrations and sit-ins led to the passage of major legislation protecting disabled people. Disability pride movements asserted the independence, dignity, and cultural uniqueness of people with disabilities.[22]

This movement "from charity to confrontation" characterizes many U.S. social movements at this step of escalation. In the woman suffrage movement, for example, national mainstream organizations led electoral campaigns state-by-state appealing to legislatures and voters to grant women the right to vote. When, at the beginning of the 20th century, that approach stalled out, a new organization, the National Woman's Party, emerged and engaged in radical and militant rhetoric and action, including picketing the White House and leading parades of thousands of women in the streets of the nation's capital. The NWP's activity pushed federal action forward, resulting in the 19th Amendment to the U.S. Constitution, which granted women the right to vote.[23]

As this case suggests, the presence and increasing militancy of some wings of a movement coalition (which define the radical flank) render the claims made by moderates more persuasive than they would otherwise have been. Recall how, in the documentary *Eyes on the Prize*, there is a telling moment when the Black nationalist Ossie

Davis (an actor later known for playing the grandfather on the *Cosby Show*) describes how movement leaders sometimes approached the powers-that-be. Addressing a hypothetical city official, he says that they probably would rather deal with him and his polite requests for modest changes because just outside the door is "the other brother"—radicals and militants who might not be so polite or patient. This is how the presence of a radical flank in movement coalition indirectly bolsters moderates' effectiveness. This process has already been happening during the period we are calling escalation and was instrumental, for example, in winning voting rights and other civil rights up to this point.

Power Language

However, it is possible to identify when the flank becomes ascendant and assumes the center of the movement. Organizationally, we see the rise of new organizations putting forward a broader system critique and advocating greater militancy in confronting existing systems of power. Rhetorically, the language of power supplants appeals to equal rights, along with visions of liberation, pride and the assertion of difference over those emphasizing equality and inclusion. At this moment, many movements split into various organizations with varying degrees of radicalism and militance. **Power language** rejects the language of equal rights in favor of language asserting the capacity of an oppressed group to take control of their futures and of key institutions in society.

In the Black freedom struggle—which had moved beyond civil rights demands—we can even identify a particular moment in the struggle during which this hand-off to the radical flank takes place. On June 5, 1966, James Meredith, the first Black student at the University of Mississippi, embarked upon what he called the March Against Fear, starting in Memphis, Tennessee and ending in Jackson, Mississippi. He was shot on the second day, and civil rights leaders decided to pick up the march from that point. There was growing tension between the SCLC and the young activists in SNCC. King's leadership was challenged by that of Stokely Carmichael, a leader in SNCC the Lowndes County (Mississippi) Freedom Organization, which had been engaged in grassroots voter registration in rural Mississippi. Carmichael's goals went beyond the vote; the suppression of Black voters led many organizers to recognize that building power was the only way that even something like the vote could be won.

FIGURE 8.4 A 1970 Black Power demonstration in the UK.

On the occasion of this march, Carmichael said, "We've got to make this march our march." When the march, with both King and Carmichael at the front, entered Mississippi, Carmichael sent other organizers ahead to gauge the political mood. The scout reported that the people he had talked to were excited about the idea of Black power. While the mainstream of the march used the slogan "Freedom Now," Carmichael gave a speech that didn't "hit too much on freedom now, but hit the need for power ... When we dropped the black power ... they responded immediately." The crowd, according to one witness, thundered "Black power, black power."[24]

The march moved forward with everyone together, although the rift represented a growing coalitional crisis. When they stopped to camp in Canton, Mississippi, they were attacked by Mississippi state troopers, who tear-gassed and beat the marchers. Carmichael channeled their rage into the argument that the state was irredeemably racist and that the demand for power was now necessary for the movement to truly challenge the existing order. Carmichael's Lowndes County Freedom Organization chose the Black Panther as its symbol (much like the Donkey symbolized the Democrats). When militant Black people began to organize in Oakland in 1966, they adopted this symbol in the formation of the Black Panther Party for Self-Defense.

Nationalism and Self-Defense

Between 1966 and 1968, new organizations emerged to give expression to a deepening radical critique of the state and white supremacy and greater militancy in the face of violent suppression. Two of these, the Black Panther Party for Self-Defense and the Nation of Islam represented the politics of **Black nationalism**. Black nationalism, with roots in the 19th century, is a tendency in the politics of social movements that argues that Black people in the United States represent a separate nation with a separate identity from the mainstream. Emphasizing African cultural history and identity, Black nationalism asserts the fundamental integrity and value of Black people against a racist society.[25] It follows that, if Black people constitute a unique and separate people, activists in this tendency demand full recognition and sovereignty over their lives and futures. The tactics of these movements are generally more militant, including armed self-defense, than integrationist wings of the struggle.

Formed in Oakland, California (and eventually with chapters across the nation), the Black Panther Party for Self-Defense organized in poor Black communities on two fronts. In the community, they cultivated a sense of pride among young Black people and provided material aid in the form of a free breakfast program and other efforts. They also argued for the right of Black people to carry guns and defend themselves against police violence. The Panthers considered themselves to be revolutionaries—activists seeking not only reforms possible within the system but the overthrow of hegemonic powers.

Rarely did any member of the Party kill police officers or others, but their militant stance drew the attention of the police and the FBI who dedicated themselves to surveilling and persecuting Panther members and offices. They cultivated a network of informants inside the organization. Based on these sources, on December 4, 1969, a tactical unit of the Chicago Police Department raided the apartment of Panther leader Fred Hampton, shooting more than one hundred bullets, killing Hampton and one other person.

Meanwhile, a Black nationalist movement had become prominent in the North. Black nationalism asserts that Black people constitute an oppressed nation and that organizing by and for Black people in their own interests should be the center of the struggle. Black nationalist movements also cultivate a sense of pride in Black identity, appearance, and African heritage. Malcolm X was the leader of the Nation of Islam in the 1960s. His rhetoric provided a counterpoint to that of Martin Luther King, Jr. Malcolm X did not preach violence, but, like the Panthers, argued for the right to self-defense. In a famous speech "*The Ballot or the Bullet*," Malcolm argued not that Black people should automatically take up armed struggle but rather that if society did not protect Black people's right to the ballot, armed struggle would be inevitable. Martin Luther King Jr., contrary to popular mythology, never condemned Malcolm's approach. Malcolm stated that he was not for violence, saying that he would be nonviolent with anyone who was nonviolent with him.[26] There is a lot of mythology in public memory of the Black Power and Black nationalist movements that equates these movements with irrational and hateful violence. It is important to recognize how reasonable the rhetoric of self-defense is given the sustained violent suppression of the movement throughout the struggle. In addition, it is important not to confuse a deep critique of the institutions and systems that preserve oppressive social relations with a violent movement strategy.

There are parallels to Black nationalism in other social movements when forces urging separation from the mainstream movement and occupying a stance of pride in difference appear on the scene. **Separatism** is a tendency in a movement toward asserting difference from the mainstream and making demands beyond integration toward freedom

FIGURE 8.5 Malcolm X in a discussion with student activists in 1959 or 1960.

and justice.[27] In the LGBTQ+ struggle, for example, activists arguing for integration of LGBTQ+ people into the mainstream of jobs and family found themselves challenged by queer liberationists insisting on difference and pride. Chicanx movements go beyond immigrant rights movements when they assert a unique Mexican and indigenous cultural heritage and demand recognition of the group's separate, proud identity.

The Economic Flank

Much more common in social movements than violence is coercive economic action in the form of boycotts or strikes. **Strikes**—or the organized, purposeful cessation of work (usually led by a union)—are the major tool of the labor movement.[28] Strikes can force an employer to the bargaining table and strengthen workers' case for winning their demands. The labor movement uniquely organizes workers into organizations that struggle to win the right to bargain on behalf of the collective and to strike for higher wages, benefits, and working conditions or for more control over the workplace and work practices. The economic power of organized workers is significant. Historically, the labor movement has been among the most militant, especially at the moments at which unions struggle to form and win recognition. Membership in unions increases workers' standard of living, but unionization rates in private industry in the United States are low. In the public sector, including education and higher education, unionization rates are higher. Because many unions in the largest labor federation—the AFL-CIO—are long-established bureaucratic institutions, activists entering member unions often find themselves in an ambivalent position with regard to the union bureaucracy and have to mount a movement inside of the union in order to press the union to defend workers' interests more reliably.[29]

Union solidarity can increase the effectiveness of aligned movements. For example, in the 1970s, the Teamsters aligned with LGBTQ activists in San Francisco, including city supervisor Harvey Milk, in boycotting and striking Coors beer. Although that struggle ended in defeat for the Teamsters, it was an important model of cross-movement coalition-building adding the economic flank to the overall movement. During the recent encampments for Palestine at U.S. universities, academic labor unions have signed on to their demands; some unions have passed cease fire and solidarity resolutions. The national organization Labor for Palestine has a growing list of member unions.[30]

Boycotts are organized efforts undertaken by consumers to reject products and services associated with oppressive interests.[31] The U.S. farmworkers sustained a decades-long grape boycott in protest against the treatment of farm workers. The instrumental effects of boycotts are more difficult to observe than those of strikes, because boycotts depend on the actions of consumers dispersed over a large area and time. The grape boycott did not stop the growers of grapes from exploiting migrant labor. Boycotts only work when significant numbers of people stop shopping at, say, Amazon. But short of a unified mass effort, boycotts are largely symbolic, personal ethical choices that can, at least, send a message to exploitative companies. There is a related phenomenon called **buycotts**, in which consumers organize themselves to purchase specific brands regarded to be behaving more ethically than others.[32]

We have already seen how the Montgomery Bus Boycott, although an early moment in the post-*Brown v. Board* civil rights struggle, mounted effective economic pressure on the city to desegregate the bus system. Economic pressure is a tactic that can serve as a powerful flank for appeals to the establishment. Another example of a civil rights action serving the function of an economic flank was the Memphis Sanitation Workers' strike in 1968, which, after two months,

FIGURE 8.6 The United Auto Workers strike in 2023 demonstrated the power of thousands of workers to disrupt industry profitability and win workers' demands.

won recognition of the workers' union and higher wages. This was also the movement campaign that Martin Luther King, Jr. was working on when he was assassinated in Memphis on April 4.

Toward the end of his life, King undertook an economic justice program called the Poor People's Campaign. (He also spoke out against the War in Vietnam.) When a movement makes economic demands, it is not only because economic pressure is a militant tactic, but also because movements become more radical when they recognize that oppression is connected to a broader economic system that should be challenged. King's last movement campaigns represent the process of radicalization.

Establishment Response: Bargaining and Suppression

As at the end of the escalation phase of the pressure cycle, established elites have choices at this moment of greater confrontation, disruption, and militancy. One response is to take advantage of divisions between moderates and militants in the movement, vilifying the Left flank in favor of the reformers. Ironically, this reaction can serve to make the reformers and their demands—even as they become more radical—more credible. Political leaders may at this point bargain with movement leaders and organizations to make new reforms or expand the ones already set into motion. As before, sectors of the movement might fold at this point, moving into mainstream electoral and legislative institutions.

At this point, the establishment may feel pressure to engage in **bargaining**, or negotiating with movement leaders over possible reforms. The major establishment response to the emergence of the radical flank, however, is intensified surveillance, policing, and violent suppression, as the case of the Black Panthers demonstrates. **Suppression** is the organized effort on the part of the state or other authoritative institution to stop the progress of a movement through coercive means. The state, its police, and its military are the resources of suppression. One could argue that the assassination of movement leaders, which happened to both Martin Luther King, Jr. and Malcolm X, is a tool in the suppression of social movements. Intense, violent suppression can constrain or defeat a movement. Although many civil rights organizations carried on after the assassinations of King and Malcolm X and after the raid that killed Fred Hampton, they did so in withered form.

In democratic societies, the policing of protest ranges between repressiveness and tolerance depending upon the situation at hand. (See Chapter 2.) The trend in democracies in the 1960s was toward escalating repression and intolerance of movements like the civil rights movement. The trend from the 1970s into the 1990s was toward softer, less confrontational, more flexible, more negotiated, and more selective forms of policing when it comes to social movements.[33] State responses to movement agitation often involves massive intelligence gathering about organizations, actions, and leaders, including the use of informants and, in recent years, the use of drones and imaging technology to identify movement participants. Legal intervention and cultural discrediting of movements are aspects of a negotiated management model of policing.

In the early 2000s, the policing of protest shifted when a movement arose to challenge corporate globalization. The anti-globalization movement built massive marches, demonstrations, strikes, and direct actions against summits of international corporate influence like the World Trade Organization and the International Monetary Fund. Increasingly militarized and technologically advanced police forces engaged in more brutal, direct repression in pursuit of the social control of dissent. In these situations, police did not engage in negotiation, but subjected demonstrators to beatings, the use of attack dogs, gassing, and indiscriminate mass arrests. In this way, the policing of protest returned in the 2000s to the escalated force model. After the attacks on the World Trade Center in 2001, the state's interest in order and security shifted the balance to harsher uses of force, but soft and hard models of policing co-exist and work to "limit protest's potential impact on the status quo."[34]

The escalated force model characterized the policing of the U.S. civil rights movement. Police, state troopers, and the National Guard regularly confronted even peaceful protests asking for even modest reforms. The image of the National Guard confronting striking Memphis sanitation workers is a case in point. The demonstration in Birmingham in 1963, when police dogs set upon youth engaged in a nonviolent sit-in as the whole world looked on, is another. The infiltration, surveillance, and police raids on groups of the Black Panther Party also exemplify the escalated force model of policing protest during that time. Assassinations, while carried out usually by non-state agents, also aim to halt the effectiveness of agitation for social change. And vigilante violence, such as that carried out by the KKK and other white supremacist groups, are also part of the process of violent control of dissent.

However, suppression and bargaining don't necessarily spell the end of a movement's challenge. In fact, the violent intervention of police or armed forces against a protest event can propel movement escalation and fuel radicalization and militancy. There is a moment in the civil rights movement when the coalition, including the SCLC and SNCC (who were reluctant), planned to march from Selma to Montgomery, Alabama. On a day remembered as "Bloody Sunday," Alabama state troopers tear-gassed and beat the marchers as they tried to leave Selma, prompting many participants to arm themselves and leading the movement to a point of crisis. At this point, the Left flank may continue to escalate pressure on the establishment, sometimes provoking a broader social crisis.

Step 5: Social Crisis

Crowds, Insurrections, and Urban Rebellions

When masses of ordinary people gather in public to express their outrage in the streets and the halls of power without having been part of an organized social movement, scholars and pundits often call such actions "riots." Participants are characterized as taking part in irrational mobs, crowds without form or purpose. The word "riot" also has the connotation of violence whether or not angry crowds cause harm to others. What is missed if we use the word "riot" are the facts that such rebellions are often reasonable responses to crisis and oppression and that they have often played a productive role in winning social movement demands, even when the crowds in question have not been active in any organized movement efforts. Jodi Dean has called our attention to how outraged crowds can pose a significant symbolic, political, and material threat to established interests, and also to how militant and organized movements can form out of such events. Dean writes that crowds have historically been denounced by elites, but that they

> have disrupted the settings given by capital and the state. Breaking with the suffocating reflexivity of contribution and critique in the mediated networks of communicative capitalism, insistent crowds impress themselves where they don't belong. Their very presence challenges the privatization of ostensibly public spaces.[35]

FIGURE 8.7 Protesters march in Dallas on June 6, 2020, against the police murder of George Floyd in Minneapolis, Minnesota.

Here we will defined **crowd**, per Jodi Dean, as a form of unplanned collective being in public space. When a crowd engages in disruptive expression against prevailing structures of power, it becomes a **rebellion**. When a rebellion becomes massive and more focused and organized, it becomes an **insurrection**.

Rebellions and insurrections point out the limits of democratic governments' defense of themselves as ruled by the people when the exploited and oppressed enter public space with a set of inchoate but pressing demands. The potential productivity of inchoate mass political action means that we need better language to describe it. Dean uses "crowd" for this purpose. The word "rebellion" or "insurrection" may also do the trick of capturing the political importance of these phenomena. Many such events take place in cities, suggesting "urban rebellion" as a useful name for such action. Whatever alternative to "riot" we take up, this expression of outrage without organization is what happened in the later part of the 1960s in cities across the U.S. North. In the days after the King's assassination, large insurrections took place in Washington, DC., Baltimore, Chicago, and Kansas City. Few people were killed or injured in these events, although there were mass arrests and significant property damage (which, for our purposes, do not fall under the heading of "violence.") Federal forces occupied major cities. The year before the King insurrections, there were more than 150 major upheavals in more than 25 cities including Atlanta, Boston, Cincinnati, Detroit, and Newark.

The rebellions were provoked by ongoing racial oppression and inequality in housing, education, employment, safety, transportation, child care, and more. In Detroit, demonstrations, burning, and looting lasted for five days, and a number of people were killed. These uprisings prompted the Johnson administration to form a commission to investigate racial disparities in U.S. cities. The 1968 Kerner Commission reported that the United States was made up of two societies, one Black and one white, separate and unequal. The authors advised the administration to take action enabling Black people to have "fuller participation in the social order and the material benefits enjoyed by the majority of American citizens." In other words, the upheavals—motivated by oppression—produced momentum toward greater reforms.

Disorganized upheavals of this kind happen wherever there are profound and widespread inequalities and injustices, which necessarily generate anger and outrage just waiting to be tapped. It may be more productive if a social movement or a political party that represents ordinary people—as opposed to the two capitalist parties we have at present—taps that anger and channels it through the cycles of organization and pressure, but there is no guarantee that any movement can contain the rage of the masses. What can happen is that people galvanized into even disorderly action can find themselves seeking organized expression for their outrage in social movements.

Counterhegemony and Revolution

If the energy of the crowd finds organized expression in mass organizations dedicated to broad systematic challenge to the status quo, a situation of counterhegemony can arise. In such a situation, the forces of challenge organize broad sectors of society and run them for themselves, for example in general strikes. At this point, the establishment will engage in ruthless suppression using the armed forces, and only if the masses are prepared for battle can they prevail in making a revolution.

Interestingly, disorganized upheavals and the social crisis they represent can be the starting point for social movements and their formation cycles. They can be the movement's constitutive spark, as in the Black Lives Matter Movement. Some movement-building had been underway when the police murder of George Floyd brought hundreds of thousands of people into the streets. Great numbers of those people sought out spaces and organizations to help educate, organize, and lead subsequent protests.

In such a situation, we can see how the pressure cycle moments of a movement can actually, to some extent, precede and motivate the formation cycle; rebellions and other social crises make the opening for people to seek meanings behind their shared experience, develop their collective identity and assessment of how society works, train up leaders and educate members, and begin to move their repertoires into the public sphere to do it all over again.

There has not been a revolution in the United States since the nation's founding—and perhaps since the Civil War, since, as Eric Foner noted, that war "completed" the American Revolution. A **revolution** occurs when a radical, system-challenging social movement is able to lead masses of people in insurrection to displace the hegemonic establishment and replace it with a new class of leaders. Revolutions can take different political forms depending on who is leading them, whom they are supplanting, and what form their government will take. In a socialist revolution, anti-capitalist social movement organizations or political parties vie for leadership of the masses during an insurrectionary crisis. It can take years or decades for a movement to build up the numbers, political analysis, and influence to take on this task. In a revolutionary moment, you will see widespread uprisings oriented toward ousting existing rulers, dismantling the government, and replacing it with something else. In other words, a broad movement can build a counterhegemonic force capable of becoming the new hegemonic leadership. This is the ultimate moment in the pressure cycle of social movements, but most movements fold before this point after either winning significant gains or being crushed.

A small social movement organization cannot achieve a popular revolution. However, right-wing and authoritarian movements can carry out coups, often replacing one dictatorial leader with another. In an authoritarian regime, there is no sphere of public debate, organization, and action, so it is difficult to build counterhegemonic movements in that context. (It does happen, however, but movements in this situation don't follow the formula for movements in at least nominally democratic societies.) Counterrevolutionary forces can decimate such a revolution.

Even a profoundly democratic revolution representing the will of ordinary people would not instantiate a utopia. So if a revolution installs a form of democratic governance with a new public sphere, then new groups of disaffected people who perceive and experience oppression and injustice will gather in common cause to share experiences, develop common identities and analysis of society, educate and train themselves in communication and leadership, and move their struggle into the public sphere, where they will put pressure on these new institutions and leaders make change in the service of equality, freedom, and justice.

Step 6: Quiescence and the Return to the Formation Cycle

Short of revolution, movements at this point can retreat, settle for reforms already won, go dormant, or cease entirely. After the peak of a movement's influence, former activists may seek electoral power, work in non-profit settings, move into the academy as intellectuals building consciousness movements, engage in cultural work (music, writing, and other arts), focus on spiritual endeavors, and/or become demoralized. We see all of these reactions in the wake of the U.S. civil rights movement, as figures like Carl Stokes (who became mayor of Cleveland), Harold Washington (who became mayor of Chicago), Maynard Jackson (who became mayor of Atlanta), John Lewis (who was elected to Congress), Jesse Jackson (who ran for president and became a Baptist minister), take advantage of the new opportunities, freedoms, and possibilities of representation that the movement produced. A wave of Black public intellectuals, including Cornel West, Patricia Hill Collins, Angela Davis (former Black Panther), Henry Louis Gates, Jr., and others have taken up the task of educating communities and students about Black history, politics, culture, and futures.[36] New political analyses tracing the intersections of oppressions based on race, gender, sexuality, immigration status, national origin, and colonial histories have emerged, especially under the banner of Black and postcolonial/decolonial feminism.[37]

As cultural studies scholar Stuart Hall explained, in moments of reaction like the 1980s in the United States and Britain, these new formations undertake the war of position, generating culture and consciousness in preparation for struggles that are sure to come. Indeed, the work undertaken by Black, queer feminism in particular lay the ground for organizing in the movements for Black lives.[38]

A number of scholars talk about movements occurring in "waves" or cycles of protest during which periods of heightened agitation alternate with periods of assessment and regrouping (which happen in the formation cycle). Indeed, we can look to the Black freedom struggle as an example of how movements unfold in waves, beginning with the movement to abolish slavery, moving through the civil rights and Black power movements, generating momentum for the movements for Black lives and the abolition of the carceral state today. The U.S. women's movement began in the anti-slavery movement and moved through the suffrage movement, the 1960s feminist movements, to reproductive justice struggles and women's marches today. These waves are often punctuated by periods of reaction or backlash that prompt a revival of struggle. Lynching and Jim Crow necessitated the civil rights movement; police violence against Black people prompted the movement for Black lives; the anti-feminist backlash of the 1980s generated struggles for reproductive justice and other variants of feminist agitation; and so on.

Conclusion: The Hegemony-Formation-Pressure Model

In this and the previous chapter, we have covered what social movements do when they enter the public sphere to influence law, politics, economics, and culture, in other words, to contest hegemonic rule in the demand for reforms. The first task of movements at this moment is to conduct publicity. Publicity calls upon activists to engage in arguments, images, slogans, and narratives to popularize their cause. Movements must use media in this process, navigating the barriers posed by mainstream mass commercial media, creating and circulating their own media, and using social media to bring people out in support of their cause. In this stage, movements petition the powers that be, asking political leaders, employers, and other institutions to take action for change. Recruitment to the movement is a key challenge, as people won to the public arguments of movements are channeled into the formation cycle for consciousness-raising and training. Meanwhile, politicians, corporate leaders, and the commercial media attempt to diminish the perception, influence, and capacity of the movement.

When the establishment is unresponsive to movement appeals, movements escalate their pressure, forming coalitions of multiple movement organizations, generating a sense of antagonism between "us," champions of justice and "them," established elites who are hostile to change. In demonstrations, marches, and other performances, activists use slogans and images to convey the identity and purpose of the movement. They also engage in public disruption, becoming more militant in their tactics such as sit-ins, other forms of civil disobedience and direct action, and strikes. The establishment at this point may bargain and offer significant reforms, or it may engage in violent suppression of the movement; sometimes it does both.

Activists and organizations frustrated with the scope, scale, and pace of offered changes, and those who have developed a deeper critique of society as fundamentally unjust, will emerge as a radical flank to mainstream movement forces, further escalating confrontation and engaging in increasingly militant and confrontational tactics. The radical flank is often provoked by establishment suppression in the form of surveillance, policing, use of the armed forces, and the injuring or killing of activists. Movement coalitions dissolve. Those organizations and people who are now interested not only in equality and freedom but also justice and power increase the pressure on the establishment. They do so by leveraging the disruptive force of bodies in public space, the economic power of workers, and the taking up of arms in self-defense. At this point, the establishment may bargain or capitulate in response to such pressure; it may also engage in further suppression and violence.

The most militant expression of contemporary social movements is the rebellion or insurrection, which involves hundreds of thousands of people protesting in the streets and disrupting the workings of an orderly society. Such uprisings can operate alongside of, in concert with, or in advance of social movement organization. When social movements can capture the wave of insurrection, revolution—the dismantling and replacing of a hegemonic order—becomes possible.

Meanwhile, the formation cycle is in continuous motion as public action brings new people into organizations. When existing authorities give in to movement demands or when they use violence to suppress movements, movement organizations can fold and the movement can go into quiescence until a new wave of grievances re-invigorates the Hegemony-Formation-Pressure cycle.

Here is a diagram putting the formation and pressure cycles together, including the strategies of the establishment at top:

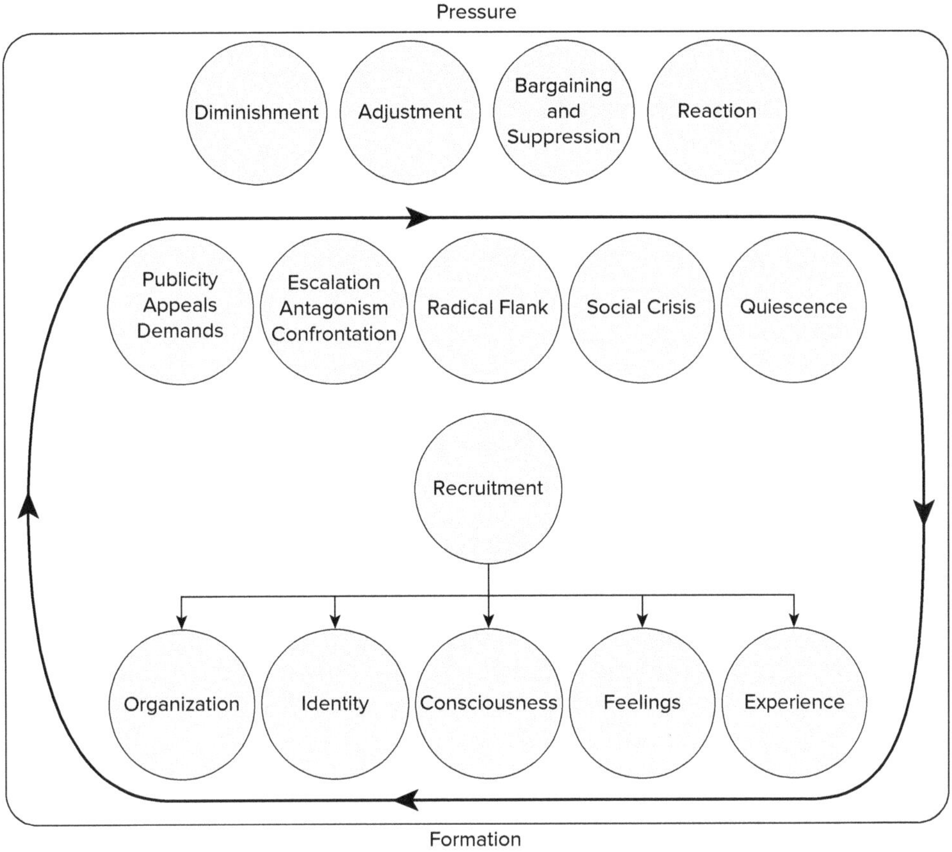

FIGURE 8.8 Hegemony-Formation-Pressure Model.

These chapters have used the civil rights and Black power movements as cases in point, but one can observe this cycle across most other U.S. social movements. The companion volume to this one, *Rhetorical Histories of Social Movements in the U.S.*, details this cycle across chapters covering most U.S. movements. While each of the movements is distinct from the others, they exhibit the patterns described in this book. What is for certain is that movements may fold and go quiet for a time, but wherever and whenever people experience injustice, there will be struggle again.

For example, the suffrage movement (for the right of women to vote) begins with literal petitions in the mid-19th century, the formation of mainstream women's rights organizations, and the escalation into protests and marches; against a recalcitrant political establishment, a radical flank in the form of the National Women's Party emerges to confront the administration of Woodrow Wilson, who (after engaging in repressive action) signs the 19th amendment in 1920. The movement subsides into quiescence until a new wave picks up the cycle in the 1960s to press for reproductive rights and the Equal Rights Amendment.

Movements by and on behalf of LGBTQ people also have followed this pattern. Interestingly, the formation cycle of these movements is extended due to conditions of illegality and secrecy such that social organizations are the first to emerge; the movement is catapulted into the public eye by the Stonewall Rebellion in 1969, which generates multiple organizations of varying radicalism and militancy to demand electoral representation, the repeal of oppressive laws and codes, and the freedom to form new kinds of families. In the struggle for marriage equality, a radical flank emerges to motivate the courts and legislature to grant that right. Since that reform was enacted, more radical and militant collectives have emerged to expand the movement's demands to include groups excluded from the activity and goals of the mainstream movement—namely, trans people, queer people of color, migrant queer people, working class and poor queer people, and others. Established political institutions and leaders have mounted a backlash against these efforts that have warranted violence and exclusion, for example, in attacks on Pride parades and Drag story hours at public libraries. The movement has taken on new shape as activists create and share new concepts of identity and demand deep changes in the treatment of queer people. In the crafting of communities of shared experience, mutual aid and care, parts of this movement linger in the formation cycle and assert the formation of such communities as enactments of liberatory change.

While queer movements orient toward the constitutive elements of the formation cycle, the labor movement lives in the moment of escalation, when already-established union organizations mobilize members to strike, taking action to compel employers to bargain. However, unions are one arena in which there can be movements inside of movements. When movement organizations like large labor unions become entrenched and bureaucratic, they can fail to represent ordinary (rank-and-file) workers, hesitating to strike in favor of high-level negotiation with employers. Since the 1990s, there have been multiple caucus movements inside of unions that respond to the union organization itself as one establishment while using that organization to challenge the broader establishment of corporate control of wages and work conditions. Those caucuses follow the formation and pressure cycles fairly closely.

The Hegemony-Formation-Pressure model of social movements is useful in describing such variations while acknowledging the overall pattern, its moments and tasks, and its rhetorical features: from petition/appeal/publicity (equality language) to escalation/coalition/confrontation (freedom and justice language) to flanking/radicalization (power language) and to insurrection/revolution and the possibility of forming a counterhegemony. The model encourages us to attend to both constitutive (formative) and instrumental (action-oriented) dimensions of social movements and to value the processes of affective investment, consciousness-raising, and organization as much as publicity and confrontation—and to recognize their cyclical interdependence. The role of establishment action or inaction in propelling the pressure cycle is also a key feature common to many social movements in the history of democratic societies. It is an irony that when the state and its forces suppress a movement in an ostensibly democratic society, it proves the movement's case that the system is corrupt, unjust, and violent, thus giving energy to agitators' efforts and motivation.

The model is meant not only to describe social movements but also to guide activists, including students, who want to engage in struggles for social justice. Wherever and whenever you decide to join with others to challenge oppression, exploitation, and injustice, you will find yourself somewhere in the formation-pressure cycle. But the cycle does not propel itself. Movements don't "just happen." They are not automatic. People like you are the prime movers of the ongoing cycle of change. An appendix to this book offers concrete advice for students looking to become involved in today's movements for social justice.

Suggestions for Further Reading

Jonathan Alexander, Susan C. Jarratt, and Nancy Welch, *Unruly Rhetorics: Protest, Persuasion, and Publics* (Pittsburgh: University of Pittsburgh Press, 2018).

Maegan Parker Brooks, *A Voice That Could Stir an Army: Fannie Lou Hamer and the Rhetoric of the Black Freedom Movement* (Jackson: University Press of Mississippi, 2014).

Karma R. Chávez and Cindy L. Griffin, *Standing in the Intersection: Feminist Voices, Feminist Practices in Communication Studies* (New York: SUNY Press, 2012).

Martin Luther King, Jr. "Letter from a Birmingham Jail" (1963), Bill of Rights Institute, https://billofrightsinstitute.org/primary-sources/letter-from-birmingham-jail.

María Lugones, *Pilgrimages/Peregrinajes: Theorizing Coalition Against Multiple Oppressions* (New York: Rowman and Littlefield, 2003).

Malcolm X, "The Ballot or the Bullet," American Radio Works, https://americanradioworks.publicradio.org/features/blackspeech/mx.html

Howard Zinn, *SNCC: The New Abolitionists* (Cambridge: South End, 1964).

Suggested Viewing

Showdown in Seattle, https://www.youtube.com/watch?v=g_XltnOjW_O.

HBO Films, *Iron-Jawed Angels* (New York: HBO Video, 2004).

Malcolm X., "The Ballot or the Bullet," *American Experience* (PBS, 1994), https://www.pbs.org/video/american-experience-ballot-or-bullet/.

Questions for Discussion

1. Did this chapter alter your perception of the value of antagonism and confrontation in social movements? How or how not?
2. What is the difference between direct action and civil disobedience?
3. How are confrontation and direct action different from violence?
4. Why do social movements escalate?
5. Describe the difference between the formation cycle and the pressure cycle. How are they related?
6. What are several things that can happen when a social movement goes into quiescence?
7. What does the establishment do when faced with escalation and why?
8. What are the various forms of the radical flank?
9. Why wouldn't we call mass uprisings "riots"?

Credits

Fig. 8.1: Martin Luther King, https://www.theattic.space/home-page-blogs/2022/1/13/mlks-epic-letter-from-birmingham-jail.

Fig. 8.2: Copyright © by Sally (CC BY 2.0) at https://commons.wikimedia.org/wiki/File:Dan_Choi_by_Sally.jpg.

Fig. 8.3: Copyright © 2024 by Aaron Amaral. Reprinted with permission.

Fig. 8.4: The National Archives UK, https://commons.wikimedia.org/wiki/File:Black_Power_Demonstration_(24284955374).jpg, 1970.

Fig. 8.5: Source: https://commons.wikimedia.org/wiki/File:Malcolm_X_in_discussion.jpg.

Fig. 8.6: Adam Schultz, https://commons.wikimedia.org/wiki/File:United_Auto_Workers_Strike_2023.jpg, 2023.

Fig. 8.7: Copyright © by Matthew T Rader (CC BY-SA 4.0) at https://commons.wikimedia.org/wiki/File:George_Floyd_Protest_Against_Police_Brutality_in_Dallas.jpg.

Appendix

Getting Involved in a Social Movement Near You

Perhaps the foregoing chapters have inspired you to seek out opportunities for social change on your campus and in your community. That's great! (And if not, that's fine too.) This brief essay offers some useful advice for doing so. It is broken down into steps that may not apply equally to every situation but that are common to many evolutions of campus and broader activism.

There are some general principles—especially for activists coming from a place of privilege—for getting involved in a social movement. (Actually, they are good principles to follow in most areas of life.) These are:

- **Demonstrating humility and respect:** The people you may meet as you get involved have already been thinking, working, educating each other and themselves, and practicing leadership and other skills. They are already committed to the cause. As a newcomer, you should communicate in ways that recognize their work and experience. For example, don't barge in telling people what the right way to do things is. Ask a lot of questions. Ask how you can help. Consider that you have a lot to learn.

  If you find yourself in a leadership position, ask yourself how that happened. Were you elected or chosen democratically by the group? Do you represent the interests of the group as a whole? Are you acting in the best interests of those whose needs and interests are at the base of the group? If not, check yourself and the practices of the organization. Suggest ways of operating in ways that might be more democratic. Be generous as you do so.

- **Doing the work:** Part of exhibiting respect is stepping up to do the work of the group. This might include attending and participating in meetings, helping with logistics (booking rooms, doing publicity, contacting media and presenters, setting up sound systems and other technology, making flyers or posters or websites, checking and answering email and social media messages, and so on). Don't be a consumer of what they have to offer; be an active participant.

- **Checking your privilege:** If you come from a group in society that is relatively privileged—for example, if you are a cisgender (gender conforming), white, affluent man who is a citizen of the United States—take care not to dominate conversations, interrupt others, or dismiss the insights of participants who have experiences different from your own. Don't assume that your priorities are the same as those of other people. They likely are not.
- Whether you should step back and allow others to lead depends on who else is participating in the group. Differences of race, gender, class, sexuality, economics, national origin, and religion mean that you may have a standpoint and perspective that is more powerful in society. Take care not to replicate that power difference in a movement organization.

  It should go without saying, but **do not harass, abuse, demean, ridicule, or otherwise harm** people you are working with. Many organizations have codes of conduct, which, when violated, can lead to discipline or expulsion.
- **Demonstrating solidarity:** A general principle about such power differences is to ask yourself continually whether the needs and agendas of the people with the least social power in the group determine the goals of the group. This is the principle of solidarity—working across differences in true common cause.

  It is crucial to consider differences of ability in the process of organizing in a social movement. We are becoming increasingly aware of how such differences—more accurately, society's neglect of those differences—can obstruct people's ability to be involved in many spheres of activity, including social movements. Best practices include making sure all rooms are accessible by wheelchairs and other assistive devices: wide doors, smooth floors, moveable furniture, accessible tables, access on first floor or by elevator, and/or virtual options for participation.

  Services like ASL interpretation or CART technology should be made available to deaf participants. All images, including the participants in the room or on screen, should be accompanied by image descriptions if there are blind participants. Audio should be available for written materials. All of these principles apply to public events like demonstrations as well. The pace of marches should be set so that people with disabilities can keep up. In general, if you are not a person with a disability, think: If I were a person with a disability, would I be able to participate in this meeting or event? If not, consider altering the group's practices. And check your language to avoid using words about disabilities in pejorative ways (like calling a fascist group "crazy" or a failed event "lame").

- **Having courage:** Embrace controversy—even conflict. Consider that you do not know as much as you think you do. Do not be afraid to ask what may seem like simple questions. Be willing to accept that you may have been wrong. As you grow in experience and knowledge, demonstrate courage by speaking in public, leading a demonstration or march, and making good arguments with people in the public sphere. Remember the principle of humility and respect.
- **Building community:** Members of historically muted groups—Black, Latine, queer, and disabled people, for example—sometimes face challenges in finding the energy (because of dealing with the burden of oppression all the time) or confidence (because of historical silencing and internalized oppression) to speak up or write. If you find yourself in this situation, one strategy is to get together with others representing a shared standpoint to workshop ideas and provide mutual support. Unfortunately, it may also be the case that activists around you are not honoring the basic principles laid out above and are not stepping back to make space for the voices of the oppressed. Know that you are

FIGURE A.1 Students participate in the climate strike on September 20, 2019.

not alone. You might be able to collectively approach leaders of the emerging social movements around you to spell out the problem and demand change. If not, it may be time to form your own activist space and bring around people who share your standpoint and embrace the knowledge and experience that you contribute as you engage in worldmaking.

With those principles in mind, here is a set of steps and questions that might guide you as you proceed.

1. Write and speak up: A first and simplest step for engagement in a movement for social justice is to write (or create art) and publish work that intervenes in public around a controversy that concerns you. Perhaps workers on your campus are organizing for better wages. Perhaps faculty and students are up-in-arms over the closure of an important cultural center on campus. Perhaps students are planning a campaign to defend transgender students from conservative efforts to silence or marginalize them. You can join their events to speak out.

   Consider writing an opinion essay or editorial for your campus newspaper. Research the issue and draft an argument. Seek out what others are already saying about the issue and try to answer their arguments. Contact the editors of your campus newspaper to gauge their interest and learn any limitations or rules for submissions. Revise and submit your work and see what evolves from there!

   You might also consider publishing on an activist website or social media outlet. It should be a place that engages audiences beyond your personal circle of friends and reaches other existing or potential activists. Consider the limitations of social media discussed in Chapter 6.

   If you have created artwork—music, visual art, performances, creative writing, etc.—find a gallery space or performance venue that might host you. Often, coffee shops and community centers are open to such contributions.

2. Find organizations on your campus related to your issue of concern: Your campus likely has campus resource centers or clubs representing groups facing injustice. For example, there may be a women's center, a queer students' center, a Black students' center, a Latine student center, and so on. Your student affairs office and website

may have a directory of such groups. There may be activist clubs on campus, too, for example, Students for Justice in Palestine, a graduate student union, or similar group.

Use the email or social media contacts that you find in a directory or on a website to reach out to leaders or contact people for the group that interests you. Explain that you would like to consider getting involved. Find out when and where their meetings are and whether they are planning any upcoming public events—forums, demonstrations, literature tables, petitioning, etc.

Ask how you can help. It is very important that you show respect, seriousness and good faith in making contact, and one way to do that is to do the work of organizing that the group is engaged in.

Attend the group's meetings and events and learn all you can about their work and the issues they are addressing. Decide whether to join based on these experiences. If you join, you will find that the group is engaged in multiple parts of the formation-pressure cycle. Observe how this process works and plug in where you fit best; you may need education and training; you may want to share your experience and stories; or you may be ready to participate in planning and leading public events. Take advice from your fellow activists as to where you should start.

3. What if there isn't a group already present doing the activist work you want to do? Consider forming your own group! Your campus' division of student affairs has information about how to get started. There are procedures and rules. Most of the time, you need to find a set number of people who are interested and make an application. You may need to write bylaws and a mission statement. Examples of these can be found at your university's website. Get advice from other organizations if you can.
4. Engage the tasks of the formation cycle:
    a. Find a space for meetings and get people together.
    b. Talk together about why you are there, what experiences you have related to the issue, what you want to achieve by getting together. Share your feelings: sadness, anger, and outrage as well as joy and excitement. Engage in consciousness-raising. Make space and time to tell and hear everyone's stories.

c. Find and choose (together) educational materials, key essays about history or theory or contemporary politics, and hold readings groups; it might help to have a leader for each to summarize readings and raise questions.

d. Work together on figuring out what your vision and analysis of the problem are. Write a manifesto or other statement announcing your analysis if people think that's a good idea. In whatever way, decide collectively what ideas, principles, and goals unite you.

e. If you haven't already, decide on a name for your group that represents those ideas, principles, and goals.

f. Set a division of labor that is egalitarian; in other words, don't always assign particular people or groups the "grunt work" of making copies or reserving rooms. Everyone should have a chance to develop intellectually and politically in the work. Movement organizations often divide labor into committees, for example, an events or logistics committee, a publicity or media committee, an education committee, a committee to liaise with the university, a social committee, and so on. Tailor your division of labor to your needs and the wishes of the group.

g. Part of dividing labor is determining leadership. Leadership can happen in a few different ways. One way is for the group to elect a steering committee (or other label) and to have regular elections open to all members to run for leadership positions. Then put major decisions of the group up for a vote as needed, deciding questions on the basis of majorities. The leadership should guide but not decide.

   Another way movements organize themselves is by consensus, in which the whole group makes every decision in real time and by discussing items until the entire group can be in total agreement, or consensus, about the way forward. This method may seem to be the most democratic, but it has the drawbacks of being extremely time consuming, working successfully only in smaller groups, and leading to pressure on dissenters to suppress opposing views. A final form of organization is informal organization, which evolves organically over time as a small group of people who take on the work and have opportunities for conversation outside the meetings increasingly take charge. That outcome may seem democratic and organic, but it excludes people who aren't in the leadership clique. It can feel confusing and exclusionary to new people.

h. Begin to plan public activity and train yourselves in how to conduct this activity. You can do this by looking at other examples, finding online and other resources for guidelines, and talking to other groups on your campus, which is then a great way to network for the future. Tapping resources to guide you is especially important with regard to nonviolent civil disobedience, which should only be undertaken after long discussion and training. Nonviolent civil disobedience is a confrontational strategy that is tremendously effective when deployed in the right circumstances for the right reasons. But it involves intentional lawbreaking and disruption, which can have consequences for participants. Having legal counsel at the ready is recommended. One resource can be found at https://actionnetwork.org/events/online-nonviolence-training-for-civil-disobedience-session-12.

i. Collectively decide your message, appeals/demands, and your target. Decide what demands are realistic in your situation. Choose your target carefully. Are they in a position to take the action you are asking for? In other words, are they agents of change? Are there pressure points? Or are they a broader audience whom you simply want to inform about the movement? Adapt your message persuasively to your target by touching on their beliefs, attitudes, and values to the extent possible; by describing negative consequences for them if they were to fail to act; and by being as clear as possible. Move forward when conditions are right.

j. Rinse and repeat. It is time to move into the pressure cycle, but all of these activities of sharing feelings and stories, developing identities and consciousness, conducting education and training, and keeping up the routines of membership become even more urgent as the organization begins recruiting newcomers who need integration into the movement. Keep in mind also that this formation cycle can be a long-term project in itself until an opportunity to take external action arises. There are long periods of history when engaging in public pressure is impossible or ineffective.

5. Engage the tasks of the pressure cycle:

    a. Keep in mind that these don't necessarily occur in tidy order. If your campus is facing a crisis, for example, confrontational strategies may be appropriate and even necessary at the get-go. Also keep in mind that the formation cycle continues as your movement grows, you recruit new activists, and engage them in the tasks of identity formation, consciousness-raising, and education.

    b. Do publicity: Spread information about your group through flyers, social media, posters, literature tables, and other tools. Develop messages for the mainstream media, keeping in mind that focusing on only a few core points gets the most effective results. You could choose a group to be media representatives at events for this purpose. Create your own media—videos, songs, literature, newsletters, magazines, and so on—and circulate widely. Tailor your materials to internal audiences and external audiences. Use social media to reach out to your networks and other activist groups to build participation and solidarity. Keep inviting people to come to your meetings and other events. You can at this point mobilize influential stakeholders to put pressure on the establishment. For example, parents of students who pay tuition and wealthy alumni can put pressure on a university administration to listen to a movement's demands.

    c. Ask your target for what you want (make appeals or demands). Present your campus officials with a petition. Have a meeting with administrators or select leaders to lay your appeals/demands on the table. Be ready to explain why reforms should happen and how they can happen. Keep asking for change at each step as you proceed. You likely will be turned down or turned away. Take heart; this is normal. It means that you need to escalate your efforts. It is likely at this point that you will take an oppositional or antagonistic stance toward the establishment and your rhetoric will take on the character of "us" and "them."

d. Develop ongoing and deepening political analysis of the situation. What is the nature of the system you are seeking to change? Who are its leaders? What are their resources? What are their weaknesses? Where can you put pressure most effectively? What are they likely to do as you escalate your movement? How do you want to characterize them as you move forward? How do you want to characterize the identity of your movement as you go forward? Now you are becoming more radical—trying to get at and target the root of the problem you are facing.

e. Consider confrontation and disruption. If your establishment target is not bargaining or considering change, you might want to talk to your group about escalating your activity to become more confrontational. Sometimes this move is not a choice, because forces opposed to your movement, including other movements and student and community groups, along with establishment representatives, are likely to come out to oppose you in public. Your membership needs to decide democratically whether to escalate in this way. You may decide to carry on with the

FIGURE A.2 Young people are a formidable force in movements for social justice today.

appeal process in the hope that the establishment will give some ground. The history of social movements teaches us, however, that abiding by the norms of civility and moderate conduct often does not work. Now you may become more militant in your orientation.

You can stage confrontation with opposing groups so as to demonstrate to others the ideas and validity of your movement. You are unlikely to change the minds of your direct opponents, so aim your messages at the audience around you and bring them around your cause. This can happen at rallies or other public events. Plan carefully if you have a chance to put forward speakers and leaders who can articulate your program most effectively. Prepare protest signs, chants, and slogans for this effort. You can also stage confrontation with establishment representatives, for example, if the Board of Trustees are meeting, you can demonstrate there and then. If the university president is speaking at a town hall, you can challenge them there. If there is a controversial speaker against social justice coming to campus, you can mount a challenge there. Be on the lookout for such opportunities.

Recall that disruption can take several forms: direct action, which is militant but often unplanned and usually small in scale; nonviolent civil disobedience, which is the product of mass organization and training and which involves disruptions of space and work; and strikes or other economic disruptions. At this point, you want to interrupt business as usual and get in the way of the system doing what it needs to do to sustain itself. Occupying intersections, offices, and hallways can disrupt traffic and the flow of the work day; striking can bring a company to the bargaining table by ceasing production and therefore profits. Often, confrontation and disruption are loud events. Security can be an issue. Prepare in advance for what you want to do if challenged by police or other authorities or by hostile and potentially violent opponents. In public events, it is sometimes good to assign marshals or people who are in charge of monitoring and responding to the security situation.

Oftentimes, interrupting the flow of business as usual will bring establishment representatives to the table to discuss making the changes that you are asking for. Perhaps they won't; in which case, you carry on to the extent that your group democratically decides.

f. Build coalitions: It is around this moment that multiple groups across a campus or a community connect and decide to build their efforts together. This is a powerful move to make because it exponentially increases your resources in terms of people power and experience. It also shows establishment representatives that you have broad support and that they are facing dissent from multiple quarters. It is also a moment of political awakening as you realize that your issues and problems are related to those of other groups. This awareness can lead to greater political radicalization, for example, when you realize, as Martin Luther King, Jr. did, that the struggle against racism is tied to the struggle of labor and the movement against the war, because it is one system that requires and enacts multiple injustices.

Remember the principles of humility, respect, and solidarity in creating coalitions. Be loving world travelers. Enable the people facing the most grievous injustice to determine the terms of mutual engagement and activity. Listen to others and step back if you find yourself wanting to dictate the way forward. Educate yourselves in how the movements and goals are interconnected. In a sense, coalition-building requires a next-level or meta-formation cycle, so be mindful to share feelings and stories, generate common ideas about problems and solutions, educate and train each other, and prepare for public-facing action.

Your organization is growing, so don't forget to invite newcomers to the formation cycle and treat them with patience, humility, and respect. They may have a great deal more experience than you do. Allow them to lead.

At this point, the establishment is likely to give some ground and negotiate over your demands. Meanwhile, they are actively suppressing the more militant confrontations. But make no mistake: They are vulnerable to your efforts. Sociologists tell us that only a weak establishment in democratic societies engages in hard repression.

If the establishment negotiates an acceptable (to your movement coalition) set of reforms, then your movement may dissolve or go quiet until the next crisis. However, if you believe that the reforms made are insufficient and the methods employed incorrect, you may find yourself in the position of the radical flank.

g. Mobilize the radical flank. Remember that every move you are making should be collectively decided to the greatest extent possible. Sometimes, one part of a coalition will either be satisfied with the promised reforms and/or comfortable with existing routines of protest. At this point, those who remain both dissatisfied and militant will agitate inside existing coalitions and/or split off and form new organizations with new names, new demands, and new methods. You may find yourself in this situation. You will likely face hostility now not only from the establishment but also from the moderates in the movement. Do not panic. This is to be expected.

Moderates fear that militancy will discredit the movement as a whole. Yet, we know from our studies that there is often a positive radical flank effect in which militancy makes the claims of moderates more persuasive and their efforts more successful.

If your group believes that pressing further with radical demands and militant (not violent) methods will be fruitful, then you all can move forward with careful assessment of opportunities and risks. Success depends upon the group's effectiveness in leading a broader movement with masses of adherents. People power gives the radical flank its strength. Be sure to weigh your strengths against risks, which may be great.

It is at this point that the establishment will accede to more thoroughgoing demands; alternatively, they will escalate the practices of suppression, potentially galvanizing broader insurrection.

h. It is unlikely that you will find yourself in a total insurrection or revolutionary situation. If you do, the tasks, questions, and problems will be more complex than this short textbook can address. You will already have learned a great deal about organization and leadership. You may be part of a thousands-, hundreds-of-thousands-, or millions-strong counterhegemonic wave that can sweep away the old rulers and replace them with new structures, institutions, and leadership. Revolutions are not initially violent but often require wars (like the American Revolution and the Civil War), because existing power is not likely to yield; they will fight back. Some scholars and activists have argued that full equality, freedom, and justice against an inherently hierarchical and unjust regime will require revolutionary change. It is up to you and your communities and organizations whether you agree.

i. At any point in this process, the establishment may give in partially or totally, the state may use resources of violence to suppress agitation, or the movement may fail to take off and remain small and isolated. In these cases, movements often go quiet, returning to the tasks of the formation cycle and building community and culture until the next opportunity for pressure presents itself. Alternatively, leaders may run for elected office or join or start NGOs. The group may dissipate. Going quiet is not a failure on your part. There are conditions beyond any person's or collective's control that shape the possibilities and constraints that will affect a movement. Avoid casting blame on your fellow activists and be generous with others and yourself.

Deciding to be an advocate for justice and an agent of change is the first, and most important, step. I hope that this book and the advice in this part might inspire you to seek out opportunities for advocacy and engagement. Happy organizing!

Credits

Fig. A.1: Minnesota Senate DFL, "Students Organizing," https://www.rawpixel.com/image/4045969/photo-image-public-domain-banner-person.

Fig. A.2: David Shankbone, "Students Engaged in Confrontation," https://www.flickr.com/photos/shankbone/6348384013, 2011.

Suggested Exercises

Chapter 1

1. In teams of two to three students, research the situation of one of the groups covered in this chapter in a particular domain of life. For example, you could investigate the situation of women in sports or the treatment of LGBTQ people in the media. Focus on specific cases and find research from credible sources with the help of your instructor or librarian, as needed. Using evidence such as statistics and examples gathered from your research, report on what you have discovered to the class. Your report might include information about the following:
   - that group's experience (or the experience of a member of that group), the institutions (like the workplace, the school, healthcare, the government, the family, the media, etc.),
   - the discriminatory rhetoric affecting that group,
   - critical statements and analysis made by members of that group, and
   - any agitation and organization they may have conducted or are conducting.
2. In pairs or teams, go to the website for *The New York Times*' 1619 project: https://www.nytimes.com/interactive/2019/08/14/magazine/1619-america-slavery.html. Watch at least one of the video chapters. Reflect and discuss the following:
   - Three historical facts that surprised you.
   - Three quotes that stand out to you.
   - Three questions you have about content in the essay.
   - Prepare and report back to class on your findings.

Chapter 2

1. As a class or in smaller groups, visit your university's library archive of the student newspaper. Read issues from a particularly agitational point in time, such as the student movement of the late 1960s or the anti-racist movements of the 2010s and 2020s. Have there been movements such as the one described in this chapter? How did they unfold? Use the questions above to guide your analysis of the movement.

Chapter 3

1. With your professor's assistance, see if your college or university library has any collections of documents from historical social movements. If so, locate one or more primary documents—speeches, newsletters, video, or audio—from a movement. If not, locate such a source online. Do research on the context of these documents: What movements do they represent? When were they made and by whom? What organizations were involved? Then describe any frames present in the document: identity frames, collective action frames, and attributional, prognostic, and motivational frames present there. How do the activists who created these documents see themselves and their actions?
2. Look at materials from a contemporary social movement, such as Black Lives Matter, the movement against sexual harassment and assault, the environmental movement, or the labor movement. Find news coverage of an event or events in that movement and describe the media frames operating there. Did the mass media attempt to enhance or diminish the appeal of the movement for its audiences? How so?
3. In one of the movements you have discovered (historical or contemporary), list the social movement organizations involved. Do they constitute a "social movement industry"? What resources did those organizations draw upon? What opportunities (historical, economic, political, or ideological) did they take advantage of to achieve their goals? What were their repertoires of contention?

Chapter 4

1. Watch the documentary *United in Struggle* (about ACT UP). Take notes on how the video depicts the movement engaging in the following:
    - Internal, constitutive rhetoric
    - External, instrumental rhetoric
    - Arguments, visual rhetoric, bodily action, emotional appeal and affect work, narratives, music and song, body rhetoric, violence
    - Confrontation moderation and militancy
    - Flanking
    - Identity frames
    - Consciousness-raising

Chapter 5

1. Discover and listen to a social movement song or set of songs and learn about their contexts. What messages and identities to these songs convey? How?
2. Discover and analyze a photographic image from a social movement event that contains images of people, signs, and banners. What messages do these images convey? How? What perspective does the photographer want to you to take on the pictured events?

Chapter 6

1. Watch "The Time Has Come (1964–1966)", *Eyes on the Prize* [video recording] (Alexandria, VA: PBS Media, 2006) and describe the differences in identity frames between the civil rights and Black power movements.
2. In your university library or online, find a social movement manifesto. A manifesto is a declarative document that lays out the identity,

demands, and strategies of a movement. The Black Panther Party's Ten-Point Program is a good example (https://www.blackpast.org/african-american-history/primary-documents-african-american-history/black-panther-party-ten-point-program-1966/), as are the numbers of radical feminist manifestoes of the 1960s and 1970s (https://www.dazeddigital.com/artsandculture/article/18674/1/the-essential-feminist-manifestos). However, any statement crafted by a movement to define its identity and lay out its program would be a good resource for you. Describe the identity frames, both ideological and tactical, of your chosen document.

3. On your campus, use the directory of student organizations to locate a campus social movement organization. Being respectful of activists' time and energy, see if you can attend meetings or interview members. If you can (and do not be surprised if group leaders are hesitant), describe the movement's organizations: people, documents, spaces, routines, leadership, and other features. What can you conclude about how this social movement organization works.

Chapter 7

1. Visit an archive of social movement media such as an archive of working-class writing, socialist literature, websites for the Black Lives Matter movement, or another case. Describe the characteristics of this literature in a report to the class. What narratives, images, arguments, and slogans are employed to make the movement's case? What identity frames can you describe based on this literature?

2. Imagine that you are active in a social movement today (or describe a movement in which you are actually active). Craft some publicity materials for that movement—songs, pictures, slogans, flyers, leaflets, opinion essays, or other types of communication. What principles will you use to draft these materials? Who are your audiences and what are your purposes?

Chapter 8

1. Watch one of the films under "Suggested Viewing" and describe the progression of escalation from antagonism to the emergence of the radical flank.
2. Find an archive of the documents of a social movement and chart the use of equality, freedom, justice, and power language.

Glossary

ableism: A rhetoric that defines people with disabilities; privileging of culturally-defined bodily ideals as measures of human worth

ACT UP: Aids Coalition to Unleash Power, the movement founded in 1987 to demand change in the government and pharmaceutical industry to respond to the needs of gay men and other sufferers of HIV-AIDS

adjustment: When the establishment gives some ground to a movement, conceding on reformist demands

affect: Pre-emotional state of intense feeling without ascribed meaning; basis in pre- or extra-cognitive bodily experience

agitation: Organized activity against established powers with the goal of social change

agitator: Those who organize to challenge established force outside the normal decision-making establishment and encounter resistance from establishment

AIDS Quilt: A massive stitched-together set of panels, each commemorating someone who died of AIDS, initiated by Cleve Jones

American War for Independence: Otherwise known as the American revolution, a war that put a new class of people—merchants and agriculturalists—in charge of society

antagonism: A relationship with the establishment, dividing society into proponents and opponents of change, an "us" and a "them"

Anti-slavery movement: Campaign against slavery in the United States beginning roughly in the 1830s and lasting through the civil war

appeal: Request or plea for something to change

archetypal metaphor: Comparisons that seem to apply universally to the human condition

argument: A proposition supported by evidence and reasoning

attributional frame: Attributes blame

avoidance: When the establishment uses tactics of delay, counter-persuasion, or otherwise ignores movement agitation in order to limit its impact

ballot or the bullet: Well-known speech of Malcolm X where he criticizes the mainstream civil rights movement for its faith in electoral politics and the possibility of reforms

bargaining: Negotiating with movement leaders over possible reforms

black freedom struggle: The set of movements from the abolitionist movement of the 19th century through the civil rights and Black Power movements and the Movement for Black Lives

black nationalism: With roots in the 19th century, is a tendency in the politics of social movements that argues that Black people in the United States represent a separate colonized nation with a separate identity from the mainstream

Black Panther Party for Self-Defense: An organization in the Black Freedom Struggle originating in voting rights campaigns but evolving into a radical, militant, and separatist organization focused on armed self-defense against police brutality and community service

body rhetoric: Theorized by Leland Griffin as a mode of protest in which activists interrupt or disrupt spaces and routines with their bodies

body-minds: Term that recognizes the interconnection among our thinking, feeling, and physical bodies and how the mind is housed in the body and that physical and neurological disabilities are of the same order and that everyone has a body-mind with specific capacities and needs; a term recognizing the wholeness of a person

boycott: Organized efforts undertaken by consumers to reject products and services associated with oppressive interests

buycott: When consumers organize themselves to purchase specific brands regarded to be behaving more ethically than others

Brown v. Board of Education: 1954 Supreme Court Decision mandating integration of public schools

capitulation: When the establishment gives in entirely to movement demands

choric communication: Rhetoric of singing that brings communities and movements into cohesion

cis-gender: Label for people whose felt identity corresponds to their gender assignment at birth

Civil society: Place of gathering, discourse, and action independent of both state and corporate power

Class/social class: Economic layer or position held in the economy by a group of people; see **class, ruling class**

Coalition: The intentional, structured coordination of activity among multiple movement groups

collective action frames: The strategic combination of **attributional, prognostic, and motivational frames** communicating the need for action; these have injustice (moral judgement), agency (capability to act) and identity components (sense of collective identity)

collective identity: A group's sense of self and purpose, developed in narratives; formation of group identification when people participate in shared efforts through interaction; development of a sense of collective solidarity

common sense: Ideas that seem natural, pre-given, and permanent and are understandable by broad audiences as such

consent: A term used by Gramsci to describe a form of rule that appears to be based on the acceptance of a population

consciousness-raising: New understandings of one's structural position accomplished through writings, speeches, documents, and interactions, productive of **oppositional consciousness**

constitutive rhetoric: Focuses on the emergence of collective identity and shared meaning in contrast to the **intstrumentalist approach**

controller: Agent of the establishment who attempts to quell agitation

counterhegemony: Resistance to and organization against established powers

counterpersuasion: When the establishment employs rhetoric counterposed to the collective identity frames of social movement groups, often involving disparaging media frames

counterpublics: Spheres of debate and deliberation organized around a particular identity, group, cause, or movement

critical race theory: A set of ideas emerging from critical legal studies stressing the salience of race in the consideration of law, politics, and culture

crowd: A form of unplanned collective being in public space

cultural turn: When social movement scholars began to focus on cultural, identity, symbolic, and affective dimensions of movements

culture shift: When a movement has so effectively challenged prevailing common sense that popular and political culture adjust to new forms of representation

cycle of contention: Evolution of movements through stages of **diffusion, radicalization, exhaustion, restabilization, and escalation**

demand: When social movement participants escalate pressure on an establishment to give ground

dialectic: A relationship between two things that are in tension but that are mutually interdependent and influential on each other

diatribe: Bitter, vituperative, counter-moral rhetoric that turns the norms of society on their head

die-in: A protest in which activists lay down as if dead, symbolizing the real death their communities experience; a form of civil disobedience common to ACT UP and Black Lives Matter

diffusion: Spread of conflict, ideas, and actions

diminishment: The attempt on the part of an establishment to use the tactics of avoidance, counterpersuasion, evasion, secrecy, and denial of access to resources in order to minimize the size, importance, power, legitimacy, and public perception of a movement

direct action: A social movement tactic in which activists, often in small groups, target institutions and public figures for disruption and damage (not violence)

disability: A cultural construct or ideological definition of people whose bodies do not conform to existing social ideas of "able-bodiedness"

dispossession: Systemic theft of land and property and the denial of access to life-sustaining resources

distributive justice: Demands actual redress of inequality in the form of economic and other goods

Ella Baker: Civil rights leader who supported the formation of the Student Nonviolent Coordinating Committee as an organization independent of the SCLC

Emmett Till: A black youth lynched in Mississippi in 1955

emotional contagion: Tendency to mimic another person's emotional experience

emotion: Coherent expression of baseline feelings as defined rhetorically in particular cultural contexts

enclave: Protected space where people can devise their identities, analyses, and plans without yet adapting to external audiences

enthymeme: A form of reasoning described by Aristotle that relies upon appeals to values and knowledge shared between a persuader and their audience

epistemic injustice: Condition of not having one's voice, experience, and realitiy recognized or included in the prevailing common sense of society

epistemic justice: When oppressed groups make themselves heard so that broader society recognizes their claims

equal rights: Core language and demand of the early civil rights movement

equality: Core term in the American political common sense appealing to the value of every person's right to participate in society at the same level

equality and rights language: When a movement couches its appeals and demands in terms of the core term of the liberal ideology, equality and argues for rights inside the system as it exists

escalation: Moment in social movement development when activists begin to deepen and radicalize their political analysis of the system and become more militant in their tactics; per sociology, when movements gain ideological hold and militancy even unto revolution

establishment: Group of people, organizations, and institutions that currently possess the preponderance of resources and determine the direction of an organization, institution, government, or society as a whole

exhaustion: Weariness and disillusionment

experience: Basic everyday knowledge of life on the part of people living it; basis for common cause and consciousness-raising

exploitation: The use of workers to earn profits for employers without being paid the full value of their work

external audience: Public audiences whom movements aim to persuade; not members of the movement itself

fascism: A form of rule in which power, achieved through mass appeals to "the people" and often warranted by racist scapegoating, openly suppresses its enemies

FDA protest: When ACT UP pressed their bodies against the fence at the Food and Drug Administration

First Nations: Tribal societies of North America colonized by Europeans starting in the early 17th century

first wave: Women's suffrage movement of the 19th and early 20th century

five kinds of emotions: Urges, reflex emotions, moods, loyalties, and moral emotions

flanking: When one part of a movement presses in more radical or militant directions, breaking with the movement mainstream and paradoxically making the mainstream more credible and effective when there is a radical flank effect

formation cycle: Process through which people come together on the basis of shared experience, foster connection among those people, cultivate emotional commitment, create shared identities, and form organizations with leadership and a method of training members in repertoires of contention; roughly corresponds to **constitutive rhetoric** and the **war of position**

formation: The constitution of movement identities and meaning

frame alignment: Resonance between movement rhetoric and the target audience

frame amplification: Accent and highlight aspects of a situation

frame articulation: Connection of a movement situation to common cultural beliefs

frame co-optation: When a contending group usurps a movement's attempt to frame its activity

frame misalignment: When movement frames depart from hegemonic ones

frames: schemata of meaning and interpretation that people use to make sense of their world

freedom language: The invocation of an ideal of freedom from oppression, violence, and exclusion and the freedom to embrace new identities and take actions challenging existing institutions and norms.

functionalism: Stresses how movements serve the function of instrumental goals

Gandhi v. guerilla: In Bowers, Ochs, Jensen, and Shulz, the stage of a social movement where parts of the movement who are more radical and/or militant split off from the mainstream of the movement and engage in more confrontational tactics

gender expression: How persons present themselves as masculine, feminine, or gender-non-comforming

gender identity: Felt identity of a person as masculine, feminine, or gender non-conforming

gender oppression: Set of institutional exclusions of, routine violence against, and cultural defamation of gender non-conforming persons motivated by the hatred and fear of gender diversity; see **transphobia**

gender: Social construction of one's identity as masculine or feminine, often assigned at birth according to perceived anatomical differences

globalization: The spread of one economic system (capitalism) around the world

good sense: Consciousness of one's own experience as related to broader social problems achieved through organizing and education

governance structures: Means by which power and authority are exercised

Gramsci, Antonio: Italian theorist of hegemony

Hamer, Fannie Lou: Voting rights activist and leader of the **Mississippi Freedom Democratic Party**

hegemony-formation-pressure model: A model that describes social movements as a combination of formation/constitutive rhetoric and pressure/instrumental rhetoric that challenges hegemonic social relations in a dialectical and recursive cycle

hegemony: Achievement of stability in economic, political, and cultural power by a particular class

hegemony frame: The structure of institutional power that is the context and target of social movements

heteronormativity: The widespread assumption that heterosexuality is the only normal and correct sexual orientation; how heterosexual is automatically assumed and valued

HIV-AIDS: A viral infection and illness transmitted via bodily fluids, originally affecting mostly men who have sex with men and consumers of illegal intravenous drugs, originally largely fatal; per Schulman, a "mass-death event"

homophobia: Oppression based on sexual orientation motivated by hatred or fear of sexual difference

i have a dream speech: Martin Luther King, Jr.'s address to the March on Washington for Jobs and Freedom in 1963

identity formation: Moment of establishing "who we are" and "who they are"

identity politics: Struggle for recognition of identity on the part of the broader society as a primary goal of movement organizing

ideology: A set of relatively stable and broadly accepted shared ideas, motivated by the preservation of power, operating in multiple domains of society, and shaping our consciousness, identities, and actions without our conscious decision to comply; dominant ideas; ideas of the ruling class; per Eagleton, "the ways in which people may come to invest in their own unhappiness"; language, beliefs, values, norms, rules, codes, and scripts that guide a population's knowledge and action; legitimates established power by making the social order seem natural, necessary, and permanent

images: Visual symbols

injustice: The lack of fairness and equal treatment and lack of the enforcement of those goals; failure of society to redress the wrongs of violence and inequality; the failure of accountability for harmful and discriminatory ideas and actions

institutional actors: Agents of power in organizations

institutional logics: Organizing principles for movements

instrumentality: How a movement uses rhetoric to achieve identified, concrete goals

instrumentalist approach: Focuses on movements as strategic rhetorical phenomena aimed at external audiences with intentional goals of making change

insurrection: When a **rebellion** becomes massive and more focused and organized

internal audience: The group of people constituting the movement rather than outsiders to be persuaded

intersectionality: Recognition that very few people have only one identity or suffer only one form of injustice

islamophobia: The fear and defamation of Muslims that justifies violence against them

justice language: Calls for radical change to the underlying systems that fuel injustice; an escalation from rights language

justice, social: State of fairness and equal treatment across the domains of social life including the nation-state, the economy, the culture, social settings, and private life

lateral deviance: When agitators dispute the entire value system itself

latine: Gender-inclusive labels for people previously called Latino or Hispanic

leaders: In social movements, those who establish their authority, facilitate identity framing, demonstrate practical organizational skills, play diver roles, and serve as symbols for the cause; people authored to guide and coordinate discussion and action in a social movement organization

Malcolm X: Leader of the Nation of Islam in the 1960s who, in counterpoint to Martin Luther King, argued for the right to self-defense

March on Washington for Jobs and Freedom: 1963 march featuring the "I Have a Dream" speech

Martin Luther King, Jr: Reverend and leader of the Southern Christian Leadership Conference

master frames: Stable prevailing cultural narratives that define social reality for most people

media frames: Per Gitlin, persistent patterns of cognition, interpretation, and presentation, of selection, emphasis, and exclusion, by which symbol-handlers routinely organize discourse, whether verbal or visual; include trivialization, polarization, emphasis on dissension, marginalization, disparagement by numbers and effectiveness, reliance on establishment sources, emphasis on outsiders or communists, emphasis on and attributions of violence

memphis sanitation workers strike: 1968 work stoppage by Black garbage collectors; famously used the slogan "I am a man" and was addressed by Martin Luther King, Jr. on the night before he was assassinated

militancy: Intention and enactment of disruptive confrontation in service of movement aims; the degree to which movements engage in confrontation, disruption, destruction, or violence

Misogyny: Literally, hatred of women/feminine people motivated by the desire to maintain the privilege and power of men/masculine people

Mississippi freedom democratic party (MFDP): A parallel Black political party to rival the white Dixiecrat domination of the South in 1964

mobilizing structures: Features of organizations enabling action

Montgomery Bus Boycott: 1955 movement in Montgomery, Alabama to integrate buses; the movement "sparked" by Rosa Parks; the movement establishing the leadership of Martin Luther King, Jr.

motivational frames: Calls to arms

Music: Important resource in social movements that aurally and physically bring participants' bodies into line with one another

muted group theory: Focuses on how marginalized groups are muted and excluded in and from language

narrative paradigm: A system of thinking about persuasion that emphasizes storytelling rather than argumentation

narratives: Stories used strategically to produce identities and bring people together in common cause; a recounting of a process in which something happens based on shared experiences and shaping beliefs, attitudes, and values

Nation of islam: First organization of Malcolm X, who later broke with the NOI to form Muslim Mosque, Incorporated as the home of radical Black nationalism

New Social Movements: Movements that put claims about identity and representation in culture to the fore

NGO (Non-Governmental Organization): Often grant-funded organization that responds to the urgent material needs of women, queer people, immigrants, workers, and the poor

nonviolent civil disobedience: A form of direct action on a large scale; it engages in intentional, systematic law-breaking; it organizes, trains, and deploys masses of bodies to disrupt the flow of business as usual in demonstrations, marches, sit-ins, and occupations; and it is designed to draw out establishment forces to reveal themselves for what they are

***Obergefell v. Hodges*:** 2015 Supreme Court decision mandating marriage equality

opportunities: Crises or gaps in an establishment's leadership, shifts in popular consciousness, and other historical events that make openings for social movement actors to make their claims

oppositional consciousness: Insight that an oppressive system should be opposed

oppression: Systematic subjugation of and discrimination against particular groups of people based on their identities

Organizations: Where resources are mobilized and momentum sustained; instrumental activities and coordination of effort

Patriarchy: Rule by men

performativity: The capacity of individuals and groups to use the resources of bodies, media, symbols, and language to engage in a politics of space and space-making based on their embodied experience and knowledge

petitioning: The act of asking the establishment to grant an appeal

Polarization: When a movement uses rhetoric to establish an antagonism between an "us" and a "them"

political opportunities: Crises that provide openings for social movements

political opportunity structure: Per Zald and McCarthy, the degree to which formal political institutions are open or closed to challengers of the status quo; the degree to which political elites are organized in stable or unstable coalitions and alignments; the degree to which movements have allies within the political elite, and the degree to which political authorities are willing to use repression against challengers

Populism: A political ideology that rhetorically creates "a people" out of otherwise disconnected groups

post-race racism: Discourse denying the continuing force of racism in society

power language: Rejects the language of equal rights in favor of language asserting the capacity of an oppressed group to take control of their futures and of key institutions in society

pressure cycle: The process in which a movement orients toward external audiences and engages in the instrumental work of persuading the establishment to change through publicity, antagonism, confrontation, and flanking prognostic frame: Articulates alternatives

promulgation: When a movement uses communication to spread its message

public sphere: All of the spaces, forums, media, and audience available to people trying to shape society where kinship and the state ideally do not interfere with the process; the sphere of debate and controversy; an audience of strangers

publicity: Entering the **public sphere** to address external audiences in support of a movement's ideas

quiescence: When movements at this point can retreat, settle for reforms already won, go dormant, or cease entirely

racism: Set of institutional exclusions of, routine violence against, and cultural defamation of minority groups in society motivated by hatred and/or fear of racial and ethnic difference; the desire to maintain the privileges afforded to white people

radical feminist movement: A movement of the 1960s and 1970s composed of women critical of mainstream feminism for failing to indict **patriarchy**; a movement targeting patriarchy, its institutions, and its expressions

radical flank effect: When a radical/militant movement split-off aids the credibility of more moderate, reformist sectors of the movement

radicalism: Ideological constructs that identify the nature and character of oppressive systems at their root; the degree to which a movement, or a particular sector of a movement, challenges the beliefs, attitudes, values, institutions, elites, and their practices of established rule

radicalization: Deepening political consciousness leading to the awareness of the need for system change

rebellion: When a **crowd** engages in disruptive expression against prevailing structures of power

recruitment: Process by which new members of a social movement are brought into the movement's activity through the persuasive activity of existing participants

recursivity: A characteristic of the HFP model that acknowledges that moments of struggle return back on themselves continually

reforms: Making of changes within a social system while leaving the system itself intact

reparative justice: Attempts to sustain community by enabling perpetrators of injustice to atone for their actions and re-establish trust

repertoires of contention: Set of skills and actions that constitute a toolkit for movements: voting, petitioning, asserting, claiming, meeting, demonstrating, striking, marching, occupying, performing, obstructing, sabotaging, and attacking; "inherited forms of collective action" per Tilly and Tarrow

resource mobilization theory: Theory that argues that movement success depends upon the organization, leadership, administration, incentives, resources, and membership

restabilization: When society returns to "normal" by repression and/or adjustment

revolution: The overturning and replacing of the existing system with something else; product of the slow organization for reforms followed by a crisis in the legitimacy of the state; when a radical, system-challenging social movement is able to lead masses of people in insurrection to displace the hegemonic establishment and replace it with a new class of leaders

rhetoric of confrontation: Per Scott and Smith, social drama in the clash between "us" and "them"

rhetoric of family values: Discourse valorizing an idealized private family; justified exclusions of Black people of equal housing, education, employment, and wealth

rhetoric of the streets: Per Haiman, civil disobedience, law-breaking, property damage, and other militant actions

rhetoric: Practice and study of how human beings use strategies of language, image, sound, and other symbols to achieve their purposes with audiences

rhetorical perspective: Focus on how social movement actors employ words, sounds, images, and bodies as symbolic resources in the struggle for influence

***Roe v. Wade*:** 1973 Supreme Court decision legalizing abortion

ruling class: Owns and controls the production, distribution, and cost of goods in the capitalist market

second wave: 1960s women's movements

separatism: A tendency in a movement toward asserting difference from the mainstream and making demands beyond integration toward freedom and justice

sexism: Set of institutional exclusions of, routine violence against, and cultural defamation of women in society motivated by the hatred and fear of gender difference; see **misogyny**.

silence: Strategic response to violence against oppressed people

simultaneity: Characteristic of the HFP model stressing how the moments or tasks of the movement do not occur in linear succession

slogan: A phrase or sentence that condenses the meaning of a movement into an immediately understood unit

Social movement industry (SMI): Entire range of social movement organizations operating at once

Social movement organization (SMO): An organization formed by and enabling a social movement

social movement: (1) collective, concerted, organized, and strategic campaign to win social change; (2) collective, concerted, purposeful, and strategic campaign on the part of non-establishment actors targeting establishment actors and institutions to reform or revolutionize parts or all of a social system; (3) from sociology, contentious collective politics, when ordinary people—often in alliance with more influential citizens and with changes in public mood—join forces in confrontation with elites, authorities, and opponents

solidarity: Consistent organizing and action alongside others in mutal support of each other's goals

southern christian leadership conference: Civil rights organization headed by Christian ministers, including Martin Luther King, Jr.

St. Patrick's cathedral protest: When ACT UP interrupted mass by lying down on the cathedral floor in a **die-in**

stages models of social movements: In rhetoric and sociology, descriptions of social movements as they evolve through stages or cycles

standpoint: Idea that the more disadvantaged are more likely to develop critical consciousness based on their social location

strategy: Broad plan or goal on the way to achieving a purpose; see **tactic**

strike: The organized, purposeful cessation of work (usually led by a union)

Stokely carmichael (kwame n'ture): Advocate of Black Power; first a leader of the Student Nonviolent Coordinating Committee, then of the Black Panther Party

student nonviolent coordinating committee: Militant group of students who broke with the SCLC and led the sit-in movement

substantive justice: When institutions and people are held accountable in meaningful ways for their actions and ideas

suppression: The organized effort on the part of the state or other authoritative institution to stop the progress of a movement through coercive means

system critique: A set of explanations of why oppressors behave as they do in terms of a broader social system

tactic: Specific means of enacting a strategy; see **strategy**

transnational activism: Resistance to **globalization** on the part of activists networked internationally

transphobia: Set of institutional exclusions of, routine violence against and cultural defamation of transgender people

vertical deviance: When agitators accept the value system of the establishment

violence: Intentional harming of human beings and other animals

visual rhetoric: Focuses on how images work differently from verbal communication, conveying perspective through visual vocabularies

undercommons: Where oppressed communities–with particular emphasis on Black, Indigenous, queer, and poor peoples–create knowledge, meaning, and resistance from below

War of maneuver: Strategic challenge to an oppressive system as a whole; mobilization of large forces to make a wholesale challenge to the existing social system including both the state and the economic system

war of position: Limited struggle in culture and politics in the process of slowly gaining and holding ground primarily in the realms of ideology and culture

worldmaking: How communicators, especially those who have been less powerful in society, co-create their identities, goals, and communities through rhetorical effort

working class: Everyone who must work for a wage in the economy and do not control their workplaces

Endnotes

Preface

1. Leah Hunt-Hendrix and Astra Taylor make this argument in *Solidarity: The Past, Present, and Future of a World-Changing Idea* (New York: Pantheon, 2024); see Astra Taylor and Leah Hunt-Hendrix, "Solidarity and Strategy: The Forgotten Lessons of Truly Effective Protest," *The Guardian* (March 14, 2024), https://www.theguardian.com/world/2024/mar/14/solidarity-and-strategy-the-forgotten-lessons-of-truly-effective-protest.
2. There is a multitude of professional non-governmental organizations (NGOs) lobbying for reform and providing material aid to communities in need, but these do not represent the kind of mass grassroots people power that shakes a nation. The Women's Marches of 2017 and 2018 were enormous but not sustained; the protests of the Arab Spring in 2011 were massive efforts that sought to depose dictators without an organized structure in place; the Occupy Movement of 2011 was largely prefigurative, as activists formed encampments in cities across the U.S. but failed to make concrete demands on powerful institutions; the #MeToo movement has done a great deal to publicize the problem, endemic to sexist society, of sexual harassment and violence. It raised consciousness and fostered identification among women who have shared the experience of such abuse, but it has not gone beyond such publicity. Even the Black Lives Matter movement—the most significant and most radical uprising in the United States since the 1960s—lacked lasting, structured organizations, leadership, and mechanisms for connecting and retaining members. It largely evaporated after its peak in 2020, opening the way to a pro-police backlash invested in combating critical theories and histories of race across public schools and universities across the United States.

Introduction

1. Southern Poverty Law Center, "Hate Map," June 5, 2020, accessed August 3, 2020, https://www.splcenter.org/hate-map.
2. Dalia Faheid, "Students at More Universities Announce Solidarity. Rallies after 108 pro-Palestinian Activists Are Arrested at Columbia," *CNN.com* (April 19, 2024), https://www.cnn.com/2024/04/19/us/palestinian-protest-columbia-what-we-know/index.html.
3. Julie McMahon, "What do #NotAgainSU Protesters want from Syracuse University? Here's a Full List of Demands," Syracuse.com, March 5, 2020, accessed August 3, 2020, https://www.syracuse.com/syracuse-university/2020/03/what-do-notagainsu-protesters-want-from-syracuse-university-heres-full-list-of-demands.html.
4. Amber Juarez, "Women's Center set to Re-open in Fall 2022," *Daily Titan*, April 20, 2022, https://dailytitan.com/news/campus/womens-center-set-to-reopen-in-fall-2022/article_a2efce2a-c034-11ec-84cf-b71793eb865b.html.
5. Bryan Sacks and Michael Reagan, "Rutgers Strike Wins Big but More is Needed to Change Higher Education," *Labor Notes*, May 11, 20232, https://labornotes.org/2023/05/rutgers-strike-wins-big-more-needed-change-higher-education#:~:-text=The%20agreement%20includes%20big%20salary,graduate%20teaching%20and%20research%20assistants.

6. This language of agitation and control comes from John W. Bowers, Donovan J. Ochs, Richard J. Jensen, and David P. Schulz, *The Rhetoric of Agitation and Control*, 3rd edition (Long Grove, IL: Waveland, 2010).

Chapter 1

1. See Miranda Fricker, *Epistemic Injustice: Power and the Ethics of Knowing* (Oxford: Oxford University Press, 2007); José Medina, *The Epistemology of Resistance: Gender and Racial Oppression, Epistemic Injustice, and Resistant Imaginations* (Oxford: Oxford University Press, 2013).
2. See Eric King Watts, *Postracial Fantasies and Zombies: On the Racist Apocalyptic Politics Devouring the World* (Berkeley: University of California Press, 2024); "'Zombies are Real': Fantasies, Conspiracies, and the Post-truth Wars," *Philosophy and Rhetoric* 51, no. 4 (2018): 441–470.
3. David Schlosberg & Lisette B. Collins, "From Environmental to Climate Justice: Climate: Climate Change and the Discourse of Environmental Justice," *WIREs Climate Change* 5 (2014): 359–375.
4. A gender-neutral alternative to "Latina" and "Latino."
5. "On Views of Race and Inequality, Blacks and Whites are Worlds Apart," Pew Research Center, June 27, 2016, https://www.pewresearch.org/social-trends/2016/06/27/1-demographic-trends-and-economic-well-being/; Rodney A. Brooks, "America's Racial Wealth Gap is Enormous and Getting Worse," *Fast Company*, August 30, 2021, https://www.fastcompany.com/90670468/americas-racial-wealth-gap-is-enormous-and-getting-worse.
6. Kenneth Shores, Ha Eun Kim, and Mela Still, "Categorical Inequalities Between Black and White Students Are Common in U.S. Schools," Brookings Institute, February 21, 2020, https://www.brookings.edu/blog/brown-center-chalkboard/2020/02/21/categorical-inequalities-between-black-and-white-students-are-common-in-us-schools-but-they-dont-have-to-be/.
7. "Wealth Matters: The Black-White Wealth Gap Before and During the Pandemic," *American Progress*, July 28, 2021, https://www.americanprogress.org/article/wealth-matters-black-white-wealth-gap-pandemic/.
8. Michelle Alexander, *The New Jim Crow* (New York: New Press, 2012); Stuart Hall, Charles Critcher, Tony Jefferson, John Clarke, and Brian Roberts, *Policing the Crisis: Mugging, the State, and Law and Order*, 35th Anniversary Edition (New York: Palgrave MacMillan, 2013); Bryan J. McCann, *The Mark of Criminality: Rhetoric, Race, and Gangsta Rap in the War-on-Crime Era* (Tuscaloosa: University of Alabama, 2017).
9. Frank Edwards, Hedwig Lee, and Michael Esposito, "Risk of Being Killed by Police Use of Force in the United States by Age, Race–ethnicity, and Sex," *Proceedings of the National Academy of Sciences of the United States*, 34 (2019), https://www.pnas.org/content/116/34/16793.
10. Dana L. Cloud, "The Rhetoric of Family Values," *Western Journal of Communication*, 62, no. 4 (1998), 387–419.
11. Sarah Banet-Weiser, Roopali Mukherjee, and Herman Gray, *Racism Postrace* (Durham: Duke University Press, 2019).
12. J. David Cisneros, "A Nation of Immigrants and a Nation of Laws: Race, Multiculturalism, and Neoliberal Exception in Barack Obama's Immigration Discourse," *Communication, Culture, and Critique* 8, no. 3 (2015): 356–375.
13. Dedrick Asante-Muhammad, Esha Kamra, Connor Sanchez, Kathy Ramirez and Rogelio Tec, "Racial Wealth Snapshot: Native Americans," National

Community Reinvestment Coalition, February 14, 2022, https://ncrc.org/racial-wealth-snapshot-native-americans/.

14. Stephanie A. Fryberg and Ariane E. Eason, "Making the Invisible Visible: Acts of Commission and Omission," *Current Directions in Psychological Science* 26, no. 6 (2017): 554–559.
15. Deepa Kumar, *Islamophobia and the Politics of Empire*, 2nd ed. Chicago: Haymarket Books, 2021).
16. Kim Parker and Cary Funk, "Gender Discrimination Comes in Many Forms for Today's Working Women," Pew Research Center, December 14, 2017, https://www.pewresearch.org/fact-tank/2017/12/14/gender-discrimination-comes-in-many-forms-for-todays-working-women/; Nikki Graf, Anna Brown, and Eileen Patten, "The Narrowing but Persistent Gender Gap in Pay," Pew Research Center, March 22, 2019, https://www.pewresearch.org/fact-tank/2019/03/22/gender-pay-gap-facts/; A.W. Geiger and Kim Parker, "For Women's History Month, a Look at Gender Gains—and Gaps—in the U.S.," Pew Research Center, March 15, 2018, https://www.pewresearch.org/fact-tank/2018/03/15/for-womens-history-month-a-look-at-gender-gains-and-gaps-in-the-u-s/.
17. Richard Reeves, "100 Years On, Politics is Where the U.S. Lags Most on Gender Equality," Brookings Institute, June 2020, https://www.brookings.edu/essay/100-years-on-politics-is-where-the-u-s-lags-most-on-gender-equality/.
18. Human Rights Campaign, "Violence Against the Transgender and Gender Non-Conforming Community in 2020," accessed August 3, 2020, https://www.hrc.org/resources/violence-against-the-trans-and-gender-non-conforming-community-in-2020.
19. Jasbir Puar, *Terrorist Assemblages: Homonationalism in Queer Times* (Durham, NC: Duke University Press, 2007); Lisa Duggan, *The New Homonormativity: The Sexual Politics of Neoliberalism* (Durham, NC: Duke University Press, 2002).
20. "Lesbian, Gay, Bisexual, and Transgender Workplace Issues," Catalyst Research, June 15, 2020, https://www.catalyst.org/research/lesbian-gay-bisexual-and-transgender-workplace-issues/.
21. Grace Hauck, "Anti-LGBTQ Hate Crimes are Rising, the FBI Says," *USA Today*, June 28, 2019, https://www.usatoday.com/story/news/2019/06/28/anti-gay-hate-crimes-rise-fbi-says-and-they-likely-undercount/1582614001/.
22. Paris Marks, "Jeff Bezos Thanks Amazon Workers for Blue Origin Launch in Revealingly Tone-Deaf Moment," *NBC News*, July 21, 2021, https://www.nbcnews.com/think/opinion/jeff-bezos-thanks-amazon-workers-blue-origin-launch-revealingly-tone-ncna1274565; Arvind Dilawar, "Amazon is the Best Argument Against Capitalism," *Pacific Standard*, February 7, 2019, https://psmag.com/ideas/amazon-is-the-best-argument-against-capitalism.
23. Geoffrey Wodtke, "Social Class and Income Inequality in the United States: Ownership, Authority, and Personal Income Distribution from 1980 to 2010," *American Journal of Sociology*, 121, no. 5 (2016): 1375–1415.
24. Katherine Schaeffer, "6 Facts About Income Inequality in the U.S.," Pew Research Center, February 7, 2020, https://www.pewresearch.org/fact-tank/2020/02/07/6-facts-about-economic-inequality-in-the-u-s/.
25. "Nine Charts About Wealth Inequality in America," Urban Institute, October 5, 2017, https://apps.urban.org/features/wealth-inequality-charts/.
26. Dedrick Asante-Muhammad, Sally Sim, and Kathy Ramirez, "Whites and the Racial Wealth Divid Snapshot," National Community Reinvestment Coalition, July 28, 2021, https://ncrc.org/whites-and-the-racial-wealth-divide-snapshot/?gclid=Cj0KCQjwtamlBhD3ARIsAARoaEy_K2uQOco90oIYCF2tqfyoFGmSgBHBCbDhoGTUQbk56VrnXfBErtoaAgrBEALw_wcB.

27. James L. Cherney, *Ableist Rhetoric: How We Know, Value, and See Disability* (University Park, PA: The Pennsylvania State University Press, 2019).
28. Keith Rosenthal, "The Political Economy of Disability," *Tempest Magazine,* June 6, 2023, https://www.tempestmag.org/2023/06/the-political-economy-of-disability/,
29. Doris James Fleischer and Frieda James, *The Disability Rights Movement: From Charity to Confrontation* (Philadelphia: Temple University press, 2011).
30. Shayda Kafai, *Crip Kinship: The Disability Justice and Art Activism of Sins Invalid* (Vancouver, CA: Arsenal Pulp Press, 2021).
31. Kimberle Crenshaw, "Mapping the Margins: Intersectionality, Identity Politics, and Violence against Women of Color," *Stanford Law Review* 43, no. 6 (1991), 1241–1299.
32. Caroline Randall Williams, "You Want a Confederate Monument? My Body is a Confederate Monument," *New York Times*, June 26, 2020, https://www.nytimes.com/2020/06/26/opinion/confederate-monuments-racism.html.

Chapter 2

1. Charles Tilly and Sidney Tarrow, *Contentious Politics*, 2nd Edition (Oxford: Oxford University Press, 2015): 7.
2. Tilly and Tarrow, *Contentious Politics*, 9.
3. John W. Bowers, Donovan J. Ochs, Richard J. Jensen, and David P. Schulz, *The Rhetoric of Agitation and Control,* 3rd Edition (Long Grove, IL: Waveland, 2010).
4. Tarrow, Contentious Politics, p. 8.
5. See Brian Doherty and Graeme Hayes, "Tactics and Strategic Action," in *The Wiley Blackwell Companion to Social Movements*, 2nd Edition, edited by David A. Snow, Sarah A. Soule, Hanspeter Kriesi, and Holly J. McCammon (Hoboken: Wiley Blackwell, 2019), 271–289.
6. Quintin Hoare, "Introduction," in Antonio Gramsci, *Prison Notebooks* (New York: International Publishers, 1971), xvii–xcvi.
7. Karl Marx, *The German Ideology* (1846), accessed September 10, 2020, https://www.marxists.org/archive/marx/works/1845/german-ideology/ch01b.htm.
8. Terry Eagleton, *Ideology: An Introduction* (London: Verso, 2007), xxii.
9. Louis Althusser, "Ideology and Ideological State Apparatuses" (1970), accessed September 10, 2020, https://www.marxists.org/reference/archive/althusser/1970/ideology.htm.
10. Marco Briziarelli and Susana Martínez Guillem, *Reviving Gramsci: Crisis, Communication, and Change* (New York: Routledge, 2016).
11. Stuart Hall, "Gramsci's Relevance for the Study of Race and Ethnicity," *Journal of Communication*, 10 (1986).
12. Antonio Gramsci, *Selections from the Prison Notebooks*, edited and translated by Quintin Hoare and Geoffrey Newell Smith (New York: International Publishers, 1971), 12.
13. Eric Foner, *Thomas Paine and Revolutionary America* (New York: Oxford University Press, 1976).
14. Perry Anderson, *The H-Word: The Peripeteia of Hegemony* (London: Verso, 2017), 1.
15. See Alan Shipman, June Edmunds, and Bryan Turner, *The New Power Elite: Inequality, Politics, and Greed* (London: Anthem Press, 2018).
16. John Dunbar, "The 'Citizens United' Decision and Why It Matters," Center for Public Integrity, October 18, 2012, https://publicintegrity.org/politics/the-citizens-united-decision-and-why-it-matters/?gclid=Cj0KCQjwnf-kBhCnARI-

sAFlg490AlCdvbNRkbNY8nmgjRsTxMrQtcgOHRA-sD-lr8OBTO-Hi25lw3EYaAjO-REALw_wcB.

17. W.E. B. Du Bois, *Black Reconstruction in America, 1860–1880* (New York: Free Press, 1998); David Roediger, *Wages of Whiteness: Race and the Making of the American Working Class* (London: Verso, 2018).
18. Bowers, Ochs, Jensen, and Shulz, *Rhetoric of Agitation*, 53–74.
19. Todd Gitlin, *The Whole World is Watching* (Berkeley: University of California Press, 2003), 27–28.
20. Nelson Blackstock, *COINTELPRO: The FBI's Secret War on Political Freedom* (New York: Pathfinder, 2000).
21. Anthony Nocella, II, Steven Best, and Peter McLaren, eds., *Academic Repression: Reflections from the Academic Industrial Complex* (Oakland: AK Press, 2010); Steven Salaita, *Uncivil Rites: Palestine and the Limits of Academic Freedom* (Chicago: Haymarket, 2015); John K. Wilson, *Patriotic Correctness: Academic Freedom and Its Enemies* (Boulder: Paradigm Publishers, 2008); Reshmi Dutt-Ballerstadt and Kakali Bhattacharya, eds., *Civility, Free Speech, and Academic Freedom in Higher Education: Faculty on the Margins* (New York: Routledge, 2021); in that volume, see Dana Cloud, "The Rhetoric of Civility as Soft Repression," 72–88.
22. Paula Chakravartty and Vasuki Nesiah, "Is This the End of Academic Freedom?", *New York Times*, April 5, 2024, https://www.nytimes.com/2024/04/05/opinion/free-speech-academic-freedom.html.
23. Anti-Defamation League, "Turning Point USA," January 25, 2023, https://www.adl.org/resources/backgrounder/turning-point-usa#:~:text=Turning%20Point%20USA%20TPUSA%20is,in%20GOP%20politics%20and%20elections.
24. Luis Fernandez, *Policing Dissent: Social Control and the Anti-Globalization Movement* (New Brunswick: Rutgers University Press, 2008), 100.
25. Fernandez, *Policing Dissent*, 33.
26. Fernandez, *Policing Dissent*, 143.
27. Constance Gordon, "Criminalizing Care: Environmental Justice Under Political and Police Repression," *Environmental Communication* 18, nos. 1–2 (2024): 138–145.
28. Antonio Gramsci, "Intellectuals and Education," in *The Antonio Gramsci Reader*, edited by David Forgacs (New York: NYU Press, 2000), 300–322; "Popular Culture," 363–378; Gramsci's point is that classes contending for power produce their own intellectuals and culture leaders to determine popular common sense; see also Eric King Watts, "'Zombies are Real': Fantasies, Conspiracies, and the Post-truth Wars," *Philosophy and Rhetoric* 51, no. 4 (2018): 441–470; see also Casey Ryan Kelly, *Abstinence Cinema: Virginity and the Rhetoric of Sexual Purity in Contemporary Film* (New Brunswick: Rutgers University Press, 2016). On the rhetoric of the religious Right, see Casey Ryan Kelly and Kristen Hoerl, "Genesis in Hyperreality: Legitimizing Disingenuous Controversy at the Creation Museum," *Argumentation and Advocacy* 48, no. 3 (2012): 123–141; Nathaniel Klemp, *The Morality of Spin: Virtue and Vice in Political Rhetoric and the Christian Right* (New York: Roman and Littlefield, 2012); Hannah Dick, "Advocating for the Right: Alliance Defending Freedom and the Rhetoric of Christian Persecution," *Feminist Legal Studies* 29, no. 3 (2021): 375–397; Matthew L. Parnell, "Rhetorics of Race and Religion on the Christian Right: Barack Obama and the War on Terror," *Quarterly Journal of Speech* 108, no. 4 (2022): 457–460; Cynthia Burack, *Sin, Sex, and Democracy: Antigay Rhetoric and the Christian Right* (Albany: State University of New York Press, 2008). Casey Ryan Kelly has argued that in such movements, a rhetoric of white masculine victim-hood that mobilizes nostalgia for a time when white men's dominance was unquestioned; see his *Apocalypse Man: The Death Drive and the Rhetoric of White Masculine Victimhood* (Columbus: Ohio State University Press, 1991); "White Pain," *Quarterly Journal of Speech* 107, no. 2 (2021): 209–233.

29. This is the insight of social reproduction theory, which posits that defining women as the domestic nurturers of families justifies the withdrawal of state support for individuals and families, the burden being placed on the private family with the justification that women should be responsible for bearing and raising families without broader social support. Regardless of the extent to which actual, embodied women fulfill that role, the discourses of women's role in reproduction serve an ideological role warranting the privatization of social responsibility—leaving the state and corporations off the hook for the provision of resources and care. See Tithi Battacharya, ed., *Social Reproduction Theory: Remapping Class, Recentering Oppression* (London: Pluto Press, 2017).
30. D.J. Mulloy, *Years of Rage: White Supremacy in the United States from the Klan to the Alt-Right* (New York: Rowman and Littlefield, 2021).
31. Mulloy, *Years of Rage*, 69.
32. Mulloy, *Years of Rage*, 184.
33. Nathan Crick, ed., *The Rhetoric of Fascism* (Tuscaloosa: University of Alabama Press, 2022), 5.
34. It is important not to be hyperbolic about any potential fascist threat Trump, a leader of a populist backlash, poses. While his rhetoric fits the rhetorical form and his base is in the middle class, his methods—employing the regular structures of elected office rather than militarizing the state—locates him in a position between more moderate Republicans and the far Right. See Daniel Steinmetz-Jenkins, "Making Sense of the Fascism Debate," *The Nation* (March 19, 2024), https://www.thenation.com/article/politics/fascism-debate/; Neil Davidson, "The Hard-Right Today: Fascists and Non-Fascists" (July 2019), Marxists Internet Archive, https://www.marxists.org/history/etol/writers/davidson/2019/07/hardright.html. Davidson writes, "Fascism is not defined simply by its recourse to extra-parliamentary or illegal activity, but by their purpose: a project of transformation which seeks the creation of a 'new' society, the final realisation of a national destiny which had hitherto been denied. But to achieve this the people—inevitably conceived in racial terms—themselves must be purified, must prove themselves worthy of the world which the fascists hope to bring into being. Fascism is never uncomplicatedly the 'tool of monopoly capitalism': it is rather that the goals of fascism overlap at certain points with that of capital, notably in the crushing of a perceived working-class threat and pursuance of imperialist goals."
35. Stanley G. Payne, *A History of Fascism 1914–1945* (Madison: University of Wisconsin Press, 2018); Martin Kitchen, "Fascism and the Capitalist System: A Marxist View," in *The Fascism Reader*, edited by Aristotle A. Kallis (New York: Routledge, 2003), 60; see also Robert O. Paxton, *The Anatomy of Fascism* (New York: Penguin, 2005).
36. Kitchen, "Fascism and the Capitalist System." See also Geoff Eley, "Fascism as the Product of 'Crisis,'" in Kallis, *Fascism Reader*, 129–136.
37. Antonio Gramsci, "Fascist Reaction and Communist Strategy, 1924–26," in *The Antonio Gramsci Reader*, edited by David Forgacs, pages 135–185 (New York: New York University Press, 1999), 138. Gramsci, "Fascist Reaction," 147–48; *contra* Alberto Toscano, *Late Fascism* (London: Verso, 2023), who argues 1) that we can understand fascism as a mass-psychological phenomenon and 2) Black Marxist and Black revolutionary scholars and activists have called our attention to the specific meaning of fascism today in the context of a specifically *racial* capitalism, in which the policing and incarceration of Black people represents a fascism not only concerned with staving off socialist revolution through an embrace of the state but also disciplining Black radicalism since the 1960s and 1970s in a form that denies the authority of the state.
38. Gramsci, "Fascist Reaction," 148.
39. Antonio Gramsci, *Prison Notebooks*, 235.

40. Marco Fonseca, *Gramsci's Critique of Civil Society* (New York: Routledge, 2016),18.
41. Peter D. Thomas, *The Gramscian Moment* (Chicago: Haymarket Books, 2009),161.
42. Gramsci, *Prison Notebooks*, 5–25; Thomas, *Gramscian Moment*, 406–417; Mary E. Triece, "The Mother Tongue as Back-Talk: Resisting Racism in Congressional Hearings," in Michael G. Lacy and Mary E. Triece, eds., *Race and Hegemonic Struggle in the United States: Pop Culture, Politics, and Protest* (Madison: Fairleigh Dickinson University Press, 2014), 103–120; Anna M. Young, "The Public Call of the Joshua Generation: Answering the Gramscian Call," in Michael G. Lacy and Mary E. Triece, eds., *Race and Hegemonic Struggle in the United States: Pop Culture, Politics, and Protest* (Madison: Fairleigh Dickinson University Press, 2014), 197–216.
43. Stuart Hall, "Studying the Conjuncture" [video lecture], Media Education Foundation, 2021, https://www.youtube.com/watch?v=bHphtlnNtB0.
44. Stuart Hall, "Gramsci's Relevance for the Study of Race and Ethnicity," *Journal of Communication Inquiry* 10, no. 2 (1986): 5–27.
45. Dennis Mumby, "The Problem of Hegemony: Rereading Gramsci for Organizational Communication Studies," *Western Journal of Communication*, 61, no. 4 (1997): 343–375, p. 348; see also Dana L. Cloud, *We Are the Union: Democratic Unionism and Dissent at Boeing* (Urbana: University of Illinois Press, 2011).
46. Shinsuke Eguchi, "Hegemonic Masculinity: The Rhetorical Strategy of 'Straight-Acting' Among Gay Men," *Journal of Intercultural Communication Research*, 38, no. 3 (2009): 193–209, pp. 195–196; Michael G. Lacy and Mary E. Triece, *Race and Hegemonic Struggle in the United States: Pop Culture, Politics, and Protest* (Madison: Fairleigh Dickinson University Press, 2014).
47. Marco Briziarelli and Susan Martínez Guillem, *Reviving Gramsci: Crisis, Communication, and Change* (New York: Routledge, 2016); see also Marco Briziarelli, "To 'Feel' and to 'Understand' Political Struggle: The National-Popular Rhetoric of Podemos," *Journal of Communication* 40, no. 3 (2016): 287–304; Dana L. Cloud, "The Critique of Domination and the Critique of Freedom: A Gramscian Perspective," *International Journal of Communication*, 14 (2020): 836.
48. Briziarelli and Martínez Guillem, *Reviving Gramsci*, 3.

Chapter 3

1. For a thorough and current introduction to all of these questions, see David A. Snow, Sarah A. Soule, Hanspeter Kriesi, and Holly J. McCammon, *The Wiley Blackwell Companion to Social Movements*, 2nd edition (Oxford: Wiley Blackwell, 2019).
2. Sidney Tarrow, *Power in Movement*, 3rd Edition (Cambridge: Cambridge University Press, 2011): 6.
3. Tarrow, *Power in Movement*, 8–9.
4. Charles Tilly and Sidney Tarrow, *Contentious Politics*, 2nd Edition (Oxford: Oxford University Press, 2015): 3.
5. Tarrow, *Power in Movement*, 24. See also David A. Snow, Sarah A. Soule, Hanspeter Kriesi, and Holly J. McCammon, "Introduction: Mapping and Opening Up the Terrain," in *The Wiley Blackwell Companion to Social Movements*, 5, 10.
6. See Doug McAdam and Sidney Tarrow, "The Political Context of Social Movements," in *The Wiley Blackwell Companion to Social Movements*, 20–21.
7. Tilly and Tarrow, *Contentious Politics*, 39–56; Charles Tilly, *From Mobilization to Revolution* (Reading, MA: Addison-Wesley, 1978), 151.
8. Tilly and Tarrow, *Contentious Politics*, 7.
9. Tarrow, *Power in Movement*, 215.

10. David Meyer and Sidney Tarrow, eds., *The Resistance: The Dawn of the Anti-Trump Movement* (New York: Oxford, 2018).
11. See Alice Echols, *Daring to Be Bad* (Minneapolis: University of Minnesota Press, 1989).
12. Carol Hanisch, "The Personal is Political," in *Notes from the Second Year: Radical Feminism*, edited by Shulamith Firestone and Anne Koedt (New York: Women's Liberation Movement, 1970), 76–77.
13. Firestone and Koedt, *Notes*.
14. Roxane Gay, "Fifty Years Ago, Protestors Took on the Miss America Pageant and Electrified the Feminist Movement," *Smithsonian Magazine*, January 2018, https://www.smithsonianmag.com/history/fifty-years-ago-protestors-took-on-miss-america-pageant-electrified-feminist-movement-180967504/.
15. *The Ladder*, newsletter of the Daughters of Bilitis, is archived at the ONE Archives at the University of Southern California. https://one.usc.edu/archive-location/ladder.
16. Kristen Hogan, *The Feminist Bookstore Movement: Lesbian Antiracism and Feminist Accountability* (Durham, NC: Duke University Press, 2016).
17. See Frances Beal, "Double Jeopardy: To Be Black and Female," in *Radical Feminism: A Documentary Reader*, edited by Barbara A. Crow (New York: New York University Press, 2000), 154–162; Cellestine Ware, "The Relationship of Black Women to the Women's Liberation Movement," in Crow, *Radical Feminism Reader*, 98–112.
18. Susan Faludi, *Backlash: The Undeclared War Against American Women* (New York: Crown, 1991).
19. Gerald F. Davis, Doug McAdam, W. Richard Scott, and Mayer N. Zald, Eds., *Social Movements and Organization Theory* (Cambridge: Cambridge University Press, 2005), 5.
20. Davis et al., *Social Movements*, 15.
21. Davis,et al., *Social Movements*, 16. See also Edward T. Walker and Andrew W. Martin, "Social Movement Organizations," in *The Wiley Blackwell Companion to Social Movements*, 167–184.
22. See Marshall Ganz and Elizabeth McKenna, "Bringing Leadership Back In," in *The Wiley Blackwell Companion to Social Movements*, 185–202. They discuss how social movement leadership has relational, narrative, strategic, structural, and collective action dimensions.
23. Gail T. Fairhurst and Stacey L. Connaughton, "Leadership: A Communicative Perspective," *Leadership* 10, no. 1 (2014): 7–35.
24. Zald and McCarthy, 164.
25. Gerald F. Davis, Doug McAdam, W. Richard Scott, and Mayer N. Zald, *Social Movements and Organization Theory* (Cambridge, UK: Cambridge University Press, 2005), 6.
26. Ibid, 45.
27. John L. Campbell, "Where Do We Stand? Common Mechanisms in Organizations and Social Movements Research," in Davis et al., p. 63.
28. Alson Morris and Carol McClurg Mueller, *Frontiers in Social Movement Theory* (New Haven: Yale, 1992).
29. See Doug McAdam, "Culture and Social Movements," in *Social Movements: From Ideology to Identity*, edited by Enrique Laraña, Hank Johnston, and Joseph R. Gusfield (Philadelphia: Temple University Press, 2009), 36–57.
30. Hank Johnston and John A. Noakes, *Frames of Protest: Social Movements and the Framing Perspective* (Lanham, MD: Rowman and Littlefield, 2005), 2.

31. William A. Gamson, "The Social Psychology of Collective Action," in Morris and McClurg Mueller, *Frontiers* (53–76), p. 57.
32. Gamson, "Social Psychology."
33. James Jasper, *Protest: A Cultural Introduction to Social* Movements (Cambridge: Polity, 2014), 115
34. Jasper, *Protest*, 123.
35. See Michelle Goldberd, "What is a Woman?", *New Yorker* (July 18, 2014), https://www.newyorker.com/magazine/2014/08/04/woman-2.
36. Quoted in Johnston and Noakes, *Frames*, 3.
37. Robert D. Benford and David A. Snow, "Framing Processes and Social Movements: An Overview and Assessment," *Annual Review of Sociology* 26 (2000): 611–639; David A. Snow, Rens Vliegenthart, and Pauline Ketelaars, "The Framing Perspective on Social Movements: Its Conceptual Roots and Architecture," in *The Wiley Blackwell Companion to Social Movements*, 392–410; Cristina Flesher Fominaya, "Collective Identity in Social Movements," in *The Wiley Blackwell Companion to Social Movements*, 429–445; Robert M. Entman, *Projections of Power: Framing News, Public Opinion, and U.S. Foreign Policy* (Chicago: University of Chicago Press, 2004).
38. Entman, *Projecting Power*, 5.
39. Benford and Snow, "Framing Processes," 615.
40. William Gamson, *Talking Politics* (Cambridge: Cambridge University Press, 1992), 7.
41. Gamson, *Talking Politics*.
42. SCUM, "The SCUM Manifesto," in *Radical Feminism: A Documentary Reader*, edited by Barbara A. Crow (New York: New York University Press, 2000/1967), 201–222.
43. Benford and Snow, "Framing Processes," 624.
44. Stephen Valocchi, "Collective Action Frames in the Gay Liberation Movement," in Johnston and Noakes, *Frames of Protest*, 53–68.
45. Doug McAdam, "The Framing Function of Movement Tactics: Strategic Dramaturgy in the American Civil Rights Movement," in Doug McAdam, John D. McCarthy, and Mayer Zald, *Comparative Perspectives*, 34.
46. Carol Mueller, "Conflict Networks and the Origins of Women's Liberation," in *New Social Movements*, edited by Enrique Laraña, Hank Johnston, and Joseph R. Gusfield (Philadelphia: Temple University Press, 2009), 235–263.
47. Mueller, "Conflict Networks," 251.
48. Carol Hanisch, "The Personal Is Political," in Crow, *Radical Feminism Reader*, 113–116.
49. Gamson, *Talking Politics*, 52.
50. Donatella Della Porta and Mario Diana, *Social Movements: An Introduction* (Malden, MA: Blackwell, 2006), 89–113; see also Sheldon Stryker, Timothy J. Owens, and Robert W. White, eds., *Self, Identity, and Social Movements* (Minneapolis: University of Minnesota Press, 2000).
51. Lori Britt and David Heise, "From Shame to Pride in Identity Politics," in Stryker et al., 252–270.
52. Verta Taylor and Nancy Whittier, "Collective Identity in Social Movement Communities," in Morris and McClurg Mueller, 104–130, 107.
53. Taylor and Whittier, "Collective Identity," 114.
54. Joshua Gamson, "Must Identity Movements Self-Destruct? A Queer Dilemma," *Social Problems* 42 (1995): 390.
55. Gamson, "Must Identity Movements."

56. Verta Taylor, "Emotions and Identity in Women's Self-Help Movements" in *Self, Identity, and Social Movements*, edited by Sheldon Stryker, Timothy J. Owens, and Robert W. White (Minneapolis: University of Minnesota, 2000), 271–300. See also Justin Van Ness and Erika Summers-Effler, "Emotions and Social Movements," in *The Wiley Blackwell Companion to Social Movements*, 411–428.
57. Taylor, V. (2000). Emotions and identity in women's self-help movements. In S. Stryker, T. J. Owens, & R. W. White (Eds.), *Self, identity, and social movements* (pp. 271–299). University of Minnesota Press.
58. Helena Flam and Debra King, eds., *Emotions and Social Movements* (New York: Routledge, 2005), 3.
59. Lory Britt and David Heise, "From Shame to Pride in Identity Politics," in Stryker, et al., *Self, Identity*, 252–270.
60. Jasper, *Protest*, 9.
61. Jasper, *Protest*, 64.
62. Jasper, *Protest*, 110.
63. Radicalesbians, "The Woman-Identified Woman," at *History is a Weapon* (1970), https://www.historyisaweapon.com/defcon1/radicalesbianswoman.html.
64. Brian Massumi, *Parables for the Virtual: Movement, Affect, Sensation* (Durham, NC: Duke University Press, 2002); Sarah Ahmed, *Cultural Politics of Emotion* (New York: Routledge, 2004); John Protevi, *Political Affect: Connecting the Social and the Somatic* (Minneapolis: University of Minnesota Press, 2009).
65. Antonio R. Damasio, *The Feeling of What Happens: Body and Emotion in the Making of Consciousness* (New York: Harcourt Brace, 1999).
66. Teresa Brennan, *The Transmission of Affect* (Ithaca: Cornell, 2004).
67. Jeff Goodwin, James Jasper, and F. A. Polletta, Eds., *Passionate Politics (Chicago, University of Chicago, 2001).*
68. Ron Eyerman and Andrew Jamison, *Music and Social Movements: Mobilizing Traditions in the Twentieth Century* (Cambridge: Cambridge University Press, 1998); Mark Mattern, *Acting in Concert: Music, Community, and Political Action* (New Brunswick: Rutgers, 1998).
69. Dana L. Cloud and Kathleen Eaton Feyh, "Reason in Revolt: Emotional Fidelity and Working-Class Standpoint in the 'Internationale,'" *Rhetoric Society Quarterly* 45 (2015): 307.
70. Cloud and Feyh, "Reason in Revolt."
71. Erin Rand, *Reclaiming Queer: Activist and Academic Rhetorics of Resistance* (Tuscaloosa, University of Alabama Press, 2014); "'What One Voice Can Do': Civic Pedagogy and Choric Collectivity at Camp Courage," *Text and Performance Quarterly* 34, no. 1 (2014): 28–51.
72. David A. Snow and Catherine Corrigall-Brown, "Falling on Deaf Ears: Confronting the Prospect of Nonresonant Frames," in *Rhyming Hope and History*, edited by David Croteau, William Hoynes, and Carlotte Ryan (Minneapolis: University of Minnesota Press, 2005), 224.
73. Snow and Corrigall-Brown, "Falling on Deaf Ears," 225.
74. Mary C. Burke and Mary Bernstein, "How the Right Usurped the Queer Agenda: Frame Co-Optation in Political Discourse," *Sociological Forum* 29, no. 4 (2014): 830–850.
75. Todd Gitlin, *The Whole World is Watching: Mass Media ion the Making and Unamking of the New Left* (Berkeley: University of California Press, 2003), 7.
76. Kristen E. Hoerl, *The Bad Sixties: Hollywood Memories of the Counterculture, Anti-war, and Black Power Movements* (Jackson: University Press of Mississippi, 2018).

77. GLAAD, "A Beginner's Guide and Brief History of LGBTQ Rights Cases in the U.S. Supreme Court," August 10 2022, https://glaad.org/beginner-guide-and-brief-history-lgbtq-rights-cases-united-states-supreme-court/?gad_source=1&gclid=CjwKCAjwoa2xBhACEiwA1sb1BM2bVPY3pTSYIkpKT-g4KGDXI_ip3RZY56gLpTSPOsbyWhdn2ec3x7BoC9A8QAvD_BwE
78. Charles Tilly, *European Revolutions 1492–1982* (Oxford, UK: Oxford University Press, 1995); Timothy Wickham-Crowley, *Guerillas and Revolution in Latin America* (Princeton: Princeton University Press, 2018); Theda Skocpol, *Social Revolutions in the Modern World* (Cambridge: Cambridge University Press, 1994).
79. Charles Tilly, *From Mobilization to Revolution* (New York: McGraw Hill, 1978), 193; Charles Tilly, *Politics of Collective Violence* (Cambridge: Cambridge University Press, 2003).
80. See Jack A. Goldstone and Daniel P. Ritter, "Revolution and Social Movements," in *The Wiley Blackwell Companion to Social Movements*, 682–697.
81. See David A. Snow, Rens Vliegenthart, and Pauline Ketelaars, "The Framing Perspective on Social Movements: Its Conceptual Roots and Architecture, in Snow et al., *Wiley Blackwell Companion*, 447–514.
82. Sidney Tarrow, *The New Transnational Activism* (Cambridge: Cambridge University Press, 2005), 6.
83. See also Donatella Della Porta, *Globalization From Below* (Minneapolis: University of Minnesota Press, 2006); John A. Guidry, Michael D. Kennedy, and Mayer M. Zald, *Globalizations and Social Movements* (Ann Arbor: University of Michigan Press, 2000); Neva Welton and Linda Wolf, *Global Uprising* (Gabriola Island, BC: New Society Publications, 2001).
84. See David Meyer and Sidney Tarrow, *The Social Movement Society* (Lanham: Rowman and Littlefield, 1998); Laraña et al., *New Social Movements*; Barbara Meil Hobson, *Recognition Struggles and Social Movements* (Cambridge: Cambridge University Press, 2003); Alberto Melucci *Challenging Codes: Collective Action in the Information Age* (Cambridge: Cambridge University Press, 1996); Su H. Lee, *Debating New Social Movements* (Lanham: University Press of America, 2007); César Augusto Rossatto, *Manifesto for New social Movements* (Charlotte, NC: Information Age Publishing, 2019).
85. See Richard Flacks, "The Party's Over—So What is to be Done?", in Laraña et al., *New Social Movements,* 330–356.
86. Nancy Fraser, *Justice Interruptus: Critical Reflections on the "Postsocialist" Condition* (New York: Routledge, 1997).

Chapter 4

1. The 20th-century rhetoric scholars who did work on social movements were not the first in our field to do so. The protests of the 1930s also inspired work by scholars working early in the field of rhetorical studies, but the decline in agitation between the Second World War and the 1960s led to a decline in scholarly attention.
2. Herbert W. Simons, "Requirements, Problems, and Strategies: A Theory of Persuasion for Social Movements," *Quarterly Journal of Speech* 56, no. 1 (1970): 1–11.
3. Michael Calvin McGee, "'Social Movement': Phenomenon or Meaning? *Central States Speech Journal* 31, no. 4 (1980): 233–44; Michael Calvin McGee, "Social Movement as Meaning," *Central States Speech Journal* 34, no. 1 (1983): 74–77; Christina R. Foust, Amy Pason, and Katie Zittlow Rogness, *What Democracy Looks Like: The Rhetoric of Social Movements and Counterpublics* (Tuscaloosa: University of Alabama Press, 2017); Raymie McKerrow, "Social Movement

Scholarship: A Retrospective/Prospective Review," in Foust, Pason, and Zittlow Rogness, *What Democracy Looks Like*, 29–45; Christina R. Foust, "Social Movement Rhetoric: A Critical Genealogy, Post-1980," in Foust, Pason, and Zittlow Rogness, *What Democracy Looks Like*, 46–74.

4. See the similar account here by Nathan Crick, ed., *The Rhetoric of Social Movements: Networks, Power, and New Media* (New York: Routledge, 2021), 13.
5. Schulman, S. (2021). *Let the record show.* Farrar, Straus, and Giroux.
6. See Sarah Schulman, *Let the Record Show: A Political History of ACT UP New York, 1987–1993* (New York: Farrar, Strauss, & Giroux, 2021).
7. Leland M. Griffin, "The Rhetoric of Historical Movements," *Quarterly Journal of Speech* 38 (1952): 184–188. Reprinted in Charles E. Morris, III and Stephen Howard Browne, *Readings on the Rhetoric of Social Protest*, 2nd edition (State College, PA: Strata, 2006), 10.
8. Simons, "Requirements, Problems, and Strategies."
9. Charles J. Stewart, "A Functional Approach to the Rhetoric of Social Movements," *Central States Speech Journal* 31, no. 4 (1980): 298–305, reprinted in Morris and Browne, *Readings*, 151–159; Charles J. Stewart, *Persuasion and Social Movements*, 4th edition (Prospect Heights, IL: Waveland, 2001).
10. John Waite Bowers, Donovan J. Ochs, Richard J. Jensen, and David P. Schulz, *The Rhetoric of Agitation and Control* (Long Grove, IL: Waveland, 2010).
11. Schulman, *Let the Record Show*, 99–135
12. Schulman, *Let the Record Show*, 136–168.
13. Schulman, *Let the Record Show*, 169.
14. Schulman, *Let the Record Show*, 227–272.
15. Schulman, *Let the Record Show*, 606.
16. Griffin, "Rhetoric of Historical Movements."
17. Franklyn S. Haiman, "The Rhetoric of the Streets: Some Legal and Ethical Considerations," *Quarterly Journal of Speech* 55, no. 2 (1967): 99–114, reprinted in Morris and Browne, *Readings*, 14–27.
18. See Amani Husain, "*No Hay Vida Sin Libertad: Testimonios* of Resistance from the #Hutto27 Hunger Strikers," *Women's Studies in Communication* 44, no. 3 (2021): 259–277, p. 259; Gerard A. Hauser, *Prisoners of Conscience: Moral Vernaculars of Political Agency* (Columbia, SC: University of South Carolina Press, 2012), 122–159.
19. Emma Graham-Harrison, "Gaza Death Toll Passes 34,000 as Israel and Iran Missile Strikes Grab Global Attention," *The Guardian*, April 20, 2024, https://www.theguardian.com/world/2024/apr/20/gaza-death-toll-passes-34000-israel-iran. For more information about the history and conflict of this context, see Noam Chomsky and Ilan Pappé, *On Palestine* (Chicago: Haymarket Boos, 2015); Ali Abunimah, *The Battle for Justice in Palestine* (Chicago: Haymarket Books, 2014); Jessica Anderson, Aline Batarshey, and Yosra El Gazzar, *Visualizing Palestine* (Chicago: Haymarket Books, 2024); Sean Jacobs and Jon Soske, *Apartheid Israel: The Politics of an Analogy* (Chicago: Haymarket Books, 2015); "Israel Gaza War: History of the Conflict Explained," *BBC* (April 5, 2024), https://www.bbc.com/news/newsbeat-44124396.
20. Robert L. Scott and Donald K. Smith, "The Rhetoric of Confrontation," *Quarterly Journal of Speech* 55, no. 1 (1969): 1–8, reprinted in Morris and Browne, *Readings*, 14–27.
21. Robert S. Cathcart, "Movements: Confrontation as Rhetorical Form," *Southern Speech Communication Journal* 43, no. 3 (1978): 233–247, reprinted in Morris and Browne, *Readings*, 95–103.

22. Theodore Otto Windt, "The Diatribe: Last Resort for Protest," *Quarterly Journal of Speech* 58, no. 1 (1972): 1–14, reprinted in Morris and Browne, *Readings*, 58–69.
23. Richard B. Gregg, "The Ego-Function of the Rhetoric of Protest," *Philosophy and Rhetoric* 4, no. 2 (1971): 71–91, reprinted in Morris and Browne, *Readings*, 45–57.
24. For example, David Zarefsky urged the historical study of specific instances of change-oriented rhetoric; David Zarefsky, "A Skeptical View of Movement Studies," *Central States Speech Journal* 31, no. 4 (1980): 245–254. Others focused their attention on the constitutive rhetoric of movements, less interested in the organization and instrumental force of movements and more in the symbolic process of creating shared conceptions of reality both internal and external to movements themselves. Sillars rejects cause-effect linearity and, intention-based critique; he sees movement as something that is made through critical compilation and observations of unfolding rhetorical events on the part of the critic. What "counts" as a movement or as movement in general becomes subjective for Sillars. Malcolm O. Sillars, "Defining Social Movements Rhetorically: Casting the Widest Net," *Southern Speech Communication Journal* 43, no. 1 (1980):17–31, reprinted in Morris and Browne, *Readings*, 106–114.
25. Alberto Melucci, *Challenging Codes: Collective Action in the Information Age* (Cambridge, UK: Cambridge University Press, 1996).
26. Constance Gordon, "Criminalizing Care: Environmental Justice Under Political and Police Repression," *Environmental Communication* 18, nos. 1–2 (2024): 138–145.
27. Michael Calvin McGee, "'Social Movement': Phenomenon or Meaning?" *Central States Speech Journal* 46, no. 4 (1980): 233–244, reprinted in Morris and Browne, *Readings*, 115–126.
28. McGee, "'Social Movement,'" 122.
29. Bitzer, L. F. (1968). The rhetorical situation. *Philosophy & Rhetoric*, *1*(1), 1–14.

Chapter 5

1. See Raymie McKerrow, "Social Movement Scholarship: A Retrospective/Prospective Review," in *What Democracy Looks Like: The Rhetoric of Social Movements and Counterpublics*, edited by Christina R. Foust, Amy Pason, and Zittlow Rogness (Tuscaloosa: University of Alabama Press, 2017), 29–45.
2. Christina R. Foust, *Transgression as a Mode of Resistance: Rethinking Social Movement in an Era of Corporate Globalization* (New York: Lexington Books, 2010). Nathan Crick, ed., *The Rhetoric of Social Movements: Networks, Power, and New Media* (Milton: Taylor and Francis, 2020).
3. Often employing an intersectional lens, rhetoric scholars have produced important articles and books on particular figures and movements. To list a number among many others, we have Stephen Browne's book-length study of Angelina Grimké, Susan Zaeske's work on women's petitions, Lisa Corrigan's work on Black movements in prisons, Lisa Flores' attention to Chicana feminism and immigration-related movements, Belinda Stillion-Southard's accounting of the National Woman's Party, Darrel Wanzer-Serrano's archival and critical work on the Young Lords movement, Robert Gutierrez-Perez's research on Latine queer worldmaking, and Sarah J. Jackson, Moya Bailey, and Brooke Foucault Welles' work on #hashtagactivism. Dan Brouwer's work focuses on queer movements around HIV/AIDS; Tiara Na'puti's research and advocacy on Indigenous (specifically Chamoru) resistance to militarism and colonialism; Catalina de Onís' work on movements for climate justice and energy sovereignty in Puerto Rico; and Phaedra Pezzullo's corpus of scholarship on environmental and climate justice advocacy. One example of this emphasis is Darryl Enck-Wanzer's study of the Young Lords, a New York Puerto Rican collective. Among other actions, the Young Lords built and burned massive barricades of trash cans to challenge "inequitable

sanitation practices." See Darryl Wanzer-Serrano, *The New York Young Lords and the Struggle for Liberation* (Philadelphia: Temple University Press, 2015); Stephen H. Browne, *Angelina Grimké: Rhetoric, Identity, and the Radical Imagination* (East Lansing; Michigan State University Press); Susan Zaeske, *Signatures of Citizenship: Petitioning, Antislavery, and Women's Political Identity* (Chapel Hill: University of North Carolina Press, 2003); Lisa A. Flores, "Creating Discursive Space Through a Rhetoric of Difference: Chicana Feminists Craft a Homeland," *Quarterly Journal of Speech* 82, no. 2 (1996): 142–156; Lisa M. Corrigan, *Prison Power: How Prison Influenced the Movement for Black Liberation* (Jackson: University Press of Mississippi, 2016); Daniel C. Brouwer, "Counterpublicity and Corporeality in HIV/AIDS Zines," *Critical Studies in Mass Communication* 22, no. 5 (2005): 351–371; Belinda A. Stillion Southard, *Militant Citizenship: Rhetorical Strategies of the National Woman's Party*, 1913–1920 (College Station: Texas A&M University Press, 2011); Robert Gutierrez-Perez, "A Return to *El Mundo Zurdo*: Anzaldúan Approaches to Queer of Color Worldmaking and the Violence of Intersectional Heteronormativity," *Women's Studies in Communication* 43, no. 4 (2020): 384–399; Sarah J. Jackson, Moya Bailey, Brooke Foucault Welles, *#HashtagActivism: Networks of Race and Gender Justice* (The MIT Press, 2020); Tiara N'aputi, "Militarization and Resistance from Guåhan: Protecting and Defending Pågat," *American Quarterly* 67, no. 3 (2015), 837–858; Catalina M. de Onís, *Energy Islands: Metaphors of Power, Extractivism, and Justice in Puerto Rico* (Berkeley: University of California Press, 2021); Phaedra C. Pezzullo, *Toxic Tourism: Rhetorics of Pollution, Travel, and Environmental Justice* (Tuscaloosa: The University of Alabama Press, 2007).

4. Foust et al., *What Democracy Looks Like*.
5. See Emily Winderman, "Anger's Volumes: Rhetorics of Amplification and Aggregation in #MeToo." *Women's Studies in Communication* 42, no. 3 (2019): 327–46.
6. See Angela J. Aguayo, *Documentary Resistance: Social Change and Participatory Media* (New York: Oxford University Press, 2019); Sarah J. Jackson, Moya Bailey, and Brooke Foucault Welles, *Hashtag Activism: Networks of Race and Gender Justice* (New York: MIT Press, 2020).
7. See Dana L. Cloud and Kathleen Eaton Feyh. "Reason in Revolt: Emotional Fidelity and Working Class Standpoint in the 'Internationale,'" *Rhetoric Society Quarterly* 45, no. 4 (2015): 300–323; Emerson (E) Cram, "Archival Ambivalence and Sensory Memory: Generating Queer Intimacies in the Settler Colonial Archive," *Communication and Critical/Cultural Studies* 13, no. 2 (2016): 109–129; Erin J. Rand, "Gay Pride and its Queer Discontents: ACT UP and the Political Deployment of Affect," *Quarterly Journal of Speech* 98, no. 1 (2012): 75–80.
8. Kimberle Crenshaw, "Mapping the Margins: Intersectionality, Identity Politics, and Violence against Women of Color," Stanford Law Review 43, no. 6 (1991):1241–1299.; Patricia Hill Collins, *Intersectionality as Critical Social Theory* (Durham: Duke University Press).
9. Jesus Cisneros and Julia Guttierez, "'What Does It Mean to Be Undocuqueer?' Exploring (il)Legibility within the Intersection of Gender, Sexuality, and Immigration," *QED: Journal in Queer Worldmaking*, 5, no. 1 (2018): 84–102.
10. Ruth Wilson Gilmore, *Change Everything: Racial Capitalism and the Case for Abolition* (Chicago: Haymarket Books, 2023); Cedric Robinson, *Black Marxism: The Making of the Black Radical Tradition* (Chapel Hill: The University of North Carolina Press, 1983).
11. Susan Koshy, Lisa Marie Cacho, Jodi A. Byrd, and Brian Jordan Jefferson (eds.), *Colonial Racial Capitalism* (Durham: Duke University Press, 2022).
12. Amani Husain, *No Hay Vida Sin Libertad: Testimonios* of Resistance from the #Hutto27 Hunger Strikers," *Women's Studies in Communication* 44, no. 3 (2021): 259–277.

13. Stacey K. Sowards, *Sí, Ella Puede!: The Rhetorical Legacy of Dolores Huerta and the United Farm Workers* (Austin: University of Texas Press, 2019).
14. See Gutierrez-Perez, "Return."
15. María Lugones, "Playfulness, 'World'-Travelling, and Loving Perception," *Hypatia* 2, no. 2 (1987): 3–19. See also her *Pilgrimages/Pregrinajes: Theorizing Coalition Against Multiple Oppressions* (New York: Roman and Littlefield, 2003). There she talks about engaging loving world-traveling across difference in the formation of coalitions among diverse communities.
16. See, for example, the work of Joshua Trey Barnett, *Mourning in the Anthropocene: Ecological Grief and Earthly Co-Existence* (East Lansing: Michigan State University Press); Sowards, "Sí, Ella Puede!" Rhetorical Agency as *Haciendo Caras* and Differential Consciousness Through Lens of Gender, Race, Ethnicity, and Class: An Examination of Dolores Huerta's Rhetoric," *Communication Theory* 20, no. 2 (2010): 223–247; Charles E. Morris III and Thomas K. Nakayama, "Paying Mind to GLBTQ Pasts," *QED: A Journal in GLBTQ Worldmaking* 1, no. 2 (2014): v-vii. This volume includes studies of various efforts to reclaim past events and archives to build community and struggle in the present, including Gerard Koskovich, "Displaying the Queer Past: Purposes, Publics, and Possibilities at the GLBT History Museum," 61–78; K.J. Rawson, "Transgender Worldmaking in Cyberspace: Historical Activism on the Internet," 38–60; Darnell L. Moore, Beryl Satter, Timothy. Stewart-Winter, and Whitney Strub, "A Community's Response to the Problem of Invisibility: The Queer Newark Oral History Project," 1–14.
17. Stefano Harney and Fred Moten, *The Undercommons: Fugitive Planning and Black Study* (New York: Autonomedia, 2013).
18. See Karma R. Chávez, "Counter-Public Enclaves and Understanding the Function of Rhetoric in Social Movement Coalition-Building," *Communication Quarterly* 59, no. 1 (2011): 1–18.
19. Walter Fisher, *Human Communication and Narration: Toward a Philosophy of Reason, Value, and Action* (Columbia, SC: University of South Carolina Press, 1989).
20. Carole Blair and Neil Michel, "The AIDS Memorial Quilt and the Contemporary Culture of Public Commemoration," *Rhetoric and Public* Affairs 10, no. 4 (2007): 596–626; Charles E. Morris, III, ed., *Remembering the AIDS Quilt* (East Lansing: Michigan State University Press, 2011); Erin J. Rand, "Repeated Remembrance: Commemorating the AIDS Quilt and Resuscitating the Mourned Subject," *Rhetoric and Public Affairs* 10, no. 4 (2007): 655–680; Daniel C. Brouwer, "From San Francisco to Atlanta and Back Again: Ideologies of Mobility in the AIDS Quilt's Search for a Homeland," *Rhetoric and Public Affairs* 10, no. 5 (2007): 701–721; Bryant Keith Alexander and Charles E. Morris, III, "Rhetorics of Loss and Living: Adding New Panels to the AIDS Quilt as an Act of Eulogy," in Morris, *Remembering*, 189; Cleve Jones, "A Vision of the Quilt," *Rhetoric and Public Affairs* 10, no. 5 (2007): 575–594; Gust A. Yep, "The Politics of Loss and Its Remains in 'Common Threads: Stories from the Quilt," *Rhetoric and Public Affairs* 10, no. 5 (2007): 681–699.
21. Nino Testa, "Duane Puryear and the Quilt Panel," *The Dallas Way*, September 19, 2021, http://www.thedallasway.org/stories/written/2021/9/19/duane-puryears-and-the-quilt-panel.
22. Quilt Panel, Leonard P. Matlovich," in Victoria Law, "The AIDS Quilt: A Photo Gallery, *Esquire*, December 1, 2016, https://www.esquire.com/lifestyle/g3077/aids-quilt-photo-gallery/.
23. See Lester C. Olson, Cara A. Finnegan, and Diane S. Hope, *Visual Rhetoric: A Reader in Communication and American Culture* (Los Angeles: Sage, 2008); Ionana Literat and Anne Balsamo, "Stitching the Future of the AIDS Quilt: The Cultural Work of Digital Memorials, *Visual Communication Quarterly* 21, no. 3 (2014):

138–149; Massimo Mariani, *What Images Really Tell Us: Visual Rhetoric in Art, Graphic Design, and Advertisement* (Barcelona: Hoaki Books, 2019); Kevin Michael DeLuca, *Image Politics: The New Rhetoric of Environmental Activism* (New York: Guilford, 1999); Dana L. Cloud, "'To Veil the Threat of Terror': Afghan Women and the <Clash of Civilizations> in the Imagery of the U.S. War on Terrorism," *Quarterly Journal of Speech* 990 (2004): 285–306; Carlos Morrison and Jacqueline Trimble, "Still Work to Be Done: The Million Man March and the 50th Anniversary Commemoration Selma to Montgomery March as Mythoform and Visual Rhetoric," *Howard Journal of Communications* 28, no. 2 (2017): 132–143; Davi Johnson Thornton, "The Rhetoric of Civil Rights Photographs: James Meredith's March Against Fear," *Rhetoric and Public Affairs* 16, no. 3 (2013): 457–488; Cara A. Finnegan, *Making Photography Matter: A Viewer's History from the Civil War to the Great Depression* (Urbana: University of Illinois Press, 2015).

24. Robert Hariman and John Louis Lucaites, *No Caption Needed: Iconic Photographs, Public Culture and Liberal Democracy* (Chicago: University of Chicago Press, 2007); Susan Sontag, *On Photography* (London/New York: Penguin 2008); Roland Barthes, *Camera Lucida: Reflections on Photography* (New York: Hill and Wang, 2010).
25. Kenneth Burke, *Language as Symbolic Action: Essays on Life, Literature, and Method* (Berkeley: University of California Press, 1966), 45.
26. On definitions of affect, see Melissa Gregg, ed., *The Affect Theory Reader* (Durham: Duke University Press, 2010). For rhetorical uptake of this concept in social movement contexts, see, for example, Josue David Cisneros, *The Border Crossed Us: Rhetorics of Borders, Citizenship, and Latino/a Identity* (Tuscaloosa: University of Alabama Press, 2014).
27. Erin J. Rand, *Reclaiming Queer: Activist and Academic Rhetorics of Resistance* (Tuscaloosa: University of Alabama Press, 2014), 127–155.
28. Amani Husain, "*No Hay Vida Sin Libertad: Testimonios* of Resistance from the #Hutto27 Hunger Strikers," *Women's Studies in Communication* 44, no. 3 (2021): 259–277, p. 259.
29. Jonathan Alexander, Susan J. Jarratt, and Nancy Welch, *Unruly Rhetorics: Protest, Persuasion, and Publics* (Pittsburgh: University of Pittsburgh Press, 2019; Dana L. Cloud, "Feminist Body Rhetoric in the #UnrulyMob, Texas, 2013," in Alexander, Jarratt, and Welch, *Unruly*, 27–44; "Body rhetoric" has been a lasting concern of rhetorical studies: see Roberta Chevrette and Aaron Hess, "The FEMEN Can Do Everything: Generating the Agentic Bodies of Social Movements Through Internal and External Rhetorics," *Communication Monographs* 86, no. 4 (2019): 416–437.
30. Cloud and Feyh, "'Reason in Revolt.'" Erin J. Rand, "'What One Voice Can Do: Civic Pedagogy and Choric Collectivity at Camp Courage," *Text and Performance Quarterly* 34, no. 1 (2014): 28–51.
31. Dana L. Cloud, "The Null Persona: Race and the Rhetoric of Silence in the Uprising of '34," *Rhetoric and Public Affairs* 2, no. 2 (1999): 177–209.
32. See Julia T. Wood, "Feminist Standpoint Theory and Muted Group Theory: Commonalities and Divergences," *Women and Language* 28, no. 2 (2005): 61–64.
33. Wood, "Feminist Standpoint."
34. See Megan Eatman, *Ecologies of Harm: Rhetorics of Violence in the United States* (Columbus: Ohio State University Press, 2020; Luis A. Fernandez, *Policing Dissent: Social Control and the Anti-Globalization Movement* (New Brunswick, NJ: Rutgers University Press, 2008); Jenet Kirkpatrick, *Uncivil Disobedience: Studies in Violence and Democratic Politics* (Princeton: Princeton University Press, 2008); Charles Tilly, *The Politics of Collective Violence* (Cambridge, UK: Cambridge University Press, 2003); Erin J. Rand, "Thinking Violence and Rhetoric," *Philosophy and Rhetoric* 12, no. 3 (2009): 461–484; Steven Salaita, *Uncivil Rites: Palestine*

and the Limits of Academic Freedom (Chicago: Haymarket Books, 2015); Anjali Vats and Mohan J. Dutta, "Locating Freedom of Speech in an Era of Global White Nationalism," *First Amendment Studies* 54, no. 2 (2020): 156–180; Dana L. Cloud and Nina M. Lozano-Reich, "The Uncivil Tongue: Invitational Rhetoric and the Problem of Inequality," *Western Journal of Communication* 73, no. 2 (2009): 220–226.

35. Morris and Browne include a number of essays studying the rhetoric of movements for internal audiences in their anthology, including Randall A. Lake, "Enacting Red Power: The Consummatory Function in Native American Protest Rhetoric," 288–303; and Mari Boor Tonn, "Militant Motherhood: Labor's Mary Harris 'Mother' Jones," 354–372. See also Karma R. Chávez, "Counter-Public Enclaves and Understanding the Function of Rhetoric and Social Movement Coalition-Building," *Communication Quarterly* 59, no. 1 (2011): 1–18.
36. Morris and Browne, *Readings*, 287.
37. Chávez, "Counter-public Enclaves."
38. In rhetoric, Karlyn Kohrs Campbell has been foundational to the study of consciousness-raising in the feminist movement: "Consciousness-Raising: Linking Theory, Criticism, and Practice," *Rhetoric Society Quarterly* 32, no. 1 (2002): 44–64; see also Elizabeth Bruner and Sarah Partlow-LeFevre, "#MeToo as Networked Collective: Examining Consciousness-Raising on Wild Public Networks," *Communication and Critical/Cultural Studies* 17, no. 2 (2020): 166–182; Dana L. Cloud, *Reality Bites: Rhetoric and the Circulation of Truth Claims in U.S. Political Culture* (Columbus: Ohio State University Press, 2018), 159.
39. Reprinted in Schulman, *Let the Record*, 113–118.
40. Morris and Browne (*Readings*) include the following as samples of externally-oriented movement rhetoric: Karlyn Kohrs Campbell, "The Rhetoric of Women's Liberation: An Oxymoron," 172–183; Kevin Michael DeLuca and Jennifer Peeples, "From Public Sphere to Public Screen: Democracy, Activism and the 'Violence' of Seattle," 244–266.
41. See also Chevrette and Hess, "'The FEMEN Body."
42. Bowers, Ochs, Jensen, and Shulz, *Rhetoric of Agitation*, 7–8.
43. Martin Luther King, Jr. "Letter from a Birmingham Jail," April 16, 1963, https://bri-wp-images.s3.amazonaws.com/wp-content/uploads/Letter-From-Birmingham-Jail.pdf.
44. Dana L. Cloud, "The Significance of the Radical Flank: The Role of GetEQUAL in the Marriage Equality Movement," in Crick, *Rhetoric of Social Movements*, 223–239.
45. Schulman, *Let the Record*, 86–89.
46. Herbert Haines, *Black Radicals and the Civil Rights Mainstream* (Knoxville: University of Tennessee Press, 1988).
47. Julian Bond, Callie Crossley, and James A. DeVinney, "Bridge to Freedom," *Eyes on Prize* [television documentary] (Public Broadcasting Service, April 4, 2021/1986).
48. Madison Davis Lacy, James A. DeVinney, "The Time Has Come (1964–66)," *Eyes on the Prize* [television documentary series], Public Broadcasting Service, 2006.
49. Schulman, *Let the Record*, 207.

Chapter 6

1. Rhetoric scholars have called our attention to the strategies of the incarcerated for agency and justice: Chris S. Earle, "Dispossessed: Prisoner Response-ability and Resistance at the Limits of Subjectivity," *Rhetoric Society Quarterly* 46, no.

1 (2016); Suzanne Marie Enck and Blake A. McDaniel, "'I Want Something Better for My Life': Personal Narratives of Incarcerated Women and Performances of Agency," *Text and Performance Quarterly* 35, no. 1 (2015): 43–61; Lisa M. Corrigan, *Prison Power: How Prison Influenced the Movement for Black Liberation* (Jackson, MS: University Press of Mississippi, 2016).

2. Peter Thomas, *The Gramscian Moment* (Chicago: Haymarket, 2011); see also William K. Carroll and Kanchan Sarker, eds., *A World To Win: Contemporary Social Movements and Counter-Hegemony* (Winnepeg, CA: ARP Books, 2016).
3. *Eyes on the Prize* [television series], Public Broadcasting Service, aired April 4, 2021, https://www.pbs.org/wgbh/americanexperience/films/eyesontheprize/.
4. Maegan Parker Brooks, *A Voice That Could Stir an Army: Fannie Lou Hamer and the Rhetoric of the Black Freedom Movement* (Jackson: University of Mississippi Press, 2016).
5. Karma Chávez, "Counter-public Enclaves and Understanding the Function of Rhetoric in Social Movement Coalition-Building," *Communication Quarterly* 59, no. 1 (2011): 1–18.
6. Jeffrey A. Bennett, "A Stitch in Time: Public Emotionality and the Repertoire of Citizenship," in *Remembering the AIDS Quilt*, edited by Charles E. Morris III (East Lansing: Michigan State University Press, 2011), 133–160.
7. Betty Friedan, *The Feminine Mystique*, 50th Anniversary Edition (New York: Norton, 2013).
8. Proposition 8 was a ballot proposition in California in 2008 that mandated marriage as being between a man and a woman. It passed, but was overturned by the California Supreme Court. It remained in effect until 2013.
9. Karlyn Kohrs Campbell, "Consciousness-Raising: Linking Theory, Criticism, and Practice," *Rhetoric Society Quarterly* 32, no. 1 (2002): 45–64.
10. Michael Morgan, *George Gerbner: A Critical Introduction to Media and Communication Theory* (Pieterlen and Bern, Switzerland: Peter Lang Press, 2011).
11. Howard Zinn, *SNCC: The New Abolitionists* (Cambridge: South End, 1964), 33–35, 59.
12. Celeste Michelle Condit and John Louis Lucaites, *Crafting Equality: America's Anglo African Word* (Chicago: University of Chicago Press, 1993).
13. See Michael Eric Dyson, *"I May Not Get There with You": The True Martin Luther King, Jr.* (New York: Simon and Schuster, 2000).
14. See Gerald F. Davis, Doug McAdam, W. Richard Scott, and Mayer N. Zald, *Social Movements and Organization Theory* (Cambridge, UK: Cambridge University Press, 2005).
15. Rachel Einwohner, "Leadership in Social Movements," *American Behavioral Scientist* 50, no. 10 (2007): 1306–1412.
16. Charles J. Stewart, Craig Allen Smith, and Robert E. Denton, Jr., *Persuasion and Social Movements* (Prospect Heights, IL: Waveland 2001), 103–127.
17. Marllyn Bordwell DeLaure, "Planting Seeds of Change: Ella Baker's Radical Rhetoric," *Women's Studies in Communication* 31, no. 1 (2008): 1–28.
18. Steven Preskill, *Education in Black and White: Myles Horton and the Highlander Center's Vision for Social Justice* (Berkeley: University of California Press, 2021).
19. See Todd Gitlin, "Occupy's Predicament: The Moment and the Prospects for the Movement," *British Journal of Sociology* 64, no. 1 (2013): 3–25.

Chapter 7

1. Martin Luther King, Jr., Speech to March on Washington for Jobs and Freedom ("I Have a Dream"), 1963, National Archives: https://www.google.com/search?q=martin+luther+king+jr+i+have+a+dream+speech&oq=martin+luther+king+&aqs=chrome.2.69i57j69i64j35i39i650j46i131i433i512j46i175i199i433i512j0i433i512j46i175i199i512j0i512.3741j0j4&sourceid=chrome&ie=UTF-8#ip=1.
2. Michael Osborn, "Archetypal Metaphor in Rhetoric: The Light-Dark Family," *Quarterly Journal of Speech* 53, no. 2 (1967): 115–116.
3. See Craig J. Calhoun, ed., *Habermas and the Public Sphere* (Cambridge, MA: MIT Press, 1992).
4. On the limits of the law in protecting political speech and specifically how the law privileges some voices and identities over others, see Anjali Vats, *The Color of Creatorship: Intellectual Property, Race, and the Making of Americans* (Stanford: Stanford University Press, 2020).
5. Robert Asen and Daniel C. Brouwer, eds., *Counterpublics and the State* (Albany: State University of New York, 2001).
6. Nancy Fraser, "Rethinking the Public Sphere: A Contribution to the Critique of Actually Existing Democracy," in *Habermas and the Public Sphere*, edited by Craig Calhoun (Cambridge, MIT Press 1992), 123; Asen argues that what makes a public "counter" is not necessarily the identities, locales, or topics of a group but rather the explicit recognition among participants that they have been excluded from wider publics and are set against the broader public in challenging its norms and ideas. Robert Asen, "Seeking the 'Counter' in Counterpublics," *Communication Theory* 10, no. 4 (2000): 424–46.
7. Fraser, "Rethinking, 123.
8. Phaedra Pezzullo, "Resisting 'National Breast Cancer Awareness Month': The Rhetoric of Counterpublics and their Cultural Performances," *Quarterly Journal of Speech* 89, no. 4 (2003): 345–365.
9. Dana L. Cloud, "Networks of Queer Care: The Privatization of Social Responsibility and the Politics of Queer Generosity," *QED: A Journal in Queer Worldmaking* 10, no. 1 (2023): 203–213.
10. Christina Foust, Amy Pason, and Kate Zittlow Rogness, eds., *What Democracy Looks Like: The Rhetoric of Social Movements and Counterpublics* (Tuscaloosa: University of Alabama Press, 2017).
11. Daniel C. Brouwer, "Counterpublicity and Corporeality in HIV/AIDS Zines, *Critical Studies in Media Communication* 22, no. 5 (2005): 351–371; "Risibility Politics: Camp Humor in HIV/AIDS Zines," in *Public Modalities*, edited by Daniel C. Brouwer and Robert Asen (Tuscaloosa, AL: University of Alabama Press, 2010), 219–239.
12. On this idea of oscillating counterpublics, see Daniel C. Brouwer, "From Vernacular to Official—and the Spaces in Between," *QED: A Journal in GLBTQ Worldmaking* 1, no 2 (2014): 181–185.
13. Todd Gitlin, *The Whole World is Watching: Mass Media in the Making and Unmaking of the New Left* (Berkeley, CA: University of California Press, 2003). For an excellent discussion of how media frames shape the public memory of social movements, see Kristen Hoerl, *The Bad Sixties: Hollywood Memories of the Counterculture, Antiwar, and Black Power Movements* (Jackson: University Press of Mississippi, 2018).
14. Downing, John. *Radical Media: Rebellious Communication and Social Movements* (Thousand Oaks, CA: Sage Publications, 2001): v.
15. Linda J. Lumsden, *Social Justice Journalism: A Cultural History of Social Movement Media from Abolition to #WomensMarch* (New York: Peter Lang, 2019).

16. Downing.
17. Downing.
18. For a list of socialist newspapers in the United States, see https://en.wikipedia.org/wiki/Category:Socialist_newspapers_published_in_the_United_States. For communist publications, see https://en.wikipedia.org/wiki/Category:Communist_periodicals_published_in_the_United_States. These are not complete lists.
19. Dan Georgakas and Marvin Surkin, *Detroit, I Do Mind Dying: A Study in Urban Rebellion* (New York: St. Martin's Press, 1975); Jack Taylor, "Revolution at the Point of Production: An Interview with Mike Hamlin of DRUM and The League of Revolutionary Black Workers," *Spectrum* 2, no. 1 (2013): 99–122.
20. Stewart Bird, Rene Lichtman, and Peter Gesser, with the League of Revolutionary Black Workers, *Finally Got the News* (Icarus Films, 1970/2003), https://icarusfilms.com/if-fin#.
21. Angela J. Aguayo, *Documentary Resistance* (New York: Oxford University Press, 2019).
22. Aguayo, *Documentary,* 27–54.
23. Aguayo, *Documentary*, 183.
24. See Allissa V. Richardson, *Bearing Witness While Black: African Americans, Smartphones, & the New Protest #Journalism* (New York: Oxford University Press, 2020). Richardson argues that "Bearing witness while black is an innovative style of protest journalism that has been centuries in the making" and represents a form of Black witnessing that "reclaims black lives and stories from the margins," making a Black visual public sphere. ii–xiii; 136–152.
25. Aguayo, *Documentary*, 222.
26. Michael D. Conover, Emilio Ferrara, Filippo Menczer, Alessandro Flammini, and Matjaz Perc, "The Digital Evolution of Occupy Wall Street," *PloS One* 8, no. 5 (2013): 64679.
27. Manuel Castells, "Communication, Power, and Counter-power in the Network Society," *International Journal of Communication* 1, no. 2 (2007): 238–266. See also Jennifer Earl, "Technology and Social Media," in *The Wiley Blackwell Companion to Social Movements*, 2nd Edition, edited by David A. Snow, Sarah A. Soule, Hanspeter Kriesi, and Holly J. McCammon (Hoboken: Wiley Blackwell, 2019), 289–305.
28. Homero Gil de Zuñiga, Isabel Inguanzo, and Alberto Ardevol-Abreu, "Introduction" to Special Issue on "Protesting While Polarized: Digital Activism in Contentious Times," *Media and Communication* 10, no. 4 (2022): 1–4; Victoria Carty, *Social Movements and New Technology* (New York: Routledge, 2018); see also Donatella della Porta, *Communication in Movement: Social Movements as Agents of Participatory Democracy* (New York: Routledge, 2012), Chapter 3; Alice Mattoni, A Situated Understanding of Digital Technologies in Social Movements: Media Ecology and Media Practice Approaches," *Social Movement Studies* 16, no. 4 (2017): 494–505; Deana A. Rohlinger and Jennifer Earl, "The Past, Present, and Future of Media and Social Movement Studies: Introduction to the Special Issue on Media and Social Movements," *Social Movements and Media* 14 (2018): 1–20.
29. Mattoni.
30. Jordana J. George and Dorothy E. Leidner, "From Clicktivism to Hacktivism: Understanding Digital Activism," *Information and Organization* 29, no. 3 (2019): 100249.
31. Helen Margetts, Peter John, Scott Hale, and Taha Yasseri, *Political Turbulence: How Social Media Shape Collective Action* (Princeton: Princeton University Press, 2015): 28.
32. Marcia Mundt, Karen. Ross, and Charla M. Burnett, "Scaling Social Movements Through Social Media: The Case of Black Lives Matter," *Social Media + Society* 4, no. 4 (2018): 1–14. See also Radhika Gajjala, "Introduction: Alternetworks and

Contrapublics in Digital Activism," *Communication, Culture, and Critique* 16 (2023): 81–82.

33. Brian G. Smith, Arunima Krishna, and Reham Al-Sinan, "Beyond Slacktivism: Examining the Entanglement Between Social Media Engagement, Empowerment, and Participation in Activism," *International Journal of Strategic Communication* 13, no. 3 (2019): 182–196.
34. Bronwyn Carlson and Jeff Berglund, eds. *Indigenous People Rise Up: The Global Ascendancy of Social Media Activism* (New Brunswick: Rutgers University Press, 2021): 109; Bronwyn Carlson and Ryan Frazer, "The Affective Economies of Indigenous Social Media Activism: Making the Personal Political," in Carlson and Berglund, 48–64; Jiyoun Suk, Yinii Zhang, Zhiying Yue, Rui Wang, Xinxia Dong, Dongdong Yang, and Ruixue Lian, "When the Personal Becomes the Political: Unpacking the Dynamics of Sexual Violence and Gender Justice Discourses Across Four Social Media Platforms," *Communication Research* 50, no. 5 (2023): 610–632; Charlotte Nau, Jinman Zhang, Anabel Quan-Haase, and Kaitlynn Mendes, "Vernacular Practices in Digital Feminist Activism on Twitter: Deconstructing Affect and Emotion in the #MeToo Movement," *Feminist Media Studies* 23, no 5 (2023): 2046–2062.
35. Nau et al., 2058.
36. Anne Kaun, "'Our Time To Act Has Come': Desynchronization, Social Media Time, and Protest Movements," *Culture & Society* 39, no. 4 (2017): 469–486.
37. Catherine Bouko, *Visual Citizenship: Communication, Political Opinions, and Emotions on Social Media* (New York: Routledge, 2024); Kevin DeLuca, "Image Events Amidst Eco-Ruins: Social Media and the Mediated Earth," *Communication and Critical Cultural Studies* 16, no. 4 (2019): 329–339.
38. Rik Smit, Ansgard Heinrich, and Marcel Broersma, "Activating the Past in the Ferguson Protests: Memory Work, Digital Activism, and the Politics of Platforms," *New Media & Society* 20, no. 9 (2018): 3119–3139.
39. Christina Foust and Craig Weathers, "Memes in Social Movement 2.0: #JeffCoSchoolBoardHistory and the Ouster of Conservative Education 'Reformers' in Colorado," in *The Rhetoric of Social Movements: Networks, Power, and New Media*, edited by Nathan Crick (New York: Routledge, 2021): 135–155; see also Christina Foust and Kate Draner Hoyt, "Social Movement 2.0: Integrating and Assessing Scholarship on Social Media and Movement," *Review of Communication* 18, no. 1 (2018): 37–55; Chris Duerringer, "Who Would Jesus Bomb? The Republican Jesus Meme and the Fracturing of Ideology," *Social Media + Society* 2, no. 1 (2015): 1–12.
40. Foust and Hoyt, 41.
41. Todd Wolfson, *Digital Rebellion: Birth of the Cyber Left* (Champaign-Urbana: University of Illinois Press, 2014), p. 17.
42. See also Sami Çöteli, *Cyber Public Sphere and Social Movements* (Baden-Baden: Nomos, 2018); Su Young Choi and YounghanCho, "Generating Counter-Public Spheres Through Social Media: Two Social Movements in Neoliberalised South Korea," *Javnost: The Public* 24, no. 1 (2017): 15–33; Kristin Peterson, *Unruly Souls: The Digital Activism of Muslim and Christian Feminists* (New Brunswick: Rutgers University Press, 2022); Laura Cervia and Carles Marín-Lladó, "#FreePalestine on TikTok: From Performative Activism to (Meaningful) Playful Activism," *Journal of International and Intercultural Communication* 15, no. 4 (2022): 414–434.
43. Mattoni, "Situated Understanding," 499.
44. Sarah Jackson, Moya Bailey, Brook Welles, *#HashtagActivism: Networks of Race and Gender Justice* (Cambridge, MA: MIT Press, 2020).
45. Jackson et al., *#Hashtag Activisim*, xxv.

46. Sarah J. Jackson, Moya Bailey, and Brooke Foucault Welles, #GirlsLikeUs: Trans Advocacy and Community Building Online," *New Media & Society* 20, no. 5 (2018): 1868–1888.
47. Phaedra Pezzullo, *Beyond Straw Men: Plastic Pollution and Networked Cultures of Care* (Berkeley: University of California Press, 2023).
48. Radhika Gajjala, "Introduction: Alternetworks and Contrapublics in Digital Activism," *Communication, Culture, and Critique* 16, no. 2 (2023): 81–82.
49. Carlson and Frazer; Marisa Elena Duarte and Morgan Vigil-Hayes, "How We Connect: An Indigenous Feminist Approach to Digital Methods," in Carlson and Berglund, *Indigenous People*, 96.
50. Nicholet A. Deschine Parkhurst, "From #Mniwiconi to #StandwithStandingRock: How the #NoDAPLMovement Disrupted Physical and Virtual Spaces and Brought Indigenous Liberation to the Forefront of People's Minds," in Carlson and Berglund, *Indigenous People*; Mohan J. Dutta and Nga Hau, "Voice Infrastructure and Alternative Imaginaries: Indigenous Social Movements Against Neocolonial Extraction," in Crick, *Rhetoric of Social Movements*, 254–267.
51. Sumru Atuka and Alyson Cole, "Bodies on the Line vs. Bodies Online: A Feminist Phenomenology of Digitally Mediated Political Action," *Women's Studies in Communication* 47, no. 1 (2024): 63–86; Shaheen Bagh, Sarah Ford, Radhika Gajjala, Padmioni Ray Murray, Design Beku, and Kiran Vinod Bhatia, "Making Sense of (Re)emerging "Subaltern" Feminist Political Subjectivities in Hashtag Publics Through Critical, Feminist Interventions," *new media & society* 26, no. 1 (2024): 473–494.
52. Smith et al., 184; Summer Harlow and Lei Guo, "Will the Revolution be Tweeted or Facebooked? Using Digital Communication Tools in Immigrant Activism," *Journal of Computer-Mediated Communication* 19, no. 3 (2014): 463–478.
53. Margetts et al., *Political Turbulence*; see also Malcolm Gladwell, "Small Change: Why the Revolution Will not Be Tweeted," *The New Yorker* (October 4, 2010).
54. Wolfson, *Digital Rebellion*, 188.
55. Wolfson, *Digital Rebellion*, 193.
56. Michael Etter and Oana Brindusa Albu, "Activists in the Dark: Social Media Algorithms and Collective Action in Two Social Movements," *Organization* 28, no. 1 (2021): 68–91.
57. See Lisa Cuklanz, *Gender Violence, Social Media, and Online Environments: When the Virtual Becomes Real* (New York: Routledge, 2023).
58. Susanne Foellmer, Margreth Lünenborg, and Christoph Raetzsch, eds., *Media Practices, Social Movements, and Performativity* (New York: Routledge/Taylor and Francis, 2018).
59. Susan Zaeske, Signatures of Citizenship: Petitioning, Antislavery, and Women's Political Identity (Raleigh-Durham: University of North Carolina Press, 2003).
60. "Mississippi Freedom Democratic Party," Digital SNCC Gateway, https://snccdigital.org/inside-sncc/alliances-relationships/mfdp/
61. Fannie Lou Hamer, *The Speeches of Fannie Lou Hamer: To Tell It Like It Is* (Jackson: University Press of Mississippi, 2011).
62. Maegan Parker Brooks, *A Voice that Could Stir an Army: Fannie Lou Hamer and the Rhetoric of the Black Freedom Movement* (Jackson: University Press of Mississippi, 2014).
63. Jo Reger, Rachel L. Einwohner, and Daniel J. Myers, *Identity Work in Social Movements* (Minneapolis: University of Minnesota Press, 2008).

64. Gerald M. Platt and Michael R. Fraser, "Race and Gender Discourse Strategies: Creating Solidarity and Framing the Civil Rights Movement," *Social Problems* 45, no. 2 (1998): 160–179.

65. Jane Rhodes, *Framing the Black Panthers: The Spectacular Rise of a Black Power Icon* (Champaign-Urbana: University of Illinois Press, 2017).

66. Celeste Michelle Condit and John Louis Lucaites, *Crafting Equality: America's Anglo-African Word* (Chicago: University of Chicago Press, 1993).

67. Carol Finnegan, "Review Essay: Visual Studies and Visual Rhetoric," *The Quarterly Journal of Speech* 90, no. 2 (2004): 234–247; Caitlin Frances Bruce and Cara Finnegan, "Visual Rhetoric in Flux: A Conversation," *Rhetoric and Public Affairs* 24, nos. 1–2 (2021): 89–108.

68. "The Murder of Emmett Till" (collection), Library of Congress, https://www.loc.gov/collections/civil-rights-history-project/articles-and-essays/murder-of-emmett-till/; Christine Harold and Kevin Michael DeLuca, "Behold the Corpse: Violent Images and the Case of Emmett Till," *Rhetoric and Public Affairs* 8, no. 2 (2005): 263–286; "The Body of Emmett Till: 100 Photos," https://www.youtube.com/watch?v=4V6ffUUEvaM.

69. Dave Tell, *Remembering Emmett Till* (Chicago: University of Chicago Press, 2019), 128. Tell provides geographical, cultural, and historical context for this event with an emphasis on public memory.

70. Jeremy Helligar, "How the Clenched Fist Became a Black Power Symbol," *Reader's Digest*, July 21, 2021, https://www.rd.com/article/history-behind-the-clenched-first-and-the-symbol-for-black-power/.

71. Livia Gershon, "How the Memphis Sanitation Strike Changed History," *JSTOR Daily,* February 9, 2018 https://daily.jstor.org/how-the-memphis-sanitation-strike-changed-history/; Photograph by Joshua Rashaad McFadden, in Ted Conover, "The Strike that Brought MLK to Memphis," *Smithsonian*, January 2018, smithsonianmag.com/history/revisiting-sanitation-workers-strike-180967512/.

72. Foellmer et al., *Media Practices*, 4.

73. Judith Butler, *Toward a Performative Theory of Assembly* (Cambridge, MA: Harvard University Press, 2015), 11.

74. O'Neill, T. (2015, January 8). Twelve cruel anti-suffragette cartoons. *The Week*. https://theweek.com/articles/461455/12-cruel-antisuffragette-cartoons

Chapter 8

1. Ernesto Laclau and Chantal Mouffe emphasize the rhetorical character of such oppositions; they may be based on experience, but they must be articulated in rhetoric by a social movement seeking to orient audiences to a cause.Ernesto Laclau and Chantal Mouffe, *Hegemony and Socialist Strategy* (London: Verso, 2001), 93–148.

2. Martin Luther King, Jr. "Letter from a Birmingham Jail" (1963), Bill of Rights Institute, https://billofrightsinstitute.org/primary-sources/letter-from-birmingham-jail.

3. Karlyn Kohrs Campbell and Kathleen Hall Jamieson, "Ronald Reagan's Enactment of the Presidency in his 1981 Inaugural Address," in *Form, Genre, and the Study of Political Discourse*, edited by Herbert W. Simons and Aram A. Aghazarian (Columbia, SC: University of South Carolina Press, 1986).

4. Christina Foust, *Transgression as a Mode of Resistance: Rethinking Social Movement in an Era of Corporate Globalization* (Lanham, MD: Rowman and Littlefield, 2010), 5.

5. Jonathan Alexander, Susan C. Jarratt, and Nancy Welch, *Unruly Rhetorics: Protest, Persuasion, and Publics* (Pittsburgh: University of Pittsburgh Press, 2018).

6. Kevin Michael DeLuca, *Image Politics: The New Rhetoric of Environmental Activism* (New York: Guilford Press, 1999); Dana L. Cloud, "The Significance of the Radical Flank: The Role of GetEQUAL in the Marriage Equality Movement," in *The Rhetoric of Social Movements: Networks, Power, and New Media*, edited by Nathan Crick (New York: Routledge, 2021), 223–239.
7. Candice Delmas and Kimberley Brownlee, "Civil Disobedience," *Stanford Encyclopedia of Philosophy* (2021), https://plato.stanford.edu/entries/civil-disobedience/.
8. King, *Letter.*
9. Erin R. Pineda, *Seeing Like an Activist: Civil Disobedience and the Civil Rights Movement* (Oxford: Oxford University Press, 2021).
10. Nadine Bloch, "Education and Training in Nonviolent Resistance," *United States Institute of Peace Special Report 394*, October 2016, https://www.usip.org/sites/default/files/SR394-Education-and-Training-in-Nonviolent-Resistance.pdf.
11. Aimee Carillo Rowe, *Power Lines: On the Subject of Feminist Alliances* (Durham: Duke University Press, 2008).
12. See Karma R. Chávez and Cindy L. Griffin, eds., *Standing in the Intersection: Feminist Voices, Feminist Practices in Communication Studies* (Albany: State University of New York Press, 2012). See also Mega E. Brooker and Davis S. Meyer, "Coalitions and the Organization of Collective Action," in *The Wiley Blackwell Companion to Social Movements*, edited by David A. Snow, Sarah A. Soule, Hanspeter Kriesi, and Holly J. McCammon (Hoboken: Wiley Blackwell, 2019), 252–268.
13. María Lugones, *Pilgrimages/Peregrinajes: Theorizing Coalition Against Multiple Oppressions* (New York: Rowman and Littlefield, 2003), 7.
14. Karma R. Chávez, "Counter-public Enclaves and Understanding the Function of Rhetoric in Social Movement Coalition-Building," *Communication Quarterly* 59, no. 1 (2011): 1–18, 4.
15. Isaac West, "PISSAR's Queer and Diabled Politics," in *Transforming Citizenships: Transgender Articulations of the Law* (New York: New York University Press, 2013), 61–88.
16. Chávez, "Counterpublic," 12.
17. Howard Zinn, *SNCC: The New Abolitionists* (Cambridge: South End, 1964), 15.
18. Maegan Parker Brooks, *A Voice That Could Stir an Army: Fannie Lou Hamer and the Rhetoric of the Black Freedom Movement* (Jackson: University Press of Mississippi, 2014), 126.
19. Rosa Luxemburg, *The Essential Rosa Luxemburg: Reform or Revolution and the Mass Strike*, edited by Helen Scott (Chicago: Haymarket Books, 2008).
20. See Deborah Macey, Kathleen Ryan, and Noah Springer, eds., *How Television Shapes Our Worldview: Media Representations of Social Trends and Change* (Lanham, MD: Lexington Books, 2014); Herman Gray, *Watching Race: Television and the Struggle for "Blackness"* (Minneapolis: University of Minnesota Press, 1995).
21. Lance Selfa, *The Democrats: A Critical History* (Chicago: Haymarket, 2008).
22. Doris Zames Fleischer, *The Disability Rights Movement: From Charity to Confrontation* (Philadelphia: Temple University Press, 2011).
23. Belinda Stillion Southard, *Militant Citizenship: Rhetorical Strategies of the National Woman's Party, 1913–1920* (College Station: Texas A&M Press, 2011).
24. Henry Hampton, Callie Crossley, and James DeVinney, "Bridge to Freedom" (video recording), *Eyes on the Prize* episode 6 (Public Broadcasting Service, 1986).
25. Dexter B. Gordon, *Black Identity: Rhetoric, Ideology, and Nineteenth-Century Black Nationalism* (Carbondale: Southern Illinois University Press, 2003).
26. Malcolm X, "The Ballot or the Bullet," 1966, *American Radio Works,* https://americanradioworks.publicradio.org/features/blackspeech/mx.html.

27. Gordon; see Michael J. Lee, *We Are Not One People: Secession and Separatism in American Politics since 1776* (New York: Oxford University Press, 2022).
28. Sharon Smith, *Subterranean Fire: A History of Working-Class Radicalism in the United States* (Chicago: Haymarket, 2018).
29. See Dana L. Cloud, We *ARE the Union: Union Democracy and Dissent at Boeing* (Champaign-Urbana: University of Illinois Press, 2011).
30. https://laborforpalestine.net/.
31. Monroe Friedman, *Consumer Boycotts: Effecting Change Through the Marketplace and the Media* (New York: Routledge, 1999).
32. On boycotts and buycotts, see Phaedra Pezzullo, "Contextualizing Boycotts and Buycotts: The Impure Politics of Consumer-Based Advocacy in an Age of Global Ecological Crises," *Communication and Critical/Cultural Studies* 8, no. 2 (2011): 124–145; Lous, Hyman, ed., *Shopping for Change: Consumer Activism and the Possibilities of Purchasing Power* (Ithaca, NY: Cornell University Press, 2017).
33. Donatella Della Porta and Herbert Reiter, eds., *Policing Protest: The Control of Mass Demonstrations in Western Democracies* (Minneapolis: University of Minnesota Press, 1998).
34. Luis A. Fernandez, *Policing Protest: Social Control and the Anti-Globalization Movement* (New Brunswick: Rutgers University Press, 2008), 23.
35. Jodi Dean, *Crowds and Party* (London: Verso, 2018), 6.
36. See Sarah J. Jackson, *Black Celebrity, Racial Politics, and the Press: Framing Dissent* (New York: Routledge, 2014); Black Public Sphere Collective, *The Black Public Sphere* (Chicago: University of Chicago Press, 1995); Patricia Hill Collins, "Black Public Intellectuals from DuBois to the Present," *Contexts* 4, no. 4 (2005): 22–27; Reynaldo Anderson, Clinton R. Fluker, Sheree R. Thomas, eds., *The Black Speculative Arts Movement: Black Futurity, Art + Design* (Lanham: Lexington Books, 2019).
37. Keeanga-Yahmatta Taylor, *How We Get Free: Black Feminism and the Combahee River Collective* (Chicago: Haymarket, 2017); Marquis Bey, *Black Trans Feminism* (Durham: Duke University Press, 2022); Jennifer Nash, *Black Feminism Reimagined: After Intersectionality* (Durham: Duke University Press, 2019); Chandra Talpade Mohanty, *Feminism Without Borders: Decolonizing Theory, Practicing Solidarity* (Durham: Duke University Press, 2003).
38. "Herstory," Blacklivesmatter.com, https://blacklivesmatter.com/herstory/#:~:-text=In%202013%2C%20three%20radical%20Black,movement%20building%20project%20called%20%23BlackLivesMatter.

Index

www.ingramcontent.com/pod-product-compliance
Ingram Content Group UK Ltd.
Pitfield, Milton Keynes, MK11 3LW, UK
UKHW050930280826
474804UK00005B/261

9 781793 517722